BOOK SELECTION
FOR
SCHOOL LIBRARIES

BOOK SELECTION

FOR

SCHOOL LIBRARIES

by

AZILE WOFFORD

Associate Professor Emeritus, Department of Library Science
University of Kentucky

THE H. W. WILSON COMPANY
NEW YORK   1962

Copyright © 1962
By Azile Wofford

First Printing 1962
Second Printing 1964
Third Printing 1967

Printed in the United States of America

Library of Congress Catalog Card No. 62-15046

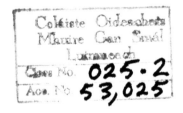

To
the nieces and nephews
twenty-two in number, equally divided as to sex
with whom
at various times and in widely scattered places
their "Aunt Iddie"
has been privileged to share
experiences with books and reading

FOREWORD

In 1927, under the impact of newly adopted standards of the Southern Association of Colleges and Secondary Schools, I entered the school library field via the high school of my native South Carolina town. My first library training consisted of a summer term at the University of North Carolina the following year, when the university first offered courses in library science.

In a class in adolescent literature I recall chiefly my introduction to the *Standard Catalog for High School Libraries,* its first edition then just two years old. I read for review Edna Ferber's *So Big* and first learned of the Newbery Medal awarded that year to Will James for *Smoky, the Cowhorse.* This brief experience fired my interest in books and reading for children and young people, an interest at which I have ever since been working. A fringe benefit of that class is a lasting friendship with the instructor, Nora E. Beust, long-time specialist in school and children's libraries in the Office of Education (at present part of the Department of Health, Education and Welfare), now my fellow retired summer neighbor in the Blue Ridge Mountains of North Carolina.

Later, at the George Peabody College for Teachers, I had a similar course in children's literature with Margaret Gramesley of the University of Illinois. As part of my work at Columbia University, I took further courses in books and reading for children and young people with Alice I. Hazeltine, Effie L. Powers, and Mabel Williams.

From 1938 to 1960, at the University of Kentucky, I taught courses in books and reading for children and young people. The arrangements of these courses varied as standards for certification of school librarians shifted and changed. For the last three years of this time, I was privileged to teach children's literature to both prospective elementary school teachers and school librarians. Scattered summers have found me teaching at Atlanta University, Emory University, George Peabody College for Teachers, and the

University of North Carolina. I have also experienced the responsibility of selecting materials for the juvenile and high school collections in the Library Science Department of the University of Kentucky.

BOOK SELECTION FOR SCHOOL LIBRARIES incorporates what I have learned through more than thirty years of experience about materials for children and young people and their selection for school libraries. In addition to studying, teaching, and reading for background, I have benefited greatly by wide reading of books for children and young people and from discussing books with students and fellow librarians.

This book is intended primarily as a guide in selecting materials for school libraries. It should prove useful in courses in book selection for children and young people. It should also help the school librarian on the job, especially as he begins his task, and teachers who exercise their responsibility for choosing school library materials. Librarians in public libraries may find the book helpful in selecting materials to supply or supplement those in schools.

In this ever widening field, any book about selection can merely open doors beyond which librarians and teachers must explore for themselves. BOOK SELECTION FOR SCHOOL LIBRARIES is offered as a key, with high hopes that its users may sense some of the joy which its writing yielded as they explore the limitless possibilities of using books with young readers.

AZILE WOFFORD

Hendersonville, North Carolina
June, 1962

ACKNOWLEDGMENTS

Many people, often unknowingly, have helped in writing BOOK SELECTION FOR SCHOOL LIBRARIES. The few names selected for acknowledgment of specific contributions could be matched by many others who likewise have here and there rendered needed services.

At the University of Kentucky, President Frank G. Dickey, Dean Martin M. White of the College of Arts and Sciences, and Maurice D. Leach, Jr., Head of the Department of Library Science, not only encouraged the undertaking of this book, but arranged sabbatical leave for its completion. A small grant was made from the Research Fund of the University, which is designed to encourage publishing among the faculty.

Readers who faithfully read and criticized material as it was being written have proved to be of immeasurable assistance. They are: Ruby Trower, Supervisor of School Libraries; Ruth Wheeler, Librarian, Morton Junior High School; Mrs. Eugene S. McConnell, formerly Anne Young LeBus, who at the time of her assistance was Librarian of Arlington and Maxwell Elementary Schools—all three in the Lexington, Kentucky, City Schools; Gertrude Coward, Director of Libraries, Mecklenburg County Schools, Charlotte, North Carolina; and Mrs. David K. Edwards, Librarian, Beverly Hills Unified School District, Beverly Hills, California.

A number of publishers and organizations have answered requests for information and supplied materials. Libraries have been generally helpful in making available a wide variety of materials for examination. Special mention should be made of the Henderson County Public Library, Hendersonville, North Carolina (Mary Kent Seagle, Librarian), for granting access even when the library was closed to the public. Two divisional executive secretaries of the American Library Association, Mildred Batchelder, Division of Library Work with Children and Young People, and Eleanor E. Ahlers, then with the American Association of School Librarians, generously supplied both information and materials.

Mrs. Louise C. Midkiff, Lexington, Kentucky, having conquered the author's handwriting through a former similar venture, typed the manuscript in preparation for the editor's eagle eye. Mrs. Frances L. Heidacker, Hendersonville, North Carolina, has aided in typing revisions for publication.

Last, but by no means least, John Jamieson, Editor of General Publications, and his coworkers of the H. W. Wilson Company have gone beyond the call of duty as they worked to bring BOOK SELECTION FOR SCHOOL LIBRARIES from manuscript into printed form. The book has benefited greatly from their corrections and been enriched by their many helpful suggestions.

Yet only the author must be held responsible for any shortcomings which this book may have. In spite of such shortcomings, however, it is hoped that it may serve as an aid to all who must select books for collections to serve children and young people in schools.

CONTENTS

PART II. MATERIALS FOR SELECTION

PART III. PROBLEMS IN SELECTION

PART IV. FACTORS RELATED TO SELECTION

CONTENTS

PART I

PRINCIPLES OF SELECTION

THE WAY OF SELECTION FOR THE SCHOOL LIBRARY

BUILDING THE COLLECTION

What school librarian has not at some time wanted to throw away the books in his collection and start all over again? Or longed to walk into a new school library with the privilege of selecting the books that make up a well-rounded collection? Or looked with pride at the books on the school library shelves which he has helped to choose? Or searched diligently among book selection aids to find just the right book to meet a specific need in the school library collection?

Many school librarians, especially in the early years of school library development, must surely have had the rare privilege of starting a school library and building the collection. Such must have been the experience of Mary E. Hall, who in 1903 became the first trained librarian in a public school in the United States, the Girls High School in Brooklyn, New York, and in 1943 retired after forty years of devoted service as librarian. Hannah Logasa, spending the twenty-five years from 1914 to 1939 at the University of Chicago High School library, must have built many of her ideas and ideals into the collection there. A similar experience must have been that of Lucile F. Fargo, who from 1909 to 1926 served as librarian of the North Central High School of Spokane, Washington, to the boys and girls of which she dedicated *The Library in the School* (A.L.A., 4th ed. rev., 1947), a book which for many years served as the standard guide to the administration of school libraries.

In the field of elementary school libraries, Anne T. Eaton had a marvelous opportunity to build the collection at the Lincoln School of Teachers College, Columbia University, to which she went as librarian when the library was established in 1917 and from which she retired at the end of the school year in 1947. It was from her rich experience in selecting materials for this collection and using them with young readers that Miss Eaton was able to write *Reading With Children* (Viking, 1940) and to compile the helpful list of books *Treasure for the Taking*, now in a revised edition (Viking, 1957). There are likewise many librarians in schools today who have remained in one situation long enough to experience the satisfaction of building a school library collection.

Other school librarians have had the opposite experience— that of being called upon to build a collection quickly. It may be that a new building is being opened and materials must be purchased and processed during the vacation months so that the library will be ready for business when school opens in the fall. Or perhaps additional funds, over and above the regular appropriation, have been made available to the library and must be spent within a limited period of time. Sometimes it happens that regular funds have not been expended and so must be spent before the close of the fiscal year. In such emergencies, although it is not recommended as regular practice, the school librarian may consider the starred and/or double-starred titles in the tenth edition of the *Children's Catalog* (Wilson, 1961) or the eighth edition of the *Standard Catalog for High School Libraries* (Wilson, 1962) and their supplements. In the case of a new collection, he might order largely from the seventh edition of *A Basic Book Collection for Elementary Grades* (A.L.A., 1960); *A Basic Book Collection for Junior High Schools* (A.L.A., 1960), now in its third edition; or the sixth edition of *A Basic Book Collection for High Schools* (A.L.A., 1957), since these lists contain titles which are considered basic for libraries on the respective levels. One new elementary school library purchased as a beginning collection every title on a list of 147 books considered by a committee working with the state school library supervisor as being minimum essentials for a newly established library.

In any case the hasty building of a collection is apt to be a frustrating experience because there is not time to give much-needed individual consideration to books being added and to determine their most useful place in the school library collection. As one school librarian who had the experience of building a collection quickly remarked: "There is no time to enjoy the books." The streamlined procedure with students, teachers, and perhaps parents helping prepare books for the shelves is not conducive to enjoyment except in the satisfaction of being expeditious. Any school librarian enjoys being able to handle a new book, become acquainted with its contents, and decide its use in the library as the book is being classified, cataloged, and otherwise made ready for use by teachers and pupils.

Most school librarians, however, inherit a library collection, the selection of which represents the judgment of many people. The librarian acquaints himself with the present collection and fits future selections into it. After some years, he probably moves to another school, another library, and another collection to which he likewise makes a contribution. Since this is the situation in which the average school librarian works, it is the situation with which this discussion concerns itself.

The Challenge of Selection

Charting a course in building a school library collection is not easy. Choosing the materials alone is a difficult task; trying to tell others how the job is best accomplished proves even more difficult. But the very difficulty of the task is itself a challenge.

In the first place, no two school library collections are identical, any more than two schools are identical. This is true of schools and their collections even in the same system. Two junior high school libraries in a city system offer a good example. One is in a school situated in one of the better residential suburbs of the city. The pupils come largely from privileged homes where they have access to books and magazines. The majority will continue through senior high school and a large percentage will eventually attend college. The courses of study are set up with this objective in mind and teachers rely a great deal on the use of library materials in their classes. The other junior high school is situated in a part of town where most of the pupils come from culturally retarded homes. Reading materials in their homes are limited and few of them use the public library. A large percentage of the pupils are slow and progress in school does not match their chronological age. Many will never complete high school; a very small number will be able to go on to college. Some are only waiting until they reach the age when school attendance is no longer compulsory. The curriculum contains some terminal courses with emphasis on the utilitarian, and teachers cannot always correlate library materials with their classwork in spite of the increased volume of low-reading-level, high-interest-level materials in many subject areas. Library collections in these two schools could not possibly be identical; indeed, they should not even be very similar.

The school library is only a part—albeit an important part —of the total school program. It has no objectives other than those of the school in which the library is located. A school library is indeed dependent on the school which supports it and which the library in turn serves. Thus the *library must always exist as a part of, never apart from, the school*. Its collection must be tailor-made to suit the individual school. This calls for a great deal of careful consideration and cooperation on the part of all concerned with selection for the school library.

There is probably no type of library in which selection is more important than in the school library. Here the collection has the dual purpose of enriching the curriculum and, at the same time, of serving the individual reading needs of the pupils. Overlapping occurs in this duality of purpose, to be sure. Often books which might be considered purely recreational serve as tools for sharpening reading skills or offer rich sources of information for a classroom situation. On the other hand, a book read for a class assignment may be of great interest to pupils. One book is sometimes chosen over another because it will serve both purposes rather than only one. Many books must be passed over, regardless of enticing reviews, because they promise to serve adequately neither purpose of the collection.

Often the school library provides the only source of reading materials to which some pupils have access. Many have very limited reading matter, if indeed there is any, in their homes. There are unfortunately many sections of the country not yet served by a public library. Where public libraries do exist, there are many children who make little or no use of their services. Unfortunately, it is also true that there are many schools which do not have libraries or offer only meager collections and mediocre service. Yet the fact remains that for many pupils the school library is apt to be their first, if not their only, contact with reading materials outside their textbooks. The school library collection *must* be good if pupils are to learn there to use materials for the enrichment of their school courses, as well as to read for pleasure, and to depend on library service, wherever it is offered, in later life.

Materials in a school library are generally on open shelves and thus easily available to young readers. There are no closed stacks—no "off limits" materials. Pupils are privileged to browse at will, especially among the books and magazines. In choosing for themselves, they get to know the materials rather intimately. Each selection for a school library constitutes a definite recommendation as to its suitability. Thus the school librarian who puts the final stamp of approval on a selection must be able to defend its inclusion in a rather limited collection.

Furthermore, the school library usually operates on a minimum appropriation and within the limits of a rather tight budget. Each piece of material must be carefully chosen for its genuine worth. It must carry its own weight. There is no place in a school library collection for dead material which merely occupies space on the shelf: reference books that fail to answer questions; books that do not circulate; magazines that are never read; pamphlets, clippings, and pictures that only fill up files; audio-visual materials that serve no real purpose. Since it is costly in both time and money to prepare materials and since weeding is a time-consuming process, it is advisable to eliminate in selection as much as possible of the only slightly useful material.

CONTINUITY AND COOPERATION IN SELECTION

Selection for the school library is a continuous process. No school librarian sets aside a day, or even a considerable part of a day, for selection. There is never a "book selection week." The librarian is not privileged to say: "Do not bother me because today I select materials." Instead he is *always* selecting. The school librarian who concentrates on selection only just before an order goes off loses half the fun of choosing materials and weakens his chances of building a strong, workable collection. Selection of materials is both warp and woof of whatever pattern of library service is provided for the school. Without a well-selected collection of materials, good library service is impossible.

The school librarian is chiefly concerned, of course, with new and recent materials. He glances over notices from publishers to see what they offer for future purchase. He eagerly checks each new supplement to the *Children's Catalog* or the *Standard Catalog for High School Libraries* wherein is concentrated the best selection of new materials. He watches for new editions of books which have proved useful but which need to be revised and brought up to date. If none seem available, the search is begun for other titles to replace the old ones in filling a particular need. Especially in the fields of the physical and social sciences, where new discoveries are constantly being made and new developments reported, it is important that materials be kept up to date. The librarian is likewise interested in additional titles by authors whose books are popular with pupils and useful to teachers. He also notes new writers who seem promising in various fields. As the latest issue of each current book selection aid arrives in the library, it is checked for new materials. The educational magazines are examined for possible additions to the collection since most of them review books. As time permits, the librarian scans the incoming general magazines which may offer free or inexpensive materials suitable for the information file or picture collection.

Often there are older titles which the library needs but has never purchased, so that the librarian occasionally looks again over standard book selection aids. This process is resorted to especially if there is need for a book on a special topic or by a given author. Indeed when a specific item of information is called for and the collection cannot supply it, the school librarian carefully combs every available source for a book or a pamphlet to meet the demand.

The school librarian welcomes every opportunity to discuss materials with teachers and other librarians. Such exchanges of ideas and pooling of knowledge are beneficial to all concerned and result in better selection. Any school librarian knows the stimulation of discussing books with other librarians and of learning about useful titles with which he is not familiar. In many school systems, city and county, the librarians are organized for the purpose of meeting regularly for book discussions, reviews, and other phases of book sharing.

North Carolina has adopted a plan of book reviewing by school librarians on a state-wide basis which might serve as a pattern for similar projects. Under the direction of the school library adviser in the state Department of Public Instruction, the state is divided into seven regions, each having a group of experienced school librarians who cooperate in reviewing. From the office of the school library adviser new books are sent to each group twice during the school year. Each book is read by two librarians who fill out a form giving all the needed information about the book. This includes full bibliographical data, coded information regarding the format of the book, and a meaningful annotation. From these review sheets, bibliographies are compiled and distributed to all school libraries in the state. In this way, new books are appraised by librarians who are familiar with the schools of the area and their needs, and the resulting information is made available to other school libraries while the books are new.

The school librarian examines books wherever they are available: on the shelves of the public library and other school libraries of the area, in bookstores and in exhibits at library and educational conventions. One of the difficulties in selection is that it is frequently impossible to see the books before they are purchased. Sometimes even books that are favorably reviewed prove disappointing when they arrive in the library. They may be good books but simply not suitable for the particular collection. Unless such materials have been received on approval, it may be difficult to return them to the dealer. Consequently, one must make every effort to see books before ordering them.

It is advisable for the librarian to make a card for the consideration file whenever he discovers a book which seems suitable for his collection. When the decision to order is made, he fills out an order card which is held with others. In the case of materials available free, or for a very small sum, he checks the source so that a pupil assistant may send a card with a printed form requesting a copy for his library. In this way, a simple routine for ordering selections may be established.[1]

Securing Cooperation from the School

Building the school library collection is not only a continuous process; it is also a cooperative venture. It might appear from the preceding discussion that the school librarian alone is concerned with selection. This is not true. While the school librarian, in the final analysis, is responsible for seeing that the selection of materials is accomplished and in many instances actually does the selection, no one person is capable of selecting materials in all fields. The wise school librarian will not attempt to do so. On the other hand, a school library collection comprising only teachers' selection will hardly prove balanced. The task of the school librarian is to coordinate all selection with the cooperation of teachers, administrators, and pupils. He must make sure that, so far as possible, all interests and needs are represented in the collection.

The librarian should, through faculty meetings and personal contacts, let teachers understand that they are not only privileged to, but expected to, select materials in their special fields. He

[1] Forms for the consideration file card, the order card, and the card requesting free and inexpensive materials are suggested in Azile Wofford, *The School Library at Work*. New York, H. W. Wilson Company, 1959.

should make available for their use all the book selection aids pertinent to various subject fields and levels of reading ability.[2] He will also keep teachers supplied with request slips which should encourage them to submit requests. He will notify teachers when orders are to be sent and give them a deadline for submitting requests. A well-organized system of selection and ordering should keep a fairly steady stream of requests coming to the library. The librarian should make a point of discussing books with teachers, calling new materials to their attention, and suggesting that they comment on new books or test materials with pupils in their classes. A faculty meeting once each semester might be devoted to a discussion of the library, including selection policies and procedures. Such a discussion would provide an opportunity to demonstrate book selection aids to teachers. It would also enable the librarian to understand the school curriculum better and so use materials more wisely in implementing it. Thus by various means the librarian can encourage cooperation in selection from all teachers.

Teachers vary widely in their attitude toward selection of materials for the school library. There are some who feel that the selection of materials in their special subject fields should be entirely in their own hands, forgetting that the school librarian also knows materials. Others seem to consider that the librarian is paid to "run the library" and therefore should select all materials. Some teachers request so many titles that the books cannot be purchased within the budget set up for their departments. Some, on the other hand, seldom if ever make any requests for purchase. Usually there is a close correlation between requests for new materials and the use made by various teachers of library materials. The teacher who knows materials, uses them with his classes, and keeps up with new publications in his field will be more inclined to work closely with the librarian in building the school library collection. Yet the librarian must be careful not to favor unduly the requests of the teacher who constantly demands materials, to the neglect of other fields in which the teachers seldom submit

[2] A bibliography of book selection aids appears with discussion in Chapter 2 and additional aids will be found in the Appendix.

requests. He must see to it that a fairly well-rounded collection of materials is available for use by all.

While administrators are not so close to the problem of selection as are the teachers, they should also cooperate in this area. Supervisors who know materials and appreciate their use in the processes of teaching and learning can prove especially helpful in building the school library collection. Perhaps their greatest contribution may come through suggesting materials and their sources to the teachers and encouraging them to request such materials for the collections in their own school libraries. Many a system of elementary school libraries owes its existence to a wide-awake supervisor who worked faithfully to secure a centralized library in each school. The school librarian will be wise to work with both general supervisors and those in special fields in the interest of building a good school library collection. The school principal should also be helpful in planning the library collection and particularly in interpreting its importance in the school program.

Pupils too should be made to feel that they have a part in the selection of materials for the school library. Request slips kept at the circulation desk may be used to record suggestions for the purchase of certain titles or of books by authors whose works are not found in the collection. The librarian should honor particular requests whenever possible. Even if the book requested does not seem suitable for the school library collection and cannot be ordered, the request does offer to the librarian a suggestion as to types of books desired or deemed suitable by pupils. Pupil requests may also indicate reading interests not already represented in the collection. It might be added that pupils may be taught to consult standard book selection aids, thus assuring their choice of standard and suitable books.

Many school libraries have benefited also from actual selection of materials by pupils in a certain grade or high school class, by pupil library assistants, or by members of the library club and other organizations in the school. Selection could be made a project directed by the teacher, the librarian, or the two working jointly. In ascertaining whether desired titles are already in the collection, pupils would have to make extensive use of the card catalog in the school library and would become better acquainted with what it already has to offer. This would also be an excellent opportunity for acquainting pupils, as well as teachers, with book selection aids, especially those prepared for readers. Pupils who are made to feel that the school library is theirs and are allowed to cooperate in selection of materials will be much more interested in the collection and will consequently use it more enthusiastically and efficiently.

As has been suggested, the process of selection in a school library is continuous and cooperative, and involves a great deal of coordination as well. This is hard to explain to anyone but a school librarian. No book should be selected for a school library simply because it is a good book or the collection does not have a copy. It must be evaluated in terms of its relation to a particular unit of study, a certain class project, a recognized group interest, or some other known need.

KNOWLEDGE OF EXISTING COLLECTION

Effective selection for a school library is based on a thorough knowledge of the existing collection. Indeed an intimate acquaintance with what is already available is a prime prerequisite for the selection of materials to be added. When the school librarian remains year after year in the same situation, his knowledge of the collection grows steadily as the collection itself grows. In the case of a change from one school to another, the librarian's first task is to become acquainted with the present collection. This in itself is no small task, however interesting.

The quickest source for consultation is obviously the shelf list. The librarian notes the number of books in each division of the Dewey Decimal Classification and checks the titles included. Some information as to the recency of the material may also be obtained from the shelf list. Study of the books on the shelves is the next step. Many titles will prove familiar, like the faces of friends in a gathering away from home. Books with which the librarian is not familiar may be removed from the shelves for additional and more leisurely examination. But a librarian can learn a great deal about books from a rather brief examination.

If the collection has been checked against the *Children's Catalog* or the *Standard Catalog for High School Libraries,* an excellent method for getting acquainted with the library holdings is already available. Many school libraries check titles in these catalogs which are already in the collection, adding call numbers beside each entry where the classification chosen differs from that suggested in the catalog. This checking enables librarians to see at a glance what proportion of the titles included in a standard list are in their library collections. It also helps teachers, when browsing through these catalogs for additional suggestions, to know what is already in the collection. Moreover, it furnishes a quick method of determining when ordering whether a desired title is already in the library. The handicap, of course, is that when the next edition of the catalog appears, the checking must be done all over again and this takes time.

As he uses the card catalog day after day in helping to locate materials for teachers and pupils, the librarian soon becomes conscious of gaps in the collection and makes the proper record, which will eventually lead to ordering certain missing titles. Soon he will feel quite at home with the new collection. Until such time, however, the librarian will find it extremely useful to study what is available in each division of the classification before adding new titles. Even when he is familiar with the collection, he must repeat this study periodically whenever he has funds for new purchases. He also gains knowledge of the collection as he classifies, catalogs, and otherwise prepares for use materials being added.

KNOWLEDGE OF THE CURRICULUM

The school librarian needs not only to know the collection, but also to be thoroughly familiar with the curriculum. This involves more than merely knowing the subjects taught and who teaches each subject in high school, or which teachers handle what grades in the elementary school. To do a thorough job of selecting materials to use with the curriculum, the librarian really needs to have a working knowledge of what the curriculum is and what materials are needed to enrich every phase of classroom work. He must understand educational objectives and be in accord with them. He also must understand the place of the school library in the modern educational program and what the librarian's relation to both is. He must know the school which his library serves, and the program which it offers. A very simple, but helpful, suggestion is for the librarian to familiarize himself with the textbooks used, especially bibliographies of materials included in these textbooks for which requests come from teachers and pupils.

It is desirable for the school librarian to serve on committees charged with discussion of the curriculum: initial planning, addition of new courses or changes in existing ones, any change of emphasis in teaching various subjects. If this is not possible, then it is the responsibility of the administration to keep the librarian informed of all curriculum developments in the school. The librarian should attend faculty meetings, especially those concerned with the curriculum or the teaching program when any discussion of library materials is involved. If he takes part in such discussions, the librarian may be able to suggest materials that are already available or may be obtained to implement the plans. On the other hand, absence or paucity of materials might result in shifting or temporarily postponing such plans. The administration deprives itself of the full service which a capable school librarian can offer if the librarian is asked only to supply bibliographies of materials or, even worse, to put references to materials into correct bibliographical form after the plans for the curriculum have been made and the resulting report is being prepared.

The school librarian should have the opportunity to visit classrooms. This is necessary if he is to know how effectively existing library materials are being used in classrooms and what types of additional materials are needed in the school library collection. Visits to classrooms are easily advised, but it is not always easy to carry them out. The question of time for the librarian is involved. Any school librarian always has more work than he will ever be able to accomplish. Duties that await attention and work that piles up are a normal part of his experience. Unless the librarian has an assistant, present usually only in large schools, it is difficult for him to be out of the library for classroom observation. When he is absent from the library, discipline problems may arise. And he always realizes that some pupils will not be able to secure needed materials without his help.

Another facet of the problem, of course, is that many teachers do not welcome what may look to them like needless observation on the part of the librarian. There is some reason for this. An additional person in the classroom may make it more difficult for the teacher and pupils to do their work in the usual way. And, unfortunately, there are some school librarians who have not yet learned how to make a meaningful visit to a classroom, or what to do as a result of their observation.

Problems inherent in classroom visits by the librarian might be solved by providing additional help for the librarian, professional or clerical. Observations should be made on a fairly regular schedule worked out cooperatively. The time would probably depend on when the librarian is free to go and when a visit would be most profitable to the class as well as to the librarian. If there is no help other than pupil assistants in the library, the librarian could probably best visit during a light period in the library when presumably pupil assistants could more easily carry on alone. Or perhaps he could get away when a teacher is available to take his place. However helpful classroom visits are, the school librarian cannot and should not make them at the expense of library service.

By working together closely, the teacher and librarian may arrange a meaningful visit for all concerned. It might be at a time when the class is beginning a unit and the librarian could introduce a group of books which should prove useful to the class, and he might also learn of other needs. He might plan with the teacher and the class a visit to the library to use materials which

may not be available elsewhere. The librarian could work with
the group there even while supervising other pupils. A high school
class preparing to write term papers might profit by a talk from
the librarian on materials available in periodicals and how to
locate them through the *Readers' Guide to Periodical Literature.*
An observation in any classroom should result in a better understanding of curriculum needs and the type of materials needed
to meet them.

The librarian will always find it helpful to observe classes
in reading when pupils read aloud or share their reading experiences. Class reports based on materials used in the library help
the librarian better understand what is involved. The school
librarian is sensitive to the effective use of library materials in
the classroom, welcomes every opportunity to observe classroom
work, and plans constantly how the school library collection may
better serve the entire school.

KNOWLEDGE OF BOOKS

In planning an adequate school library collection, the librarian must know books themselves—really know them. This applies
equally to the books that are already in the collection and to
those which are constantly being added. When all is said and
done, nothing quite takes the place of actual reading, especially
when working with children. With more adult readers, the librarian can often resort to quotations from reviews or statements of
opinion from those who have read the book. However, the young
reader wants assurance from the school librarian that he knows
what the book is about from actually having read it. How often
a pupil puts the librarian on the spot with the very simple but
realistic question: "Have you read it?" To be sure, no librarian
can read all the books offered to school library users, but he makes
an effort to read as many as possible. He keeps a book always
at hand for the extra minutes of waiting or for time at night
when sleep will not come. Even so, he can read only a sampling
of the many books available: an older book which he has never
read but about which some question has been raised, a book illus-

trated by a newcomer in picture books to observe his characteristic style, the latest book by a well-known author to see if he is upholding his usual standard of excellence in writing, a teen-age book, another science fiction tale, a book for lower grades on a technical subject, the newest medal award book, a mystery story for younger readers, an adaptation of a well-known classic, one of the new books for the beginner in reading, an adult book which promises to appeal to young people. In nonfiction, the librarian can learn a great deal from examining the book and reading portions here and there. It is almost necessary, however, to read in its entirety a book of fiction or biography in order to know the contents and test the book's flavor.

The busy school librarian also uses legitimate substitutes for actual reading. He discusses with pupils and teachers books which they have read, sometimes at his request. He listens to what readers returning books have to say about them. He reads reviews of new books in current book-reviewing periodicals and scans annotations in book selection aids. For still older books, a tool like Helen Rex Keller's *Reader's Digest of Books* (Macmillan, 1929), while not to be lent to pupils meeting reading requirements or writing book reports, can be very helpful for teachers and librarians who cannot find time to read all the books or who wish to refresh their memories of books already read.

School librarians will find especially helpful several books by Elizabeth Rider Montgomery which in chatty style furnish interesting facts regarding the writing of a selected number of books. Their titles are *The Story Behind Great Books* (Dodd, 1946), *The Story Behind Great Stories* (Dodd, 1947), and *The Story Behind Modern Books* (Dodd, 1949). Books for children and young people discussed in these range in time of publication from *Robinson Crusoe* by Daniel Defoe (1719) to the Petershams' *The Rooster Crows* (Macmillan, 1945), which won the Caldecott Medal. In age level, the appeal of the books discussed extends all the way from Robert McCloskey's picture book *Make Way for Ducklings* (Viking, 1941) to Owen Wister's *The Virginian,* which was first published in 1902. The latter has been labeled the first western and is still read by modern high school boys if they are introduced to it. Teachers also will find the Montgomery books helpful in interesting pupils in particular books by certain authors. Often something personal about the author or an interesting story as to how the author happened to write the book will encourage a reluctant reader to give it a try. Anecdotal material from the books which are recommended for grades six and up could also be used profitably by pupils to enrich reports about books which they have read.

The librarian also reads books about books and reading for children and young people [3]—books like *"Bequest of Wings"* (Viking, 1944), relating a mother's experience in introducing her own children to books and reading, and *"Longer Flight"* (Viking, 1955), which continues such family experiences into the adolescent years. Both of these are by Annis Duff, herself a former children's librarian. Lillian H. Smith, in *The Unreluctant Years* (A.L.A., 1953), and Amelia H. Munson, in *An Ample Field* (A.L.A. 1950), each gives a librarian's viewpoint on working with young readers, the former with children in the public library of Toronto, Canada, and the latter with young people in the New York Public Library. Two more recent books are Nancy Larrick's *A Parent's Guide to Children's Reading; For Parents and Teachers of Boys and Girls Under Thirteen* (Doubleday, 1958) and *A Teacher's Guide to Children's Books* (Merrill, 1960). The subtitle indicates that the former is more than a parent's guide. Both of these books have implications also for librarians working with elementary pupils. Such guides mention many books of interest to children at various ages and suggest ways to use them. Unfortunately, book lists tend to become outdated, though such guides are not extremely helpful without them. However, the principles of selection remain sound, and the librarian who reads them will gradually build up knowledge about many books which he has not had time to read. All of this is grist for the mill when the school librarian faces the task of selecting for the library.

[3] A comprehensive list of books about books and reading for children and young people will be found in the Appendix.

Biographies of Authors

Another rich source of information about books is found in biographical and autobiographical sketches of authors who write books for boys and girls. The autobiographical accounts especially give the reader a feeling of interviewing the author in his own living room, and having him explain how he became an author and how he happened to choose the subjects, regional backgrounds, or historical periods about which he has written.

Elizabeth Janet Gray, for example, reflects her father's Scottish ancestry in the biography *Young Walter Scott* (Viking, 1935), as well as in *Meggy MacIntosh* (Viking, 1930), a book of fiction about a Scottish girl, incorporating the story of Flora MacDonald in the early days of North Carolina history. The Quaker faith of Miss Gray's mother and eventually of herself is reflected in the biography *Penn* (Viking, 1938). It was largely because she was a Quaker that this author was chosen by the Emperor of Japan as a tutor for the Crown Prince following the Second World War. This experience resulted in her book *Windows for the Crown Prince* (Lippincott, 1952), which was written under her married name, Elizabeth Gray Vining, and was intended for adults, though it is read by many high school pupils. A fringe benefit for librarians in this biography consists of the books mentioned, which the author, herself a former librarian, used in helping the Japanese Crown Prince learn about America and the underlying principles of democracy. Her choice of titles proves stimulating even though other librarians may sometimes wonder at the selection.

The respect of school librarians and teachers for the many good books on science by Herbert Spencer Zim grows even stronger when they realize that the author has had experience as a science teacher in high school and later on the university level helping to prepare many prospective teachers in the science field.

The books on the Orient by Cornelia Spencer become more meaningful when the school librarian learns that the author's real name is Grace Sydenstricker Yaukey and that she is a sister of Pearl Buck. She was also reared in China and writes of it with authority.

Eleanor Estes and Doris Gates, both former children's librarians, are no doubt better able to write books enjoyed especially by girls because of the many small girl readers for whom they have chosen books. Both have drawn on incidents from their own childhood experiences to give their books a warm feeling of family security even when dealing with present-day problems such as are found in Gates' *Blue Willow* (Viking, 1940) and *The Hundred Dresses* (Harcourt, 1944) by Estes.

Robert McCloskey's first interest was music, then mechanics, both of which appear in his books. Finally he settled on art which, combined with his own stories, produced such picture books as *Blueberries for Sal* (Viking, 1948), *Make Way for Ducklings* (Viking, 1941), and *Time of Wonder* (Viking, 1957).

The most obvious source of materials about authors and the books which they have written for children is *The Junior Book of Authors,* second edition (Wilson, 1951). This book gives an interesting sketch, often autobiographical, of each author, usually accompanied by a photograph and a list of his books. It also includes many biographical sketches of illustrators of children's books. Each issue of the *Wilson Library Bulletin* features sketches of two recent authors. The school librarian should not only read these sketches of the authors of books for children and young people, but should build an alphabetical card file of their names and the issues in which each sketch appears, so that the material may be located quickly when needed again. There should also be a section of the vertical file reserved for authors, in which biographical material clipped from book jackets, newspapers, and magazines is kept in alphabetical order by name of the author.

Current Biography, published monthly except August by the H. W. Wilson Company, includes sketches of recent authors, many of which are of interest to high school students. The sketches appearing in the monthly issues are reprinted in a single alphabet at the end of each year in the annual *Current Biography Yearbook.* In the index by professions at the back of each yearbook, authors are listed under the heading "Literature."

Similar material on illustrators of children's books, many of whom are authors as well, is found in *Illustrators of Children's*

Books, 1744-1945, compiled by Bertha Mahony Miller (formerly Bertha Everett Mahony) and others (Horn Book, 1961), and in *Illustrators of Children's Books, 1946-1956,* compiled by Ruth Hill Viguers and others (Horn Book, 1958).

More recently Bertha Mahony Miller and Elinor Whitney Field have compiled a wealth of material about a selected group of authors and artists under the titles *Newbery Medal Books: 1922-1955* (Horn Book, 1955) and *Caldecott Medal Books: 1938-1957* (Horn Book, 1957). These books constitute volumes one and two of the Horn Book Papers containing the "acceptance papers and related material chiefly from the *Horn Book Magazine.*" Librarians working with children and young people look forward after the medals are awarded each year to reading this material in *Horn Book Magazine.* It is most helpful to have it gathered together between book covers with additional material and editorial comments. The various awards for books for younger readers and their significance in selection of materials for school libraries are discussed in Chapter 19.

The alert school librarian will also watch for biographical material on authors of books for young readers in other sources, such as collections of biographies, books discussing periods of literature, and books dealing with careers. He will probably want to make analytics for the card catalog for material on authors found in such books.

An excellent source for information about authors is obviously any individual biography of an author of a book for young readers. Some years ago a surprisingly large number were listed in a brief study of this field.[4] A similar study made now would undoubtedly produce a bibliography more than twice as long, since many such biographies have been written in recent years, including some for elementary readers. Pupils themselves should be encouraged to read these and the librarian will find them enlightening.

[4] Azile Wofford, "List of Biographies of Authors of Books Read by Young People." *English Journal.* 30:377-82. May, 1941.

READING ABILITY OF PUPILS

Another factor which enters strongly into selection for the school library is the reading ability of the pupils who use the library. Selection must be made, for example, not only for fifth grade readers but for the fifth grade readers of a particular school, be they retarded, normal, or superior, or more likely a combination of the three. The librarian, to be sure, knows the levels which his library serves: elementary, junior high, senior high, or any combination of these. He needs also to know the percentage of those who are reading on their normal grade level and of those reading below or above. Pupils in the same grade vary widely in their ability to read. After pupils learn to read, there are at least three levels of reading ability in any one grade: those reading below the normal, those reading at the expected grade level, and those reading at a higher level. Teachers of the fourth and fifth grades find that pupils in their classrooms may read all the way from the first grade level to the ninth. Books selected for one grade may always be expected to be read by at least three grades. Books at the fourth grade level, for instance, will be read by normal fourth grade readers, by slow readers in the fifth and sixth grades, and by good readers in the third grade. This is one outstanding advantage of the centralized school library as opposed to classroom libraries where the materials are available only to pupils of one grade. The fact that several reading levels may use the same material tends to widen their use; it also makes for more material in the given collection. All of this has significance for librarians and teachers building a school library collection designed to satisfy the reading needs of all pupils.

The school librarian makes every effort to ascertain the reading level of individual pupils who use the library. Though it may prove a difficult task, the librarian should if possible learn the names of all pupils. Through experience he should also attempt to identify pupils as normal readers, slow readers, or superior readers. Such knowledge of reading ability comes from visiting classrooms, from conferences with teachers, and from school records showing the level of pupils' reading achievement.

One experienced librarian, visiting a fourth grade reading class, discovered what the inexperienced teacher had not been told and had not yet realized, namely that the entire group was retarded in reading. The librarian and teacher, in the light of this realization, were better able to work together in finding materials that the pupils could read. As a result, before the school year had closed, many were no longer retarded. Elementary school pupils are often asked to read for the librarian a portion of a book before taking it from the library. This not only helps the librarian choose a book that the pupil can read successfully; it also indicates to him the level at which the pupil is reading. On the high school level, the librarian should analyze the pupils' requests for books as an index of the level at which they can read.

The librarian should certainly have access to any of the pupils' tests—IQ tests, tests to determine reading ability, even personality tests—which might throw light on the pupils' performance in reading. The file of folders in the principal's office about individual pupils also proves helpful to the librarian in understanding reading problems. The librarian is fortunate also in being able to talk with teachers about the children's reading.

If individual reading records are kept in the school library, they should also furnish much needed information. Both the IQ and the reading ability of each child may be indicated in code on his reading card. The record of materials borrowed from the school library will to some extent indicate the pupil's reading ability and interests. Knowledge of both is extremely helpful to the librarian building the collection.

The junior high pupil, by way of example, who continues reading biographies in the Childhood of Famous Americans series, published by Bobbs-Merrill Company and intended for grades four to six, is almost certain to be a retarded reader. One of his classmates looking for a biography of Einstein, because of his interest in mathematics in general and Einstein's theory in particular, gives every indication of being a superior reader in interest if not in ability—probably in both. These and other signs point the way in book selection.

READING INTERESTS

Reading interests of pupils must also be considered carefully in any program of selection. The beginning librarian will have learned during his training that certain group interests seem common to all children at various stages of their development. He will learn from experience, however, that no reader follows a set pattern and that no two are identical in their reading interests.

Pupils in the first three grades are normally interested in nursery rhymes, picture books, easy books, and simple stories. These books should be about animals, especially dressed-up animals and talking beasts; familiar objects, like their toys and pets, children and their families; and community helpers, such as the milkman, fireman, and policeman. The eight-year-olds, especially girls, never seem to get enough of fairy tales, and boys begin to show interest in hero stories, tall tales, and simple legends. While at first this group must be read to and told stories, they are aided in becoming more independent by the recent trend of publishers to produce books expressly for the beginning reader.

In grades four to six, the world in which the pupils live expands and, while they are still interested in stories about children like themselves, they also like books about children of other countries. The past becomes significant and they progress from tales of their parents' childhood to days of long ago, the pioneer days in America, and back to the first men in their rude caves. This is also the age of interest in cowboys and Indians. Both boys and girls enjoy books of adventure, true and fictional, especially if there is a slight element of mystery. They enjoy almost any type of folk tales to which they are introduced: fairy stories, fables, myths, and legends. An early interest in nursery rhymes will transfer naturally to poetry, especially if parents and teachers fan this interest by reading poetry with them. Both boys and girls enjoy stories of family life and school, though boys prefer the stories when they have an added element of sports. Books about animals, ranging from domestic pets to wild animals in their natural habitats, are very popular. Informally written biographies appeal to children of this age group and they read simple books of nature and science. About the age of twelve, unless they are retarded readers, they are apt to read widely and constantly, as if there might not be time for all the books waiting to be read.

During junior high school days (grades seven to nine) reading interests expand quite naturally to include biographies of people who have lived heroic lives or made some outstanding accomplishment. In fact, biographies are popular at almost every level and children read them like fiction. Pupils in junior high school are interested in actual history, and travel in books to faraway places. Their interest in animals is apt to concentrate on fewer animals, especially dogs and horses, though they still enjoy reading about jungle animals and the adventure of bringing them back alive. In books of fiction, they continue to enjoy adventure, mystery, and home, school, and sports stories. Pupils in grades seven to nine, especially the boys, are avid readers of war stories, some junior high school librarians reporting that they cannot supply the demand. The girls enjoy teen-age stories with ever so slight a romance, and some begin to explore the more adult love stories. Boys ask for science fiction and for both books and magazines about hot rods. Reading of career fiction, formerly a high school interest, now occurs largely at the junior high level, though interest in career stories generally seems on the wane. Boys do serious reading in science also, with emphasis on atomic energy, outer space, and space travel. Both boys and girls seek books that will help them with their problems of growing up and their relations with the opposite sex.

On the senior high school level (grades ten to twelve) reading interests gradually tend to become more adult. By the age of sixteen, so far as is known at present, reading interests and reading habits are rather well fixed and fairly comparable to those of adults. More magazine reading will normally be done by high school pupils, both for reference work and for pleasure. They read various types of literature: poetry, plays, short stories, and the more objective type of essays. Interest in essays, however, seems to be waning. High school pupils read adult biographies, books of history and travel, books promoting international understanding and eventual world peace. Boys explore the various branches of pure science and the girls find new interests in books on music, art, and other creative subjects. Both are interested in reading books on human relations, a reading interest from fourth grade up when books are available, and are concerned with finding their place in a complex civilization. The budding interest on the part of most girls during junior high school in books about etiquette, dating, and other topics involving the opposite sex expands into more serious reading concerning going steady, marriage, and family life, now that early marriages are more common. In recent years there has been a trend toward standardization, with pupils showing interest in the same subjects regardless of age or sex. This is probably due to the universality of television programs viewed by all ages. Some of the subjects appealing to most readers of school age are heroes, western life, and various phases of space travel.

With experience, the school librarian will learn also that there are individual reading interests among pupils in addition to, or often as a substitute for, group interests. These interests sometimes spring from some project in the classroom which sends a boy to read everything the library offers on chivalry, Indians, or space ships. Such interests may be encouraged by a trip the pupil has made, a collection he is building, or an insect he finds on a leaf. They are often stimulated by programs heard over the radio or seen on television. A movie based on a book or one portraying places in distant parts of the globe may be the current incentive for reading. An individual reading interest may even be without rhyme or reason. Usually interests of this type are not long lived and present problems in the selection of materials to meet needs that may be of brief duration.

There are also some reading interests that are peculiar to the region in which the school is located, for example, the avid interest in horses in the bluegrass region of Kentucky, marine life in many parts of Florida, and skiing and mountain climbing in the Rocky Mountains.

The librarian in schools in which pupils of minority races or from foreign countries are enrolled may discover reading interests that are national, or cultural, in nature. For example, Negro children in the South normally seem to read more material of a religious nature than do white children. They also seem to enjoy modern fairy tales and stories of a similar nature. Negro children generally do not seem to prefer books with characters of their own race and tend, as do all other children, to shy away from books which include dialect because of its difficulty. The school librarian will find stimulation in discovering reading interests which seem peculiar to any group. Sharing his findings would also help other librarians in reading guidance with pupils of various races and nationalities.

Reading interests of pupils in each individual school should be studied whenever possible by the librarian. Such interests are evident from circulation records, from cards in the readers' file, when one is used, and from requests for reading guidance which reach the librarian. They are also indicated by the request slips submitted by pupils for material to be purchased by the library. The librarian senses reading interests when talking to the pupils and to their teachers regarding the books which they are reading and enjoying. The librarian new to a given school situation might well have each pupil fill out a one-page questionnaire regarding his reading and sources from which reading materials are available. This questionnaire might include a checklist of subjects about which children like to read so that each pupil could indicate his preference. Such a device might be used at other times, though not so often as to become routine and thus defeat the purpose of the survey.

School librarians interested in studies of reading interests of school age children may wish to consult *What Boys and Girls Like to Read,* by George Whitefield Norvell (Silver, 1958). This book offers more practical help than the author's earlier book, *The Reading Interests of Young People* (Heath, 1950), which studied reading interests in the rather limited selections offered by high school texts for the study of literature.

A BACKWARD AND A FORWARD LOOK

Building the school library collection is one of the most interesting of many tasks which the librarian undertakes. It is also one of the most important. Selection is basic to all library service, for without a good collection neither reference work nor reading guidance functions well and no adequate teaching of the use of the library is possible. To direct selection, the librarian needs to know as much as possible about the books available for young readers, the people who write and/or illustrate these books, and the publishers who produce them. He must fully understand educational objectives and be thoroughly acquainted with the curriculum of the particular school of which the library is an integral part. To choose adequate materials for use in classrooms, the librarian needs to understand classroom procedure and the contribution of library materials to the learning process. He must be aware of reading interests, both group and individual, and be able to select books to meet the demands. He must also realize that interest in reading is often curbed by the child's inability to read at the normal level for his age and grade. The collection must take cognizance of the needs of retarded readers. At the same time, it must offer material suitable for superior readers who are too often neglected in the school library program.

To this end the librarian should know and use as many standard book selection aids as are available, including the current book-reviewing periodicals. He should not only use them himself but make every effort to acquaint teachers with their availability and their value, and to encourage them to use the standard aids. The annotated list of book selection aids which follows in Chapter 2 should help the school librarian to evaluate and choose those aids deemed indispensable in his own library. While it is true that much good material for school libraries is not included in book selection aids, the bulk of the collection will consist of choices from standard lists. The beginning school librarian is well advised to rely heavily on book selection aids, at least until he is better acquainted with readers and materials.

At the same time, the school librarian needs to understand the criteria for the selection of materials applied to books which are included in standard aids. These are largely the same criteria which must be applied to a book which the school librarian examines without benefit of the opinion of others. These criteria are discussed in Chapter 3, and should prove helpful to the selector.

The way of selection in the school library as presented here may seem long and difficult. Yet in essence the process is fairly simple. The teacher needs a book of a certain type, about a given subject, for a particular grade. Together the teacher and librarian exhaust every means at hand until they find what seems to be the best book available for the stated purpose. When the librarian finally checks the entry to be ordered, back of its selection lie years of study and training, a knowledge of books and their producers, experience in selecting books for young readers, and a deep sense of intrinsic values in reading for boys and girls. The pupil who reaches for the book on the shelves, who pores over the pages at the library table, or curls up on the window seat to enjoy it, and announces on its return that this is the best book he has ever read makes the task of building the school library collection seem all the more worth while.

AIDS FOR SELECTION

The Role of Aids in School Library Selection

In the preceding chapter, the school librarian was advised to make every effort to examine materials before purchasing them. The average school librarian, however, has all too little opportunity to do this.

Bookstores offer the most convenient opportunity to examine current materials. Yet many schools are located in small towns or in rural areas where there are no bookstores, or where existing ones carry a relatively limited stock. Even in adequate bookstores the school librarian hesitates to examine very many books when the chances are he will not make large purchases there because bookstores generally cannot compete with book jobbers in the amount of allowable discount.

In some instances, the office of the state department of education, or that of the local city or county superintendent, maintains a collection of books to which teachers and librarians have access. However, such a collection, made up most frequently of review copies from publishers, can never be complete or up to date. Also there is usually little or no evaluation of the collection for potential use in school libraries.

Other library collections in the area offer some opportunity for examination, but one school library will not be likely to have current materials much earlier than the others, and the collections of books for children and young people in a public library, because of their somewhat different function, will not contain some materials essential in the school library.

At annual conventions of teachers or librarians, the publishers' exhibits are always helpful, provided there is time to give them more than a cursory examination. The Combined Book Exhibit, Inc., with headquarters at 950 University Avenue, New

York 52, New York, supplies for conventions a comprehensive collection from the recent output of many publishers, including books for children and young people, of interest to school libraries.

Books on Exhibit, Irvington, New York, has a nation-wide service which supplies several hundred junior library books, kindergarten through high school, representing recent publications of a number of publishers. This service is free of charge, except for shipping charges to the next place, to any school or library agreeing to make the exhibit available to others in the local area. The exhibit is usually scheduled for at least a week on the understanding that a minimum of one hundred teachers and/or librarians will avail themselves of the opportunity to examine the books. In addition to the book collection, printed catalogs of titles with bibliographical data and brief annotations are available for distribution. An exhibit of mounted book jackets for display purposes is also included.

Since books in such exhibits have not been evaluated as to their suitability for school library collections, librarians and teachers must select from them with care.

Book dealers offer the privilege of "books on approval," but usually only to libraries which submit large orders and only when other books are ordered.

While school librarians are always urged to make every effort to see and examine materials before selecting, most selection for the school library is made from lists of books. Fortunately, there are now available a number of excellent lists of materials compiled by experienced teachers and librarians, which include sufficient information to serve as guides in selection. School librarians who have recently come into the profession can hardly realize, as can the pioneers in school library development, the problems of building a collection without present-day book selection aids. Selection made entirely from standard aids would assure a creditable school library collection, although much good material is not included in any of them. The inexperienced librarian should adhere closely to the recommendations of standard book selection aids and even the experienced librarian relies heavily on them.

A rather fully annotated list of book selection aids is presented here for several reasons. It is a fairly complete list of the best and most recent general aids.[1] There is a discussion of the contents and arrangement of each which makes the list intelligible to the uninitiated. The specific help offered by each book selection aid is indicated. The school librarian should consequently be able to decide which aids should be most helpful in building the collection in his own school library.

GENERAL SELECTION AIDS

Children's Catalog; a Catalog of 3,310 Selected Books for Public and School Libraries, ed. by Dorothy Herbert West and Rachel Shor. 10th ed. New York, H. W. Wilson Company, 1961. 915p. $12.00.

In existence since 1909, the *Children's Catalog* provides a list of books for school libraries on the elementary and junior high school levels and for children's collections in public libraries. Inclusion in the *Children's Catalog* is determined by votes of consultants selected in cooperation with two divisions of the American Library Association in Chicago: the American Association of School Librarians and the Children's Services Division. Cataloging, classification, and preparation of the annotations are done by the editors, who are on the staff of the H. W. Wilson Company in New York City.

There are two main parts: Part 1, "Classified Catalog," and Part 2, "Author, Title, Subject, and Analytical Index." These are followed by Part 3, "List by Grades," and Part 4, "Directory of Publishers." The classified section includes books in all ten divisions of the Dewey Decimal Classification, with additional sections for "Fiction," "Easy Books," and "Story Collections." Because of their rather ephemeral nature, pamphlets are not listed.

Each entry in the classified part contains full bibliographical data: author's name as it appears on the title page; the title and any subtitle; the edition if other than the first; the name of the joint author, illustrator, translator, or compiler; the publisher,

---

[1] An additional list of book selection aids will be found in the appendix.

date, and series, if the book belongs to one. The number of pages in the book, the price, and the grade level are also given. There is a suggested Dewey Classification number; subject headings and analytics are designated. There are annotations, often quoted from other sources, for every entry in Part 1.

A star beside an entry shows that the book is especially recommended by the consultants and a double star that the book is most highly recommended. The preface of the *Children's Catalog* explains in some detail how the consultants vote for titles to be included and the basis on which certain books are starred or double-starred.

The index, in addition to listing each book by author, title, and subject, where a subject is necessary, includes analytical subject entries for parts of books when these have not been brought out by the general subject, title analytics for all folk tales and fairy tales in collections, and both author and title analytics for all short stories and plays in collections.

In alphabetical place in the index section of the *Children's Catalog* will be found lists of books which have won the Caldecott and Newbery awards.

The *Children's Catalog* is kept up to date by supplements that appear annually. The entire catalog is revised every fifth year, at which time all books in the main catalog and in the supplements which are still in print are considered for inclusion in the new edition· along with more recent titles.

The *Children's Catalog* is an indispensable aid in selecting and ordering school library materials. It is also very helpful in classifying and cataloging them. A copy of the latest edition should be in every elementary school library. Because it covers materials through the ninth grade reading level, it is helpful in junior high school libraries as well.

Standard Catalog for High School Libraries; a Selected Catalog of 4212 Books, ed. by Dorothy Herbert West, Estelle A. Fidell, and Rachel Shor. 8th ed. New York, H. W. Wilson Company, 1962. ca 1060p. $15.

Since its first edition in 1926, the *Standard Catalog for High School Libraries* has served as a guide in the selection of materials for junior and senior high school libraries and for collections serving young people in public libraries. The same method of selecting for inclusion by vote of consultants is used in this list as in the *Children's Catalog*.

The arrangement in two main parts is likewise the same. There is, of course, no section of "Easy Books" in the "Classified Catalog" or "List by Grades" in the back of the *Standard Catalog*. There is, however, a "Directory of Publishers," and, on the inside back cover, a list of sources from which annotations have been taken, with an appropriate abbreviation for each source. At the beginning of Part 3, "Directory of Publishers," there is a selected list of pamphlet and paperback series which the consultants found useful.

The reading level is designated by *j* to indicate usefulness for junior high school, and by *s* for senior high school use. Those titles having neither designation may be considered useful at both levels. Material especially suitable for trade schools is designated by *t*. Stars and double stars are used as in the *Children's Catalog*.

Standard Catalog for High School Libraries is kept up to date by annual supplements. The latest edition should be in every junior high and senior high school library. The junior high school library should also have a copy of the *Children's Catalog*, as was mentioned earlier.

A Basic Book Collection for Elementary Grades, comp. by Miriam Snow Mathes, with the assistance of consultants from the American Library Association, Association for Childhood Education International, Association for Supervision and Curriculum Development, Department of Classroom Teachers of the National Education Association, National Council of Teachers of English, and National Science Teachers Association. 7th ed. Chicago, American Library Association, 1960. 136p. $2.00.

A Basic Book Collection for Junior High Schools, ed. by Margaret V. Spengler, with the assistance of consultants representing the American Library Association, Association for Supervision and Curriculum Development, National Council of Teachers of English, Department of Classroom Teachers of the National Education Association, and the National Science Teachers Association. 3d ed. Chicago, American Library Association, 1960. 136p. $2.00.

A Basic Book Collection for High Schools, comp. by a subcommittee of the American Library Association Editorial Committee, Mariana Kennedy McAllister, Chairman, with the assistance of consultants from the Association for Supervision and Curriculum Development, National Council for the Social Studies, National Council of Teachers of English, and the Department of Classroom Teachers of the National Education Association. 6th ed. Chicago, American Library Association, 1957. 186p. $2.75.

The three "Basic Book Collections" are valuable for several reasons. They are indispensable in choosing books for a new library collection where *basic* materials are of prime importance. These lists are fairly simple for the uninitiated in school library work to use. They are valuable in checking a collection, either for the purposes of evaluation or in making decisions when materials are to be weeded. Many school librarians find it helpful to check their holdings with the appropriate list, placing a check mark beside each title in the library and indicating the classification number beside the entry when the library has not used the classification number suggested by the "Basic Book Collection."

The arrangement is approximately the same for each list. There is a section for each of the ten main classes of the Dewey Decimal Classification system with a separate section for "Fiction." The list for elementary grades includes a special section, "Picture Books and Easy Books." Each of the lists for high schools includes "Short Story Collections." There is in each list a directory of publishers and an index in which the listed numbers refer to entries rather than to pages. Each volume contains a section on magazines suitable for the appropriate grade level. The list for senior high schools also contains a section on "Aids for Selection of Audio-Visual Materials and Equipment."

Each entry carries the usual bibliographical data and an annotation. It suggests a classification number and subject headings. The symbol (W) indicates availability of Wilson printed cards and the list for senior high schools also includes the Library of Congress card number. Only the volume for elementary grades designates the grade level of books included.

In addition to the titles—about a thousand—listed in each "Basic Book Collection," others are mentioned in the annotations.

Bibliography of Books for Children. 1960 Edition. Washington, D.C., Association for Childhood Education International, 1960. 134p. $1.50.

This list of books, compiled by a committee of which Elizabeth Hodges, Supervisor of Library Service, Baltimore County Board of Education, Towson, Maryland, is chairman, aims "to suggest a limited group of quality books on a variety of subjects for children from four through twelve years of age"—chosen because of the "probable appeal of each book to its potential readers."

It is arranged alphabetically by broad subjects, beginning with "Animals of All Kinds" and extending to "Science," each subject having many subdivisions. There is a special new section of "Books for Beginning Readers" including both "Stories" and a brief list of "Fact Books."

There is also a list of Newbery and Caldecott medal winners, and at the end of the book are title and author indexes.

BOOK SELECTION AIDS INTENDED FOR USE BY AND WITH READERS

Adventuring with Books, prepared by the National Council of Teachers of English, Elementary Reading List Committee, Muriel Crosby, Chairman. Champaign, Ill., National Council of Teachers of English, 1960. 146p. 75c.

Your Reading; a List for Junior High Schools, by the Committee on the Junior High School Book List, Alice C. Baum, Chairman. Champaign, Ill., National Council of Teachers of English, 1960. 109p. 75c.

Books for You; a List for Leisure Reading for Use by Students in Senior High Schools, by the Committee on the Senior High School Book List, Anthony Tovatt, Chairman. Rev. ed. Chicago, National Council of Teachers of English, 1959. 130p. 60c.

These lists, intended for use by pupils, emphasize books for leisure reading rather than for curriculum use. The arrangement of entries is alphabetical by author under broad subjects of interest and appeal to the group of readers for which each list is intended.

Bibliographical data are kept to a minimum. *Books for You* includes only the author and title. *Adventuring with Books* gives the reading level by ages. *Your Reading* has two special signs: A star means that the book seems to be very easy to read; a dagger indicates a book which seems challenging to young readers. Annotations are rather brief but generally adequate.

Each list has both an author index and a title index. *Adventuring with Books* includes a form for explaining the Dewey Decimal Classification to children.

Book Bait; Detailed Notes on Adult Books Popular with Young People, comp. for the Association of Young People's Librarians; ed. by Elinor Walker. Chicago, American Library Association, 1957. 88p. $1.25.

Prepared primarily for librarians who work with young people in public libraries, *Book Bait* contains help also for the school librarian both in book selection and reading guidance. Miss Walker is the librarian in charge of work with young people in the Carnegie Library of Pittsburgh.

The arrangement is alphabetical by author and the list includes both fiction and nonfiction, some old and some new titles.

Each entry gives, in addition to the usual bibliographical data, "a summary of the story, suggested uses for the book, notes on material for book talks and individual reading guidance, information about special features, and suggestions for follow-ups."

The annotations are sufficiently long to refresh the memory of the librarian about books which he has already read and to acquaint him with books which he has not read.

At the end of the list are the section "Suggestions for Using This List" and a title index, including books mentioned in addition to the ninety-three books which are analyzed fully.

Patterns in Reading; an Annotated Book List for Young Adults, by Jean Carolyn Roos. 2d ed. rev. Chicago, American Library Association, 1961. 127p. $2.25.

This list is designed to be used by young people and the adults who work with them in any relation connected with books and reading. It is arranged alphabetically by seventy-five subjects suggesting reading interests of young people, ranging from "Adventure and Mystery" to "World War." Under each subject, the arrangement is by title in a suggested progressive order, usually beginning with a simple book and leading to others with the same general interest that are more difficult or more adult. In addition to bibliographical data, each entry has a fairly brief annotation suggesting the nature of the book. Both fiction and nonfiction are included. In the second edition, three fourths of the titles are new and nearly thirteen hundred are adult books. There is an author and title index.

The chief use of this list for school librarians is in the field of reading guidance. It may also provide suggestions of additional books to purchase when more material on a given subject is needed.

Miss Roos, now retired, was for many years Supervisor of the Youth Department of the Cleveland Public Library and lecturer in the field of young people's literature at Western Reserve University's Library School.

Treasure for the Taking; a Book List for Boys and Girls, by Anne
Thaxter Eaton. Rev. ed. New York, Viking Press, 1957. 322p.
$4.

A rather comprehensive guide designed to help adults—
parents, teachers, and librarians—choose books for children, first
for a collection either in the home or in a school or public library,
then to find "the right book for the right child" from either
collection.

From her long experience as librarian of the Lincoln School
(elementary) of Teachers College, Columbia University, Miss
Eaton has chosen many books, both old and new, which children
continue to read and enjoy. Most of the titles included are still
in print; a few older ones are included, though marked out of
print.

The list is arranged alphabetically by title under broad subjects, such as "Ancient Civilizations" and "Wild Animals Everywhere." Each entry includes, besides the bibliographical data, a
fresh, helpful annotation and statement of reading level by age,
preschool through fifteen, rather than grade. There is an index
of authors and titles.

AIDS FOR SELECTION OF MATERIALS BY SUBJECT

Subject Index to Books for Primary Grades; comp. by Mary K.
Eakin and Eleanor Merritt. 2d ed. Chicago, American Library
Association, 1961. 167p. $4.50.

Subject Index to Books for Intermediate Grades; comp. by Eloise
Rue. 2d ed. Chicago, American Library Association, 1950.
493p. $6.00.

This series of subject indexes began with the 1939 *Subject
Index to Readers* (now out of print) in which more than 300
readers and some 250 books of the nonreader type were analyzed.
Much of this material was later incorporated in the first edition
of the *Subject Index to Books for Primary Grades,* but the original
index is still useful for older titles in school library collections.

These indexes are arranged alphabetically by subjects used most often in schools, ranging from aardvark to Zuni Indians. Under each subject will be found the author, title, and paging of the books which are analyzed and in which material on the given subject will be found. The grade level for which the material is best suited is also noted.

The generous use of "see" and "see also" references is helpful. By a series of letters and combinations of letters, the indexes call attention to some special uses of certain books that many teachers may find valuable. On the primary level stories are included for reading aloud, with indication of the groups for which they will be suitable.

At the beginning of each volume is a "List of Books Indexed" arranged alphabetically by author. This list may be used as a purchasing guide when material on certain subjects is needed. The asterisk beside many entries in the *Subject Index to Books for Primary Grades* indicates that material is of a fictional nature.

Types of books listed are readers, picture books, song books, handicraft books, easy stories and collections of stories, and other books of information, especially in science and the social studies.

These subject indexes are helpful in school libraries for two purposes: (1) to locate material on various subjects for units being studied; (2) to select books on subjects needed in the collection.

AIDS FOR SELECTION OF CURRENT MATERIALS

The Booklist and Subscription Books Bulletin; a Guide to Current Books. Published semimonthly, September-July, and only once in August, by the American Library Asociation. $6.00.

The editor of the above-named publication is Edna Vanek. The book reviewing sections of most interest to school librarians are: "Children's Books," Helen E. Kinsey, editor; and "Books for Young People," edited by Barbara Joyce Duree. The latter section is intended for readers aged fourteen to eighteen and includes both adult books especially suitable for this age group and books written for teen-agers. There are frequent cross references to books reviewed in the section for younger readers and in the section for adults.

In addition to bibliographical data, there is included a brief descriptive annotation based on a reading of the book. A classification number is suggested for nonfiction and subject headings are given for all books. Availability of Wilson printed cards is indicated and the Library of Congress catalog card number is given.

An additional section, "List of Free and Inexpensive Material," is cited here as being of particular interest to school libraries.

The first section of *The Booklist and Subscription Books Bulletin* is generally devoted to reviews prepared by the Subscription Books Committee of the American Library Association and the views expressed represent the collective opinion of this committee.

Each issue features one or more rather extensive reviews of books, usually in sets, that are sold on subscription, that is, subscriptions for which are often taken before publication and which are obtainable directly from the publishers or their agents. Generally speaking, the types of books reviewed include dictionaries, encyclopedias, atlases, expensive reference books, and expensive sets of books for family use, especially for children.

The review gives a rather full description of the publication, including scope, authority, and other criteria, and notes its good points and shortcomings, its special features, and its potential use. The title is either recommended or not recommended and, in case of a recommendation, the type of library collection is specified. Inclusion for review, therefore, does not constitute a recommendation. When there is a new edition, the Subscription Books Committee again includes the title for review, with reference to any former reviews.

School libraries should also find helpful a new publication, *Subscription Books Bulletin Reviews, 1956-1961,* a compilation of reviews from *The Booklist and Subscription Books Bulletin* (A.L.A., 1961).

Before purchase, every title of a reference nature should be checked in *The Booklist and Subscription Books Bulletin.* If not available in the school library, this selection aid should be consulted in the local public or college library. Administrators also need to be aware of this valuable guide against which to check books offered by agents in the school office. This is also a valuable aid to use with parents who consult the librarian about sets of books offered for sale in the home.

For reference books in general, other than large sets, the section "Current Reference Books" in each issue of the *Wilson Library Bulletin* is valuable. For a number of years this has been written by Frances Neel Cheney of the Library School of George Peabody College for Teachers.

Bulletin of the Center for Children's Books. Published monthly except August by the University of Chicago Press for the University of Chicago, Graduate Library School. $4.50.

This current book reviewing publication of about fifteen pages includes some sixty to seventy-five entries in each issue. The present editor is Mrs. Zena Bailey, and Sara I. Fenwick is acting supervising editor. The title of the book reviewing section is "New Titles for Children and Young People."

Each entry gives full bibliographical data, with price and an annotation. The reading level is normally given by grades, kindergarten through grade nine, except that occasionally it is designated instead by age.

Not all the books included are recommended. By means of a code, it is indicated whether or not each book is recommended, whether it is considered as marginal, or for use only if additional material of its type is needed. The code also indicates two special categories: (1) books whose subject matter or treatment limits their use to special collections, and (2) books whose appeal is to the unusual reader, so that purchase is recommended for the special few who will use them.

The Horn Book Magazine. Published six times a year by the Horn Book. $5.

This is the oldest magazine devoted exclusively to the field of books and reading for children and young people. Principally devoted to book reviews, it is edited by Ruth Hill Viguers and several assistants. Some fifty or more books are covered in each regular issue.

Reviews are divided into the following groups: "Picture Books"; "Stories for the Younger Children" (ages 6-8); "Stories for the Middle Years" (ages 8-11 or 12); "Stories for the Older Boys and Girls" (ages 11 or 12-14 or 15); "Of Interest to Adults." In addition, within each of these groups the reviews are sub-divided by subject interest. All reviews are signed, with initials when done by regular staff members, with full names of guest reviewers. All books included are recommended with certain qualifying statements as to the readers for whom the book might have special appeal or prove of unusual value.

A separate section, "The Outlook Tower," edited by Margaret C. Scoggin, Director of Young People's Services, New York Public Library, highlights current adult books which interest high school pupils and a few books written for teen-agers.

The lack of indication as to specific age or grade level has always been a handicap in using the *Horn Book Magazine* in the selection of materials for school libraries though there has been an improvement since June 1959 with the inclusion of boxed notices, "Booklist Groupings," which give the age levels noted above. The value of the magazine, however, would be further enhanced by the citation of proper age level with each review.

Library Journal. Published twice a month, September-June, monthly in July and August, by R. R. Bowker Company. $10.00.

School Library Journal. Published monthly, September-May, as part of the *Library Journal,* but paged and obtainable separately. $3.50.

School Library Journal, which prior to September 1961 was called *Junior Libraries,* is one of the most helpful periodicals for the school librarian, especially in the field of book selection. The editors of the book review section, "Junior Books Appraised," are

E. Louise Davis and Patricia H. Allen, assisted by a Book Review Advisory Committee which acts "as a board of review of the appraisals and especially of the stars used" in each issue.

All new juvenile books, except textbooks, are examined and those chosen for review are as follows: (1) books distinguished by high literary or artistic quality or outstanding presentation of factual material, (2) otherwise average or mediocre books unique or unusual in some respect, and (3) books from generally reliable sources of such poor quality as not to warrant purchase.

The reviews are in three sections: "Preschool and Primary Grades"; "Grades 3-6"; and "Junior High Up." They are written (and signed) by school and public librarians who work with children and young people, chosen because of special knowledge in the fields of the books which they evaluate. Each review attempts to supply "information on scope or background, age or grade level, authenticity, uniqueness or relative standing among other books on the subject, curriculum applications, suitability of format, serviceability of publishers' bindings, etc."

A star is used to indicate books recommended; a double star indicates books that even the smallest collection will want. In addition to being starred a book may be noted as "recommended," "highly recommended," or, in some instances, "not recommended." This indicates that both favorable and unfavorable reviews are included. Occasionally under the heading "Difference of Opinion" is another review of the same book. The Book Review Advisory Committee may state a different opinion from that of the book's reviewer. These "Difference of Opinion" reviews and those designated as "Supplementary Opinions" prove useful for school librarians wavering in their choice and unable to examine the book.

The book reviewing service of the *School Library Journal* is especially helpful in the matter of format, since a code of letters is used in the description of each book to show its physical make-up. For example, CSm designates a cloth-bound book which has been Smyth sewn. A "Key to Symbols" explaining the code used is included in each issue.

An additional section, "Books for Young Adults," is in the charge of a special committee. The reviews are brief and unsigned, with frequent references to books reviewed for adults in the "New Books Appraised" section of the *Library Journal*.

At this point, mention should also be made of the *School Library Journal's* annual list of *Best Books for Children,* which many school librarians find useful. Published by the R. R. Bowker Company, the 1961 edition was edited by Patricia Allen, one of the publication's book review editors.

Saturday Review. Published weekly by Saturday Review, Inc. $7.

The section "Books for Young People" appears once a month, usually in the third issue of the month. Mary Gould Davis was the first editor and, after her death in 1956, the section was edited by Frances Lander Spain, Director of Children's Services, New York Public Library, until September 1959.

Following Mrs. Spain's retirement, this section was edited by members of the faculty and of the Publications Department of the Bank Street College of Education in New York City. Beginning July 15, 1961, Alice Dalgliesh became editor of "Books for Young People." Editor of books for young readers at Scribners from 1934 to 1960, Miss Dalgliesh has taught both in elementary schools and at Columbia University. She is also the author of several books for children and young people.

There are usually two pages, one consisting of a discussion of new books on a special subject, the other of brief reviews of about twelve to fifteen new books. The March 19, 1960, issue, for example, featured an article on encyclopedias, "Riches for Youthful Research," by Irma Simonton Black, author of books for children. The reading level of each book is indicated by age, rather than grade, and extends through junior high school. Not all of the books included are recommended.

SELECTION FROM SOURCES OTHER THAN BOOK SELECTION AIDS

The book selection aids previously discussed, certainly when taken in combination, present, both in quantity and quality, the "cream of the crop" in materials for school libraries. At the same time, much good, usable material never finds its way into any book selection aid. Often it is obvious why certain titles are not included; others may seem just as good, or even better, than titles which are included. Any experienced school librarian could compile his own list of overlooked titles.

To find acceptable material not included in standard book selection aids, the school librarian must have a firm sense of values in books and must apply his judgment rigorously; otherwise, he may weaken the collection with mediocre, even shoddy, material. He must check every possible printed source: bibliographies in textbooks and other books, suggested materials in educational periodicals, lists compiled by school librarians and often available through the state department of education, and material mentioned in articles about books and reading for children. The school librarian also examines materials available outside his own library. He welcomes suggestions from teachers and fellow librarians. In other words, the school librarian leaves no stone unturned in the effort to unearth every bit of material useful in building the school library collection.

○

CHAPTER 3

CRITERIA OF SELECTION

When a school librarian holds in his hands a book which he has never before seen, of which he has read no review, and which has not yet been included in any book selection aid, he faces the same problems that confront the reviewers of books for library publications or book selection aids. For what shall he look? What criteria of evaluation must any book meet to pass the acid test of suitability for the school library collection?

AUTHORITY

The school librarian, like others of the library profession, is interested primarily in the author of the book. Like Clifton Fadiman, he probably holds the theory that "a book is not as good as its subject, but only as good as its author." If the author is already well known and highly regarded, the book immediately recommends itself for serious consideration. If the author is not well known, the title page, foreword, or introduction will probably offer some clue to his qualifications for writing. This will be indicated by any position he holds or has held, organizations with which he is identified, or a statement about other books which he has written. As time permits, the school librarian will undoubtedly look for further information about the author in the biographical sources described in Chapter 1. In any event, a mental note of the unknown author's name will be made and the librarian will watch for information about him.

As the librarian checks the author's qualifications, he will also look for an account of sources of information used in writing the book. Statements of sources are apt to be less conspicuous in books for young children than in those for high school pupils. At the same time, any bibliography of sources will be indicative of materials accessible to the author and consequently should be noted. Sources are also sometimes mentioned in the part of the book devoted to acknowledgments.

It is important, for instance, that the author of a biography have had access to the person's letters and other writings, and if possible have talked with those who knew him. In the case of a book about a foreign country, it is important to know whether the author has traveled or lived in the country and has first-hand knowledge of the things about which he writes. Even the simplest book of science should be based on the author's years of study and perhaps experimentation in the field. Authority, or the lack of it, shows up quickly on close examination of a book.

There are many excellent writers of books for children and young people. In Part II, "Materials for Selection," there are introduced what may seem to the uninitiated an overwhelming number of authors. Many make a career of writing for young readers. Others are subject specialists, in one or several fields, who prefer to write on the level of elementary school or high school pupils. Sometimes they are outstanding writers of adult books with an occasional book of interest to high school readers. Many books in high school libraries are written by professional writers who are accurate researchers with an innate ability to choose and use their original authorities with discrimination. The one thing which these writers all have in common is that their books ring true with a note of authority.

SCOPE

To the selector for the school library collection, the book's scope is very important. The first source of information as to scope is the table of contents with its chapter headings and other subdivisions. In some books, a collection of literature for example, the table of contents would very quickly indicate the scope of the volume without need for further examination.

In history the scope may be as broad as the world or as narrow as the boundary of the reader's own state. It may be confined to ancient times or cover only the history of the past decade. A book of biography may be collective biography, including brief sketches of many persons, or a full-length biography of only one person. In the case of an individual the biography may cover his entire life, tell only of his childhood (a rather popular trend in biography for the very young), or emphasize the accomplishments of the biographee's productive years, especially his contribution to the life of his own times. A work on science may deal with general science or it may treat only one small facet of science. In social studies the scope of the book may fall into any one of the many subdivisions of this wide field: folklore, government, social life and customs, to mention three.

The scope of a book of fiction would probably place it as to type: an adventure story, a book about animals or children of other lands, science fiction, historical fiction, or a book involving some modern social problem, a rather common subject on any reading level.

Determination of scope is furthermore a guide in the consideration of the potential use of the book, discussed later.

RELIABILITY

There are two main facets of reliability, part and parcel of each other and of the book itself, both important in evaluation: accuracy and up-to-dateness. Accuracy in statement of fact is important in any field; up-to-dateness is most important in science, the social studies, and other subjects involving rapid change and/or growth.

The copyright date of a book offers some clue as to the recency of material. It is not the only criterion. Authors often face the problem of having material become outdated even as they write, and time is needed for publication. Nevertheless, pupils even in elementary schools should have the latest information available on such subjects as atomic energy, electronics, and space travel. Books in these and other fields in which there is rapid change should be as current and accurate as possible when they are added to the school library. New or revised editions of books already in the collection should be considered as they are published. Weeding of outdated material should also be a continuous part of building the school library collection. In checking a book for recency, the school librarian will do well to note dates of books cited in bibliographies and dates of information given in charts and diagrams.

For accuracy of statement, the school librarian will make an effort to check material on some phase of the subject against a well-known authority. He should also consult the teacher in the school who is a specialist in the field. This practice gives the librarian an opportunity to call new materials to the attention of teachers. Besides, no librarian has time to keep up fully with all fields, even if he should have the background and the interest for such an effort.

TREATMENT

Related to consideration of the book's scope and reliability is the question of how the material is treated. This can be determined only by some study of the contents.

In nonfiction, especially if the book is informational in nature, the librarian would do well to read a few passages at the beginning, the middle, and the end of the book. Another helpful test is to read part of the book dealing with a subject with which the selector is familiar: Argentina in a book on South America, stars in a book on science, the librarian's native state in history or geography, the Civil War in American history, one's own profession in a book on vocations.

The selector also needs to be conscious of any bias displayed by the author, prompted by sectionalism or political affiliation, prejudice in favor of or against the subject in hand, and the like. This is most important in books of a controversial nature or on debatable subjects. It will also be a stronger factor in selection for high school than for elementary school libraries.

While fiction needs to be read in its entirety to obtain the full flavor of the book, the busy school librarian seldom has time to do so when selecting. He therefore devises ways and means of determining how the author handles the plot and whether he is able to make the characters come alive. One dips into some books, skims others, hunts the high spots, ferrets out the climax, and scans the final chapter.

One of the most important aspects of treatment is the author's purpose in writing the book. Is it intended for general reference, factual information, pure recreation, or inspiration? Other factors to be considered are whether it is brief or full, simple or technical in language, practical or theoretical.

READABILITY

This phase of evaluation holds a more prominent place in selection for a school library than for other types of libraries because both teachers and the librarian are accustomed to thinking in terms of "reading level" or "grade level." Also, the school library serves all pupils and must provide for each grade materials on various levels of readability.

As the librarian evaluates a book, he determines the approximate grade in which pupils normally would be able to read the book. He constantly checks the grade levels suggested for books under consideration that are included in book selection aids. In discussing books with teachers and in selecting books for individual pupils, the librarian must always consider the grade level, especially in elementary schools. Some school librarians when cataloging indicate by an inconspicuous code, for the benefit of teachers and the librarian, the grade level of each book. It is most unwise, however, to label and shelve books by grades and to require pupils to read only from books intended for their grade level, as is done in some school libraries. There is too much variation in reading abilities of pupils in each grade for this to be a sound practice, however much it may seem to simplify the librarian's task or meet with the approval of teachers.

While the subject of readability is too broad for full discussion in a limited space, some very simple suggestions may prove helpful in checking a book for readability.

For the very young, the print should be fairly large. Some authors resort to writing in script as being simpler for beginning pupils to read, though some teachers and librarians feel that script in some books is confusing to the pupil learning to read. A few modern books are printed in all large capital letters, a feature which may also confuse the beginning reader. Rather short lines of type with plenty of space between the lines are helpful. The sentences themselves should be short and fairly simple. The words should be within the range of those who will read the book and new words should be introduced gradually. The unfamiliar words used should not be too numerous and should be repeated as often as is possible without resulting in monotony.

There should be a generous use of storytelling pictures which amplify the text, even as the text amplifies the pictures. Little children are attracted to pictures that are in color, have a childlike humor, and are free from a great deal of detail. Being attracted by the illustrations, they ask questions about them, listen to the story, and eventually read the books for themselves. (A fuller discussion of picture books and their illustrators will be found in Part II.) Books for older children naturally devote less space to illustrations and more to reading material. Well-chosen pictures supplementing the text continue to enhance the value of books for the elementary school library, but become less essential as the reading level approaches high school.

The vocabulary should continue to include words with which the children to whom the book is addressed are largely familiar. At the same time, the book should include words which stretch the ability of pupils to read if they are to develop reading skills. The print should be good in all books for school libraries and the leading between lines sufficient to avoid a crowded appearance on the page. This is especially important for pupils who have any difficulties with vision as well as for slow or retarded readers who hesitate to choose a book with "so much reading on a page," since the printed word is for them a deterrent.

SUBJECT INTEREST

Whether a pupil will actually read a given book depends not only on his ability to read but also on his interest in its subject matter. Any experienced school librarian has seen a slow reader plow through a book difficult for him because of his interest in the subject. On the other hand, a good reader will soon put down a book if the subject does not appeal to him. Interest depends both on the choice of subject matter in relation to the group for which the book is intended and on the skill of the author in presenting the subject. A good rule of thumb is that any child's book interesting to an adult will also probably interest the child. Reading interests of children, both group and individual, were discussed for various ages in Chapter 1; experience in school library work makes the selector conscious of these reading interests, and helps him discover others.

Good writing is no less necessary in books for children than in adult books. That is one reason why school librarians are "author conscious." Pupils want books of information to be straightforward, not sugar-coated. They want books of fiction written for them, but not written down to them. They want all books for children and young people to be genuinely good, honestly written, and of special appeal to their interests.

When the school librarian is evaluating any book, he mentally notes the group for which the book will have the greatest appeal. Sometimes, he thinks in terms of an individual pupil or the class of a certain teacher. He considers grade level and interest level, which may coincide for average readers. Gifted pupils are not only able to read, but would probably be interested in reading, material beyond that intended for pupils of their grade. The retarded reader, on the other hand, because of his need for information, will often be interested in material beyond his ability to read. This poses a problem in selection and causes the school librarian to search for books combining high interest level with low level vocabulary. Further discussion of this will be found in Chapter 16.

FORMAT

All books intended for school library use should be reasonably attractive in format. This implies a bright, colorful cover, preferably with some decoration in addition to the author, title, and other information necessary to identify the book. The cover should somehow entice the young reader to investigate its contents, whether the book is located on the shelves or on a reading table.

The paper should be of good quality. Cream or an off-white color is better for the reader's eyes than glaring white. The print, as mentioned earlier, should be fairly large, especially in books for pupils in grades one to three.

Firm sewing should be used when the book is bound into its covers, or else the book should be reinforced before being put into circulation. Many publishers now furnish books with some type of reinforced bindings, variously known in the trade as "library editions," "library bindings," etc. Otherwise, books may be secured in reinforced bindings from book dealers, both regular jobbers and those who specialize in prebound books, and from some binderies. Many school librarians, especially on the elementary level, purchase all their books prebound or specify certain ones to be furnished with reinforcement. If books are to be rebound satisfactorily after use, they should have sufficiently wide margins on the inside of each page to allow trimming and resewing.

Illustrations should be numerous in all books for children in grades one through three and in books of an informational nature, especially in science and the social studies, for older pupils. In books of a recreational nature, illustrations should have a story-telling quality. In informational books, illustrations should add to the teaching value of the text. Diagrams are very useful in books of the "how-to-do-it" type. Photographs showing social life and customs are very helpful in books about people of other countries, especially as regards costumes. Drawings based on careful research serve the same purpose in books about early times in our own country. The practice of placing all photographs together in the front, back, or the middle of a book is deplored since they are more useful in school libraries when interspersed through the text.

Special Features

The school librarian looks for special features which would make the book even more useful to teachers and pupils. Examination for special features always includes the index, without which no book of nonfiction is very useful as a reference tool. Special features also include such things as: bibliographies for each chapter or for various sections and/or at the end of the book; questions and answers, though these are remindful of the textbooks; a list of suggested things to do, including experiments or an assortment of possible projects; a glossary of terms, especially in books using foreign or other unusual words, giving pronunciation and explanation of meaning and use; charts and diagrams; maps and other atlas features; and any other helpful material of an appendix nature. In a school library, where collections are too often limited and demands are both wide and heavy, special features may contribute beyond the expectations of authors and publishers.

Through experience the school librarian will find that certain publishers are well known for producing superior materials in certain fields and will check the publisher as part of the evaluation of any book.

Potential Use

Any discussion of criteria of selection leads inevitably to the potential use of the book in the particular collection for which it is being considered. The school library is probably concerned more than other types of libraries that no book be added which is not calculated to make a distinct contribution to the school for which the library exists. Potential use is therefore one of the considerations of paramount importance in selection for the school library.

While many potential uses necessarily overlap, the following uses suggest themselves. Books, pamphlets, and magazines are needed in a school library to:

1. Meet the needs for reference work, either as a part of the special reference collection or as a good book with an index in a subject field.

2. Offer factual information on a given subject from the historical standpoint, as background reading, or for specific facts in developing a variety of classroom units.

3. Help pupils with their personality problems and with their adjustment to today's world.

4. Serve as a source of material which teachers and librarian may use for reading aloud or telling stories to children.

5. Widen knowledge and understanding of other lands and other peoples and the conditions under which they live and work.

6. Offer understanding of cultures other than the pupils' own and eventually expand their sphere of understanding.

7. Furnish material for programs, especially relating to holidays and their meaning.

8. Help pupils and teachers keep informed about current events.

9. Open fields for exploration in connection with hobbies or other special interests.

10. Answer needs for recreational reading of many types.

11. Help develop esthetic tastes, either through writing or illustrations.

12. Give inspirational values.

13. Serve the needs of retarded readers because of low vocabulary, high interest level.

14. Furnish more mature reading for young adults, especially the superior readers.

PART II

MATERIALS FOR SELECTION

CHAPTER 4

o

"LET'S LOOK IT UP": REFERENCE BOOKS

It would not be practical or even desirable to include a complete list of reference books for the school library collection in this volume. Reference books vary from school to school, as do other materials, according to needs. Besides, space limitations prevent a full discussion of reference materials. In any school librarian's preparation there will be a course dealing with reference books, including those for school libraries. There are also reliable selection aids for reference books, as discussed in the last section of this chapter. This chapter merely aims to consider the general types of reference books needed in any school library, with some suggestions as to desirable titles.

A word might be inserted here as to the criteria that determine whether a book belongs in the reference collection. Generally speaking, all books containing information so general that they cannot be classified elsewhere belong in the reference section. Books which provide brief factual answers to many questions are also often found in the reference collection. In fact, almost any book of nonfiction with a good index may be regarded as a reference book.

Increasingly in the school library constant need is an important factor in deciding that a book should be placed in the reference collection where it will be available at all times. Teachers should prove helpful in advising about certain books in their own fields. Occasionally a book on a special subject is kept in the reference section because its size or cost make it unsuitable for circulation. It is assumed, to be sure, that such a book lends itself to reference use, either because of the nature of the material included, or because of some special feature, such as numerous or outstanding illustrations. It is also assumed that other books on the subject would be available for circulation to those interested. However, there is nothing against having one copy of a book in the reference collection and another copy for circulation, and this is done in many school libraries.

ENCYCLOPEDIAS

The backbone of any school library reference collection consists of encyclopedias on the various levels of reading ability. When any reference question is presented to the busy librarian, the first response is apt to be: "Have you used the encyclopedia?" The school librarian often consults the encyclopedia first when looking for information on an unfamiliar topic. The teacher is likely to suggest at the beginning of a unit of study that background material be obtained from the encyclopedia. In learning to use the library, pupils are usually advised to begin with the encyclopedia on almost any topic studied, though even simple research will eventually lead to other types of material.

The elementary school library will need the latest edition of one, or more, of the following: *Britannica Junior; the Boys' and Girls' Encyclopaedia* (Encyclopaedia Britannica), *Compton's Pictured Encyclopedia and Fact-Index* (Compton), and *The World Book Encyclopedia* (Field Enterprises). The high school library, certainly on the junior high level, will also need *Compton's* and *The World Book,* and some senior high school libraries include them as well for readers who cannot easily read the more adult encyclopedias. High school libraries will also include *Collier's Encyclopedia* (Collier), *Encyclopedia Americana,* published by the Americana Corporation, and perhaps the *Encyclopaedia Britannica; a New Survey of Universal Knowledge* (Encyclopaedia Britannica) for the more advanced pupils. School librarians are advised to purchase the latest printing of each encyclopedia used in the library about every five years, staggering purchases so as not to buy more than one new set in a given year. Most multiple-volume encyclopedias now follow the policy of "continuous revision," with some revising and updating in each new printing.

Lincoln Library of Essential Information (Frontier Press, 1961), which has gone through twenty-five editions, will prove useful in any school library. The subject divisions contain some information not easily available elsewhere, and the full index quickly locates desired topics. Some high school libraries may also want to include the one-volume *Columbia Encyclopedia* (Columbia University Press, 1956), now in its second edition with a supplement added in 1959, for brief information on many subjects. Neither of the one-volume encyclopedias, however, can take the place of a set of multiple-volume encyclopedias.

DICTIONARIES

For the very young children in elementary schools, the library should provide, by way of introducing dictionary use, some good first dictionary of the picture book type. A good title is *The Golden Dictionary*,[1] by Ellen Wales Walpole (Simon & Schuster, 1944), with 1,030 words arranged alphabetically with pictures in color. Under some words, for example animals, there are pictures of many kinds of animals, each of which is named. For an older group, grades two to four, there is available *The Rainbow Dictionary*, by Wendell W. Wright, assisted by Helen Laird (World Publishing, 1959), first published in 1947, consisting of over 2,000 entries of words, listed alphabetically, which children should recognize. Its chief value lies in the definitions of words, since neither pronunciation nor plural forms are indicated.

For upper elementary pupils, there should be one or more of the abridged dictionaries published by Funk and Wagnalls, Merriam, or Holt, Rinehart & Winston. Some teachers prefer one of the dictionaries prepared under the direction of the late Edward L. Thorndike, psychologist and educator of Teachers College, Columbia University, and compiler of the Thorndike word lists. Titles are *Thorndike-Barnhart Beginning Dictionary* (1959) for younger elementary school pupils; *Thorndike-Barnhart Junior Dictionary* (1959) for upper elementary school pupils; and *Thorndike-Barnhart Advanced Junior Dictionary* (1957) for junior high school pupils. These dictionaries are published by Doubleday but are also available from Scott, Foresman.

[1] Since 1960 new printings of this and other publications in the Golden series have borne the Golden Press instead of the Simon & Schuster imprint.

Though unabridged dictionaries are found in elementary school libraries, inclusion might be questioned on the ground of their difficulty for pupil use. However, some school librarians insist that an unabridged dictionary be included in any elementary school library for the good students and as a final authority for the teachers.

High school libraries, on the other hand, will need the latest edition of either or both unabridged dictionaries: *Funk and Wagnalls' New Standard Dictionary of the English Language* and *Webster's New International Dictionary of the English Language,* the latter published by Merriam. Some high school librarians select either the second edition of *Webster's* as "the oldest and most famous American Dictionary," or *Funk and Wagnalls'* because of its emphasis on the current, rather than the historical, meaning of words, and do not consider it necessary to have both unabridged dictionaries. Other librarians, who feel that high school pupils need to know both dictionaries and to learn how to use them, purchase a copy of each. The fact that the second edition of *Webster's* is now available in two volumes (Merriam, 1959) may affect the choice. Although more expensive than the one-volume edition, this does have the advantage of allowing more than one pupil to use the dictionary at the same time. The most recent edition of *Webster's,* with the full title *Webster's Third New International Dictionary of the English Language,* published late in 1961, is radically different from the earlier editions of this work, omitting such encyclopedic features as the gazetteer and the biographical dictionary and basing the inclusion and definition of words solely on current usage rather than on traditional standards of correctness.

There should also be a selection of good abridged dictionaries on the high school and college level for ordinary dictionary use in high school libraries. Among the best known are the *American College Dictionary,* edited by Clarence L. Barnhart (Random House, 1956); *Funk and Wagnalls' New College Standard Dictionary,* edited by Charles Earle Funk; and *Webster's New Collegiate Dictionary* (Merriam, 1960). The last one is the largest abridgment of the second edition of *Webster's New International Dictionary of the English Language,* with 125,000 entries, many illustrations, and several supplementary sections.

In addition to English language dictionaries, a high school library will need at least one dictionary for each foreign language taught in the school. This is also true of the libraries in elementary schools which offer courses in foreign languages. Junior and senior high school libraries should have the new, revised edition of *Roget's International Thesaurus; the Complete Book of Synonyms and Antonyms in American and British Usage* (Crowell, 1959), or some book of a similar nature. *The New Roget's Thesaurus of the English Language in Dictionary Form* (Putnam, 1961) may prove even more useful in school libraries because it is much easier to use. This volume was edited by Norman Lewis and is "based on C. O. Sylvester Mawson's alphabetical arrangement of the famous Roget system of word classification." Elementary school libraries which encourage word study may also need a thesaurus. Some librarians may also classify with the reference books some titles on words, their origin and use, suggested in the section "Words and Their Use" in Chapter 6.

YEARBOOKS

For quick information, a yearbook is probably the reference tool most often consulted. Practically all of the major encyclopedias keep their publications up to date with some form of annual supplement, usually called a yearbook. Some school librarians prefer not to include this service with the purchase of an encyclopedia because the yearbook is often different from the set of encyclopedias, both in the nature of its contents and the arrangement, and thus proves difficult for pupils to use. If the yearly supplement consists of loose-leaf pages, there is the further problem of keeping it available for use. Other librarians select one encyclopedia with a good yearbook and exclude this annual feature with other encyclopedias.

Two other yearbooks, usually referred to as almanacs, are used as often in school libraries as encyclopedias and dictionaries.

They are the *World Almanac and Book of Facts,* published continuously since 1868 (New York World-Telegram), and the *Information Please Almanac* (McGraw). Though these books are obtainable in paper covers, it is recommended that all reference books, because of their constant use, be purchased in cloth bindings or be rebound before being made part of the collection. A copy of the *World Almanac* is indispensable in any school library, elementary as well as high school, as a source for statistics and general information. The older volumes continue to help with subjects omitted in succeeding volumes. The *Information Please Almanac* contains much information about events of the year not easily obtainable elsewhere.

Two other annuals are useful in high school collections: *Statesman's Year-Book,* a manual of information about governments of the world (St Martin's), and *Statistical Abstract of the United States,* obtainable from the Superintendent of Documents in Washington, D.C. In addition to the *Statesman's Year-Book,* some school libraries may also wish to consider the latest edition of *International Year Book and Statesmen's Who's Who,* published in London by Burke's Peerage. Larger and more attractive in format than the *Statesman's Year-Book,* the latter contains, in addition to information about international organizations and the countries of the world, a biographical section of brief "sketches of some eight thousand world leaders in government, church, commerce, and industry."

Biographical Reference Tools

The most quickly available source of biographical material is that found in the unabridged dictionaries. In the older *Webster's* this is located in a separate section at the back, while in *Funk and Wagnalls'* the names are included in the regular vocabulary of the dictionary. There is a wealth of biographical material, of course, in all of the general encyclopedias. Useful also is *Webster's Biographical Dictionary; a Dictionary of Names of Noteworthy Persons with Pronunciations and Concise Biographies,* edited by William Allan Neilson (Merriam, 1961). Still useful for older names is *Thomas' Universal Pronouncing Dictionary of Biography and Mythology* (Lippincott, 1930), formerly known as Lippincott's. This book will probably be in many of the older high school libraries though it is at present out of print. More recent is the *New Century Cyclopedia of Names* in three volumes, edited by Clarence L. Barnhart with the assistance of William D. Halsey (Appleton, 1954). This book contains geographical and biographical names, names of organizations, and titles of such things as national songs, paintings, operas, and books. For larger high schools with adequate budgets, the *Dictionary of American Biography,* in twenty-two volumes (Scribner, 1928-1944), should prove helpful for information about people no longer living.

For information about outstanding living men and women, high school libraries will probably want *Who's Who in America,* published every other year by Marquis. For many years this was kept up to date by *Who's Who in America Monthly Supplement,* with a cumulative index. This was discontinued in 1959.

Because of the demand in schools for information about people who are currently prominent in the news, a useful publication is *Current Biography,* published monthly except August by Wilson. For each year a cumulative yearbook includes in one alphabet all biographies in the monthly issues, with an index by professions and a necrology. Many school libraries wait to purchase the annual volumes rather than subscribe to the monthly issues. This practice is strongly recommended for school libraries with limited budgets. Some libraries subscribe to both the current issues and the yearbook and permit each year's monthly issues to circulate after the yearbook has been received.

Especially helpful for information about authors and illustrators of books is the Kunitz-Haycraft authors series, also published by Wilson. Since all books in this series are listed with full bibliographical information in the *Standard Catalog for High School Libraries,* school librarians can easily locate them. Probably the most useful are *Twentieth Century Authors* (1942) and its *First Supplement* (1955), and *The Junior Book of Authors* (1951), now in its second edition. The latter, which includes illustrators as well as authors, will also prove useful in an elementary school library. Each entry in these volumes provides an interesting sketch, often autobiographical, about the author or illustrator, usually accompanied by a photograph.

Available also are several biographical dictionaries of outstanding persons in various fields, such as music or science, which may be needed in high school libraries in which much reference work on these subjects is done.

INDEXES

Essential in school libraries will be indexes to materials of various kinds according to the grade levels served by the library: fairy stories, plays, poetry, quotations, and short stories. Because school libraries are called upon to supply so much material on various subjects, subject indexes are always helpful. Special attention is called to the second edition of *Subject Index to Books for Primary Grades* (American Library Association, 1961), compiled by Mary K. Eakin and Eleanor Merritt. A similar book, *Subject Index to Books for Intermediate Grades,* compiled by Eloise Rue, is now in its second edition (1950); it too is published by the American Library Association, which reports plans for further revision. These indexes are discussed in Chapter 2, above. Every school library which keeps back issues of magazines for reference work will need either the *Readers' Guide to Periodical Literature* or the *Abridged Readers' Guide to Periodical Literature,* depending on the number of magazines to which the school library subscribes. Both of these indexes are published by Wilson.

ATLASES

Two atlases which will prove useful at any level are *Goode's World Atlas,* formerly *Goode's School Atlas,* now in its eleventh edition (Rand McNally, 1960), and *Hammond's Ambassador World Atlas* (Hammond, 1960). An elementary school library may prefer *Hammond's Illustrated Atlas for Young America* (Hammond, 1960), the subtitle of which reads "Full Color Maps and Up-to-Date Facts with New Concepts About Our Physical and Political World." A senior high school library might wish to include *Encyclopaedia Britannica World Atlas* (Encyclopaedia Britannica, 1961). For the junior high school which can afford only one atlas, the *Rand McNally International World Atlas* (Rand McNally, 1961) will prove a good choice. Senior high school libraries which can afford a copy of the *Columbia-Lippincott Gazetteer of the World* (Columbia University Press, 1952) will find it very helpful. This volume lists in one alphabet the names of, and information about, most geographical features of the world.

REFERENCE BOOKS IN OTHER FIELDS

In addition to reference books of a general nature, there are a number of individual reference books in various fields that almost any school library would need. Only a few can be noted here, though examples could be multiplied many times over. The United States Department of Agriculture's *Yearbook of Agriculture* contains a wealth of material useful in courses on agriculture. Each yearbook has a different subject; *Grass* (1948), *Soils* (1957), and *Seeds* (1961), are examples. They are all obtainable from the United States Superintendent of Documents. A free copy is usually obtainable on application to the congressman from the district in which the school library is located. *American Red Cross First Aid Textbook; Prepared by the American National Red Cross for the Instruction of First Aid Classes*, now in its fourth edition revised (Doubleday, 1957), is useful in any senior high school library. The junior high school library, and perhaps the elementary school library will find useful the second edition of *First Aid Textbook for Juniors* (Doubleday, 1953). *Henley's Twentieth Century Book of Formulas, Processes and Trade Secrets* is considered a must in many high school libraries. Originally edited by Gardner Dexter Hiscox, it has been revised and enlarged by T. O'Connor Sloane (Books, Inc., 1957). The high school chemistry teacher should help to decide whether to purchase a copy. The third edition of *Van Nostrand's Scientific Encyclopedia* (Van Nostrand, 1958) covers a wide variety of scientific subjects from aeronautics to zoology, which are called for often in high schools.

Because of the demand for simple science experiments in the elementary school, a book dealing with this subject will prove acceptable. Of several available, two may be mentioned. *Science Experiences; Elementary School,* by Bertha Morris Parker (Row, 1959), offers a great many suggestions for teachers, yet is simple enough for children to use as well. *Making and Using Classroom Science Materials in the Elementary School,* by Glenn O. Blough and Marjorie H. Campbell (Holt, 1954), may be mentioned as a practical book for the science teacher.

Used often by clubs and other groups studying parliamentary procedure is *Robert's Rules of Order,* by Henry Martyn Robert, in a revised edition (Scott, Foresman, 1956). Any high school library will want a good book of etiquette in its reference collection, such as Emily Post's *Etiquette, the Blue Book of Social Usage,* now in its tenth edition (Funk & Wagnalls, 1960), or Amy Vanderbilt's somewhat less formal *Complete Book of Etiquette; a Guide to Gracious Living* (Doubleday, 1958). One can hardly picture a school library without a copy of George Earlie Shankle's *State Names, Flags, Seals, Songs, Birds, Flowers, and Other Symbols,* so often do questions about these arise in schools. The revised edition of this book (Wilson, 1938) is now out of print but a new work on the subject is in preparation. Dr. Shankle compiled another book, *American Nicknames; Their Origin and Significance,* which the school library may need. This book is now in its second edition (Wilson, 1955).

AIDS FOR SELECTION OF REFERENCE BOOKS

While there is not a special section of reference books in the *Children's Catalog* and the *Standard Catalog for High School Libraries,* they, as well as many other book selection aids, list books of the type to be labeled reference, kept in a separate collection, and used only in the school library. For example, encyclopedias are included under the 030 classification; statistical books, such as the *World Almanac* in 317.3; English language dictionaries in 423; biographical dictionaries in 920.03; and dictionaries of United States history in 973.03. In other words, reference books may be found under many classifications in the standard book selection aids.

For older standard reference materials, the school librarian is referred to *Basic Reference Sources: An Introduction to Materials and Methods*, by Louis Shores (American Library Association, 1954), though many titles included are not suitable for reference work in school libraries. This book is helpful for a full analysis and evaluation of reference books which the school librarian may know only by title. It may also suggest titles which would prove useful for reference purposes in the school library. For librarians needing additional suggestions, the seventh edition of *Guide to Reference Books*, by Constance M. Winchell (American Library Association, 1951), and its supplements may prove useful.

The chances are that a list of reference books for school libraries will be available to most school librarians from their state department of education. Under the direction of school library supervisors, committees of school librarians in various states have compiled bibliographies of various kinds. Two very helpful aids for the selection of reference books have been prepared under the direction of Cora Paul Bomar, Supervisor of School Library Services in North Carolina, and are available from her office at the Department of Public Instruction, Raleigh, North Carolina. One title is *Evaluation of Sets of Books for School Libraries*, now in its third edition (1957). In addition to the evaluation of some seventy sets of books, there is a preface which offers excellent advice to superintendents, principals, and teachers who may be examining sets of books for possible purchase for school libraries; it should be equally helpful for the beginning librarian. A more recent (1959) and more comprehensive publication issued by the same office is *Reference Materials for School Libraries*, which includes some seven hundred titles of reference books of various types for grades one to twelve. The first chapter, "Reference Materials in the School Library," contains some very practical advice in brief form.

Before the selection of sets of books with which the school librarian is not familiar, as well as new editions of known books, titles should be checked in the "Subscription Books Bulletin" section of *The Booklist and Subscription Books Bulletin,* published semimonthly, September-July, and once only in August, by the American Library Association. A description of this aid and its service in evaluating and recommending books sold by agents in sets on the subscription basis was given in Chapter 2. A copy of *The Booklist and Subscription Books Bulletin* should be available to every school librarian, probably through the office of the school library supervisor if the individual school does not subscribe to it. Otherwise, the periodical will doubtless be available at the public library or a nearby college library. Teachers and administrators, as well as school librarians, not only should be aware of this service but are urged to use it before recommending the purchase of *any set* of books.

For reference books not sold on the subscription basis and hence not evaluated in *The Booklist and Subscription Books Bulletin,* each issue of the Wilson Library Bulletin carries a section, "Current Reference Books," which gives a brief description and evaluation of a number of books suitable for reference use. This is an excellent source from which the school librarian may learn about new and current reference books; it tells enough about each title to help the school librarian judge its suitability for his library.

FOR THE VERY YOUNG:
PICTURE BOOKS AND EASY BOOKS

Books in this category are specifically, of course, for elementary school libraries. They are usually shelved separately on low shelves easily accessible to pupils of the first three grades. Because of a variety of odd sizes and because they are all apt to be thin, books for the very young are laid out on sloping shelves, stacked in bins, or housed on special shelves with frequent uprights. Even so, it is well-nigh impossible to keep them shelved in an orderly fashion, and school librarians devise ways and means by which picture books may easily be selected for reading by the pupils.

Classification of picture books and easy books also leads the librarian into confused waters. In the *Children's Catalog* the section of "Easy Books" includes:

1. Books with little text, widely spaced or scattered, with extra large print and simple vocabulary for the beginning reader.

2. Picture books with very little text and simple enough vocabulary to be read by the child himself.

3. Picture books with a larger amount of text or text of greater difficulty to be read to the child.

Picture books with definite subject content are classified in the *Children's Catalog* with other nonfiction according to subject. When this arrangement is followed in elementary school libraries, it helps the teachers find material for their classes. It seems especially important that easy science books should be classified as, and shelved with, nonfiction. A few picture books, such as *The Great Geppy* (Viking, 1940) by William Pène Du Bois, *Lentil* (Viking, 1940) by Robert McCloskey, and all of Maj Lindman's books are included in the "Fiction" section.

Whatever arrangements are made for handling such books, every elementary school library will need picture books and easy books—lots of them. They constitute the main collection for use by the first three grades. They are helpful in getting beginning pupils accustomed to handling books and to associating books with both information and enjoyment. They are useful in developing reading skills as pupils learn to read and in establishing early the important habit of reading. The present trend toward supplying simple material which the beginning readers can read will be discussed in Chapter 15. Librarians find by experience that carefully selected primers and readers, not used as texts in their schools, prove useful in supplementing the more expensive trade books. This applies especially to those on a special subject.

Picture books by the older illustrators, especially those whose work was finished largely by the turn of the century, are now rather outdated for modern-day children. However, it would be a pity if any child failed to become acquainted with *Johnny Crow's Garden* (Warne, 1903), with delightful pictures by L. Leslie Brooke to accompany the rhymes recited to him as a child by his own father, and the other books of the Johnny Crow series, though none quite so good. This is also true of the small books by Beatrix Potter, published by Warne, and always with pictures by the author. *The Tale of Peter Rabbit* remains the favorite of succeeding generations of children, though Miss Potter herself expressed a preference for *The Tailor of Gloucester*. In these delightful books, the text and the pictures complement each other perfectly.

Illustrators during the first half of the twentieth century brought illustrations for children's books to a high degree of excellence and most of their products are still available. Included in every elementary school library collection should be books by Edgar Parin d'Aulaire and Ingri Mortenson d'Aulaire, who began their career with *Ola*, a picture book of Norway (Doubleday, 1932), and have produced many books with historical or biographical background, most of them for children older than the picture-book age. All of these were illustrated with lithograph drawings in black and white and in color. Ludwig Bemelmans has contributed a series of several books, beginning with *Madeline* (Viking, 1939) and depicting life in a school for girls in Paris, which appeal to girls as does his *Hansi* (Viking, 1934) to boys. In *Madeline in London* (Viking, 1961) Madeline and her friends fly to London where they are shown in Bemelmans' colorful paintings. Margaret Wise Brown, writing under several pseudonyms, especially Golden MacDonald, produced a number of very simple books which children like, illustrated by a variety of artists. Among books of hers which have great appeal are *Goodnight Moon* (Harper, 1947) and *Runaway Bunny* (Harper, 1942), both illustrated by Clement Hurd. Virginia Lee Burton, in such books as *Katy and the Big Snow* (Houghton, 1943) and *Mike Mulligan and His Steam Shovel* (Houghton, 1939), delights small children with her gay illustrations of mechanical objects. The Caldecott Medal was awarded to Miss Burton for *The Little House* (Houghton, 1942), which appeals to adults as well as to children.

James Henry Daugherty, who writes and illustrates books of history and biography which appeal largely to older boys, has one book, *Andy and the Lion* (Viking, 1938), a modern version of the old tale "Androcles and the Lion," which pupils in grades one to three enjoy. A later book, *The Picnic; a Frolic in Two Colors and Three Parts* (Viking, 1958), in a similar vein, is a modern rendition of the old fable "The Lion and the Mouse," with illustrations unlike those in his earlier style. Roger Antoine Duvoisin, who has written and illustrated a few books of his own, is also known for his pictures in books by Alvin R. Tresselt and in the Happy Lion books by Louise Fatio, the first of which was published by McGraw in 1954. The Tresselt-Duvoisin *White Snow, Bright Snow* (Lothrop, 1947) was awarded the Caldecott Medal in 1948 and has proved popular with children.

No child should miss Marjorie Flack's delightful books, especially the series about a lovable Scotch terrier puppy, beginning with *Angus and the Ducks* (Doubleday, 1930). Children should also know books by Wanda Gág, for example *Millions of Cats* (Coward-McCann, 1928). These have a folk-tale quality because of the author's interest in folk literature, nurtured by her German grandmother. Theodor Seuss Geisel, under the name of Dr. Seuss, has contributed a long list of books of pure nonsense written in verse with gay pictures which delight children. His first book, *And To Think That I Saw It on Mulberry Street* (Vanguard, 1937), is still a favorite and most of his books are very popular with children. More recently Dr. Seuss has done *The Cat in the Hat* (Random House, 1957) and its sequel, *The Cat in the Hat Comes Back* (Random House, 1958), for beginning readers, using fewer than 250 words of which at least half are familiar to first grade pupils. (Other books for beginning readers will be discussed in Chapter 15.) Hardie Gramatky has the knack of taking some mechanical object, for example a tug-boat in *Little Toot* (Putnam, 1939) or an old-fashioned fire engine in *Hercules* (Putnam, 1940), and, to the delight of young readers, giving them real personality through text and pictures.

Lois Lenski, probably best known for her regional books written for older boys and girls, has written and illustrated a number of popular books for children. Among these are her "little books," so called not only because of their size, but because one series deals with the Small family and the little things which are theirs. Children should by all means have access to Robert McCloskey's books published by Viking Press: *Make Way for Ducklings* (1941), which won the Caldecott Medal in 1942; *Blueberries for Sal* (1948); and *One Morning in Maine* (1952). The pictures are large and very simple and there is childlike humor both in them and in the text. His *Time of Wonder* (1957), the first of his books to be done in full color and the second to win the Caldecott Medal (in 1958), is more likely to appeal to older readers, possibly even adults. Attention should be called to the fact that McCloskey was the first person to receive the Caldecott Medal twice.

Feodor Rojankovsky, illustrator for several authors, seems to have hit his stride in books of folk tales as retold by John Langstaff. Rojankovsky's illustrations in *Frog Went a-Courtin'* (Harcourt, 1955), winner of the Caldecott Medal in 1956, and in *Over in the Meadow* (Harcourt, 1957) are delightful and appealing. Mention must be made of *The Biggest Bear* (Houghton, 1952) by Lynd Ward, joint author and illustrator of several books with his wife, May Yonge McNeer, and illustrator for several other authors. Awarded the Caldecott Medal in 1953, *The Biggest Bear* is a favorite with readers from the picture-book set and those somewhat older. The book appeals to the imagination and has the humor which children like.

The work of a considerable number of contemporary illustrators of children's books is replacing that of older illustrators whose books are somewhat outdated for modern-day readers. The more recent illustrators are supplying a steady stream of picture books and easy books for school libraries. Some of these show the impact of modern art in their departures from realism and in the unusual use of color. Entirely new to children's books are combinations of vivid color used as background for an entire page with text printed in a contrasting color. These books are, however, new and fresh and of interest to school librarians using them with children and studying their reaction to the pictures.

Outstanding among those by younger illustrators, Don Freeman's books, especially *Fly High, Fly Low* (Viking, 1956), are good for young children. Marcia Joan Brown suits her pictures to the various folk tales which she retells. Among her books are *Cinderella* (Scribner, 1954), the 1955 Caldecott Medal winner, with intentionally unrealistic pastels, and *Dick Whittington and His Cat* (Scribner, 1950), which is illustrated with linoleum blocks. Marie Hall Ets sometimes draws very daintily as in *Play With Me* (Viking, 1955), in which a little girl learns to sit quietly until the meadow animals, which she has tried to catch, come to her. At other times she draws boldly as in *Mister Penny* (Viking, 1935) and *Mister Penny's Race Horse* (Viking, 1956). The third in this series is *Mister Penny's Circus* (Viking, 1961), about a circus formed by farm animals and two animals who have run away from a circus. The illustrations in *Nine Days to Christmas* by Marie Hall Ets and Aurora Labastida (Viking, 1959), which won the Caldecott Medal in 1960, seem to combine the two types of picture work by Miss Ets.

Horn Book Magazine has described the books of Virginia Kahl as being both entertaining and original. She is perhaps best known for her *Duchess Bakes a Cake* (Scribner, 1955), which is perfect nonsense told in rhyme and illustrated with colorful and imaginative pictures. Jun Iwamatsu, whose earlier books were published under the pseudonym of Taro Yashima, has written *Crow Boy* (Viking, 1955) and several other unusual picture books depicting present-day life in Japan. Elementary school children should also know the picture books by Leo Politi which, using a California background, depict foreign children, usually Mexicans, and the stories with a French background, including those about Jeanne-Marie, by Françoise Seignobosc, who writes under the name Françoise.

William Lipkind and Nicolas Mordvinoff, collaborating as Will and Nicolas, have produced a number of unusual books, the best known of which is *Finders Keepers* (Harcourt, 1951), the story of two dogs and one bone, which was awarded the Caldecott Medal in 1952. Children often choose Hans Augusto Rey's stories of an engaging monkey introduced in *Curious George* (Houghton, 1941) and brought up to date in *Curious George Gets a Medal* (Houghton, 1957) in which the monkey makes a flight into space. The space age is featured also in *Little Bear* (Harper, 1957), an I-Can-Read book for the beginning reader (see Chapter 15) by Elsie Holmelund Minarik with delightful pictures by Maurice Sendak. This little bear would win his way into the heart of any child—or adult—without a trip to the moon. He appears again in sequels, *Father Bear Comes Home* (Harper, 1959) and *Little Bear's Visit* (Harper, 1961) which takes him to see his grand-parents.

The elementary school library needs a variety of picture books on a wide range of topics. The subjects generally are simple things in which very young children take delight: animals of all kinds, toys, things about the home, children like themselves and of other countries, and mechanical objects including anything on wheels. There is usually added appeal in nursery rhymes and simple folk tales, which lend themselves to pleasing illustrations.

Pictures should generally be large and simple, uncluttered with detail. The text also should be brief, simple yet interesting. Children prefer color, usually the primary colors, combined simply. They like repetition, in both text and picture, and rhythm, even when the words do not rhyme. Appeal to the imagination is a strong feature in picture books, which should in large measure contain humor of a childlike nature, hard to characterize but easy to detect.

CHAPTER 6

SOCIAL SCIENCES AND OTHER CLASSES

OF THE MIND AND OF THE SPIRIT: 100 AND 200 CLASSIFICATIONS

Material on philosophy and allied subjects does not rank high in importance for the average school library. Standard book selection aids generally include very few books in these fields for elementary school libraries. Also, teachers find very little need for such material with elementary school pupils. Two books which will be found in many school library collections, however, are *A Girl Grows Up* by Ruth Fedder, now in its third edition (McGraw, 1957), and *A Boy Grows Up* by Harry C. McKown (McGraw, 1949), in its second edition. Both are for grades seven to nine and contain sound advice and help for boys and girls growing into adulthood.

Two phases of modern-day high school life demand some books on philosophy and allied subjects in libraries serving junior and senior high schools. In the first place, the curricula of some schools now include courses in psychology and/or ethics, or units on these two subjects in various courses related to living in the modern world. Consequently, library materials are needed to supplement classwork in these areas. Also, the high school deans of boys and of girls, the guidance counselor, the coach, or the teacher of home economics or of other subjects who must help with the guidance program often use materials on these subjects for classwork or on an individual basis in an effort to help the growing adolescent understand himself, his parents and other adult relatives, his brothers and sisters, and other adolescents. In addition to these uses, pupils ask for and read on their own books designed to help them make the most of their own possibilities. Girls are particularly interested in books that will help them in dealing with problems inherent in "the facts of life," going steady, marriage, and other topics regarding relations with the opposite sex. Such books are important to pupils in light of the present-day trend toward early marriages. Evelyn Ruth Millis Duvall and Frances Bruce Strain write books along these lines addressed primarily to the teen-age audience, while the more adult slant is furnished in books by such writers as the late Ernest Rutherford Groves, Paul Henry Landis, and Judson Taylor Landis, the last with the collaboration of his wife, Mary Green Landis. *You, the Person You Want To Be* (McGraw, 1957) by Ruth Fedder, author of the above-mentioned *A Girl Grows Up,* contains a wealth of common-sense advice about growing into maturity. A new book, *Your Teens and Mine* by Eleanor Roosevelt with Helen Ferris (Doubleday, 1961), talks about problems of growing up that are pertinent in any age, using some of Mrs. Roosevelt's own experiences as examples.

Books in the 200 classification on both the elementary and secondary school levels divide themselves naturally into books that are purely religious in nature and books of mythology. Amateur librarians are usually puzzled at the presence of myths in the 200 classification until they realize that mythology grew out of man's early efforts to explain natural phenomena, e.g., the sun passing across the sky and the roll of thunder during a storm. Thus it constitutes the religious material of the earlier cultures.

Every school library will need a good copy of the Bible. While the King James Version is probably still the most popular choice, the Revised Standard Version is now available for both Testaments and is preferred in some school library collections. In schools where classes in the Bible are taught, examples of other modern translations may also be desirable. In school libraries serving communities that are predominantly Catholic, an authorized Catholic translation of the Bible should also be available.

For younger children, interestingly told Bible stories are always acceptable for reading aloud or for the children to read for themselves. Walter Russell Bowie's *The Bible Story for Boys and Girls: Old Testament* (Abingdon, 1952) and *The Bible Story for Boys and Girls: New Testament* (Abingdon, 1951) furnish a good example. To be avoided are retellings of the Bible that have lost the flavor of biblical language and are so modern in spirit as to prove confusing to children. Among the picture books in the elementary school library should be some with religious background and lovely illustrations by outstanding artists such as Elizabeth Orton Jones, Dorothy P. Lathrop, Maud and Miska Petersham, and Helen Sewell. Leonard Weisgard has done some of his best illustrating work in *A Book about God* (Lothrop, 1953), prepared for the picture-book age by Florence Mary Fitch. With the fairly recent development of sectarian publishing houses representing major denominations and issuing children's as well as adult books, the school librarian must exert more than usual care in the selection of religious books.

On both elementary and secondary school levels, Miss Fitch's *One God; the Ways We Worship Him* (Lothrop, 1944) and *Their Search for God; Ways of Worship in the Orient* (Lothrop, 1947) are acceptable for readers of grade six and up. The former describes ways of worship for Catholics, Jews, and Protestants; the latter describes the leading faiths of the Orient: Buddhism, Confucianism, Hinduism, etc. These books are useful not only in any consideration of comparative religion but in history classes concerned with religion and its various impacts upon the cultures of people. Some senior high school libraries might have need for such a book as *A Guide to the Religions of America*, the *Look* magazine series on religion, which was edited by Leo Rosten (Simon & Schuster, 1955). This book gives in alphabetical order a brief account of eighteen different religious beliefs. It also has a section of "Facts and Figures on Religion in the United States." A similar series of 1959 and 1960 articles, reprinted under the title *The Story of Religions in America*, is available in the form of pamphlets from *Look*.

Since mythology is usually taught in schools in connection with the study of Latin and ancient history there will be less demand for books on this subject in elementary schools than in junior and senior high schools. However, many schools now offer a course on Greece and Rome in the sixth grade and need books about myths for this unit. Furthermore, there will be some teachers at all levels who use myths as a type of literature to be read or told to younger children and to be read by older pupils. There are also many pupils who enjoy reading myths for pleasure, especially if folk tales appeal to them or if they lean toward the fantasy type of tale.

Consequently, any high school library will probably find need for an adaptation of *The Age of Fable* by Thomas Bulfinch. A useful one is *A Book of Myths; Selections from Bulfinch's Age of Fable* with illustrations by Helen Sewell (Macmillan, 1942). A more recent rendition is *The Age of Fable; or, Stories of Gods and Heroes* (Heritage Press, 1958), with an introductory essay by Dudley Fitts. It would be difficult to imagine a school library without copies of *A Wonder Book* and *Tanglewood Tales* by Nathaniel Hawthorne, who retold the classical myths for his own children, then decided to share them with other children of all ages. Both these titles are available in the Children's Illustrated Classics, published by Dutton, with line drawings and color plates. Sally Benson's *Stories of the Gods and Heroes,* based on Bulfinch (Dial Press, 1940), has appeal for teen-agers both because of her informal style and because the readers are already acquainted with this author through her *Junior Miss* and short stories in collections, yet it is also simple enough for use by elementary school pupils.

For older pupils, the stand-bys are *Classic Myths in English Literature and in Art,* edited by Charles Mills Gayley, in a new edition revised and enlarged (Ginn, 1939), and *Classical Myths That Live Today,* also in a revised and enlarged edition, by Frances Ellis Sabin (Silver Burdett, 1958). *The Golden Treasury of Myths and Legends* is a good collection adapted from the world's great classics by Anne Terry White (Golden Press, 1959).

For younger readers, myths selected and retold by Padraic Colum are simply written and interestingly told. His *Golden Fleece and the Heroes Who Lived before Achilles* (Macmillan, 1921) and *Children of Odin* (Macmillan, 1920) are representative examples. The former deals with myths of Greece and Rome while the latter retells the Norse sagas. Another older book still available which presents Norse stories in an attractive way is *In the Days of Giants* by Abbie Farwell Brown (Houghton, 1930).

THE FIELD IS WIDE: 300 CLASSIFICATION

The 300 classification, Social Sciences, probably covers a wider variety of materials than any other of the ten main divisions of the Dewey Decimal System. A succinct statement of the divisions of the 300's is enough to show its scope:

    300—Social Sciences; 301—Sociology
    310—Statistics
    320—Political science
    330—Economics
    340—Law
    350—Public administration
    360—Social welfare
    370—Education
    380—Public services and utilities
    390—Customs and folklore

Few fields of materials for children and young people have in the past decade grown in volume and variety as have the social sciences. Many factors have contributed to this expansion. New trends in education stress the child and his needs in a complex society. There is widespread interest in the problems that confront mankind. Many new phases of the social sciences have developed since World War II, with the present problems of survival in a shrinking world. More people manifest an interest in government and its workings, an interest demanding understanding of various types of governments. Knowledge of what constitutes a democracy and how to make the democratic way of life work in countries having recently acquired the privilege of self-government has become increasingly important, even to young readers. School pupils, surrounded by printed materials, television, radio, and the movies, are conscious as never before of world problems. Finally, there is a present general trend to provide reading materials at all levels on many difficult subjects, some of which are found in the 300 classification.

Problems in the selection of materials for school libraries, especially on the high school level, probably appear in greater proportion in the social sciences than in any other field. There are fairly obvious reasons for this statement:

1. It is difficult for the book selector to know books in the 300's as a unit since there is such a vast variety of materials on widely different topics. In the 500's, for example, the selector is dealing with materials on various divisions of one main subject, namely pure science. Even in the 900's, another broad field covering the three subjects of biography, geography and travel, and history, there are close relations between the subjects.

2. Though the experienced book selector can supply an impressive list of writers of several books in other fields, this feat is difficult in the social sciences. Instead there are many writers who contribute some material in this field. Often outstanding authorities in other fields write one book on an allied subject in the 300's. For example, Charles Austin Beard, authority on United States history, has contributed *American Government and Politics* (Macmillan, 1949), now in its tenth edition. Paul Henry Landis, mentioned earlier as an author in the field of family relations, has written *So This Is College* (McGraw, 1954).

3. Social sciences is one of the fields in which material becomes outdated quickly. Science, of course, shares this disadvantage and materials in any field do eventually become outdated. While it is important that pupils have a variety of new and fresh materials, the school librarian hesitates to tie up limited funds in materials that may lose some of their value when they cease to be current. The use of clippings and pamphlets, of which there are many in the 300's, will help, but not all subjects are treated in such ephemeral form. *Vertical File Index,* published by Wilson, is a good source of information about pamphlets. This is especially important since book selection aids tend not to list pamphlets because of their ephemeral nature.

4. Materials in the social sciences are often of a controversial nature. In this classification may be found materials on various forms of government, including the "isms," management and

labor, minority groups, race relations, and other similar topics. The school library, to be sure, needs material on controversial subjects but it must be well selected. Examples of good material in a controversial area are two books edited by Richard Ketchum, *What Is Democracy?* and *What Is Communism?*, both published by Dutton in 1955. The discusion of material is clear and unbiased, the photographs and drawings supplement the discussion and tie the text together, and a helpful list of questions and answers for further clarification is found at the end of each book. Another useful volume is *Communism in Our World* by John Cope Caldwell (Day, 1956), though the author so simplifies the problem that the book appeals chiefly to the junior high school level. John Edgar Hoover's *Masters of Deceit; the Story of Communism in America and How To Fight It* (Holt, 1958), although classified in United States history, should also be mentioned in this connection.

5. There is considerable propaganda in one form or another in the social sciences. Propaganda is not easily dealt with, especially where pupils have been encouraged by the use of textbooks to believe that the printed word is "law and gospel." Material which would prove useful in helping high school pupils develop sensitivity to propaganda and its appeal is practically nonexistent.

6. There appears to be a greater variety of values in material on the social sciences than in some other fields. The field of social sciences seems almost to invite the "soap-box" type of publication which expresses the author's enthusiasm for, or prejudice against, the subject in hand. Classes in high school discuss freedom of speech and allied topics. Pupils need to be exposed to a variety of opinions, if they are to learn to assess other people's points of view and opinions. At the same time, they need guidance as they seek to evaluate the opinions of others and to formulate opinions of their own.

7. While this may not loom too large in the picture, many books in the social sciences are not personally interesting to pupils and are used entirely for curriculum purposes. Moreover, the selector finds less pupil response to available materials, which

leads to the inevitable conclusion that material in the social sciences should be chosen with great care. Both librarians and teachers will need to examine and read materials on controversial issues if possible before purchasing, certainly before using them with pupils. They will also depend to a large extent on standard selection aids, especially where examination before purchase is not feasible.

Elementary school pupils and their teachers constantly demand material in the 300's on transportation and communication for units on a variety of topics. They are also interested in books on safety, conservation of plant and animal life, and the broad subject of community living. There are calls, as the various holidays appear on the calendar, for material to help celebrate them. Folklore material in 398 (nursery rhymes, fairy tales, fables, and legends) constitutes a considerable portion of what the pupils read on their own.

In the early days of book selection aids for elementary schools, most of the books listed in the 300's were either collections of stories for reading or telling, holiday material, or folklore. Now, however, although those subjects account for a large number of entries, most of the subjects included for use in high school library collections are also suggested for elementary school libraries. There is, to be sure, a noticeable difference in the treatment of materials for the different levels. Community helpers (firemen, policemen, postmen, and the like), for example, are presented for elementary readers as friends of children in the community role. On the high school level, there are books on crime, juvenile delinquency, and the FBI, showing how policemen help control crime in modern society.

Today's builder of the school library collection is indeed fortunate in finding materials for all levels on many subjects. A good example is the United Nations. Outstanding on the high school level is *UN: Today and Tomorrow* by Eleanor Roosevelt and William S. DeWitt (Harper, 1953); for junior high pupils, Lois J. Fisher's *You and the United Nations* (Childrens Press, 1958) simplifies the complex organizations; and, for the very young, the idea of nations working together is presented by *A Garden We Planted Together,* adapted from a filmstrip of the same title prepared by the United Nations Department of Public Information (McGraw, 1952). Another book on the high school level is *Workshops for the World; the Specialized Agencies of the United Nations,* by Graham Beckel with an introduction by Benjamin A. Cohen (Abelard-Schuman, 1954), which teachers and librarians find useful. School libraries may also find useful the latest pamphlet (1960) entitled *Teaching about the United Nations in the United States,* prepared every four years by the United States Department of Health, Education and Welfare. There is a helpful section on materials in public school libraries.

Frequent calls come to the high school library for material on government—local, state, and federal—with special interest in international government, specifically the United Nations, discussed above. Attention is called to a very practical book, *Know Your Government* (Rand McNally, 1959) by George E. Ross, in spite of the lack of an index, because of divisions with subheads and inclusion of charts and tables. Another good book is *Our Federal Government: How It Works* by Patricia C. Acheson (Dodd, 1958). This book includes some historical background. The most helpful part consists of separate chapters on the functions of each of the executive departments.

Now that preparedness for preventing war seems an accepted part of modern life, there is interest, especially among the boys, in military service—air force, army, navy, and marines—and the newer types of training, equipment, and methods of warfare. Boys about junior high school age and older find both interesting and helpful in satisfying this interest the picture stories by John T. Engeman published by Lothrop. Examples are *West Point, the Life of a Cadet* (1956); *Annapolis; the Life of a Midshipman* (1956); *Coast Guard Academy; the Life of a Cadet* (1957); *U.S. Air Force Academy; the Life of a Cadet* (1957). Another book is *From Submarines to Satellites; Science in Our Armed Forces* by Margaret O. Hyde (McGraw, 1958). The author, former science consultant at the Lincoln School, Columbia University, and Head of the Science Department at the Shipley School, Bryn Mawr, Pennsylvania, tells of experiments by the armed forces in missiles and submarines, as well as in some phases of science in jungles and polar regions.

Among high school pupils, both those who plan to continue their education in college and those who do not, there is a perennial interest in materials on careers: jobs that are open, required preparation, probable salary, and opportunities for advancement. An interesting observation is that career material is now probably as popular with junior high as with senior high pupils. This may be the result of a unit on careers in the curricula of many junior high schools. There is even some vocational interest among pupils in elementary schools. However, interest in careers seems not so intense at any level as some years ago. *Vocations for Boys* by Harry Dexter Kitson and Edgar Morgan Stover, now in a revised edition (Harcourt, 1955), and *Vocations for Girls,* also published by Harcourt, by Mary Rebecca Lingenfelter and Harry Dexter Kitson, though it has not been revised since 1951, seem to remain as stand-bys. These books present in an interesting manner the salient points about careers in which young people are most interested. There are, to be sure, many other good books on careers, some covering a variety of careers, others only one career.

Librarians and teachers offering vocational guidance to pupils will also make use of biographies stressing particular careers, fiction with a vocational interest, plus books on etiquette, personality development, and similar material to correlate with factual information about careers. Many school libraries maintain extensive collections of pamphlets about a variety of careers, such as those published by the Occupational Information Division of Science Research Associates (57 West Grand Avenue, Chicago 10). Because material on careers and vocations goes out of date so quickly, it is wise to depend on pamphlets instead of books as much as possible in this area. These pamphlets are used extensively if and when the school has a Vocational Day or Career Week, or when a class concentrates on a vocational unit during which pupils study careers in line with their individual interests.

Those pupils planning to go to college will need not only books like Landis' *So This Is College* (mentioned above), but the eighth edition of *American Universities and Colleges,* edited by Mary Irwin (American Council on Education, 1960), and the latest edition of the *Lovejoy-Jones College Scholarship Guide* published by Simon and Schuster. High school libraries also keep a file of current catalogs from colleges in the area.

Every high school library should have access to the latest edition of *Occupational Literature; an Annotated Bibliography* by Gertrude Forrester, published by Wilson, and *Occupational Outlook Handbook; Employment Information on Major Occupations for Use in Guidance,* published every other year by the United States Bureau of Labor Statistics.

While space does not permit discussion of many subjects in the social sciences, some consideration should be given to books by and about Negroes. In the past few years, particularly since the Supreme Court decision declaring segregation in schools unconstitutional, there has been increased interest in books recounting the history of the Negro race and outstanding accomplishments of its individual members. Classified under number 325.2 are such books as *The First Book of Negroes* (F. Watts, 1952) for elementary pupils and *Pictorial History of the Negro in America* (Crown, 1956) for high schools, both by the well-known Negro poet Langston Hughes. Milton Meltzer collaborated with him on the latter. Arna Wendell Bontemps, Librarian of Fiske University, a successful writer of several books of fiction about Negro children, has contributed *Story of the Negro* (Knopf, 1958), now in its third edition, which proves helpful with high school pupils. Hildegarde Swift is the author of *North Star Shining; a Pictorial History of the American Negro* (Morrow, 1947), a moving record of the race done in blank verse with fitting lithographs by Lynd Ward. For younger readers, there are Jane Dabney Shackelford's *The Child's Story of the Negro* (1956) and *My Happy Days* (1944), both issued by the Associated Publishers.

Fairly complete lists of books by and about Negroes, not only in the 300's but also in the fields of biography, poetry, and fiction, may be found in *Books about Negro Life for Children,* a pamphlet by Augusta Braxston Baker (New York Public Library, 1961), and *We Build Together* in its revised edition (1948) prepared by Charlemae Rollins for the National Council of Teachers of English and published by the Council. In 1961 Mrs. Baker succeeded Frances Lander Spain as Coordinator of Children's Services, New York Public Library. Mrs. Rollins is Children's Librarian, George C. Hall Branch of the Chicago Public Library. In both lists, an introduction offers helpful information as to the reaction of Negroes themselves to books written about their race. Before selecting materials in this area, school librarians and teachers should read especially Mrs. Rollins' introductory article "Criteria for Judging Books about Negroes for Young People." Although this publication is reported as currently out of print, many school libraries will have a copy or can borrow one.

A further word should be said about folklore as it is related to school libraries. Most of the older collections, both in public and school libraries, contain folk material in generous quantity. Practically every book about books and reading for children includes a full discussion of folklore. The book selection aids continue to offer a wide variety of folk material, with the addition of new titles in each revision.

Nevertheless, school librarians seem generally agreed that, with a few exceptions, there is less and less demand for folklore. This is true in spite of the fact that a general upsurge of interest both in folk tales and folk music seems evident, if radio and television programs are reliable criteria. A rather cursory study of this problem shows that educational leaders tend to shift their opinion regarding the value of folklore in education with every generation. The fact that many present-day parents, teachers, and librarians are products of schools which have stressed utilitarian books and neglected folklore may account in part for the current lack of interest in folklore among the children.

There should be in elementary school libraries some picture books based on folk tales, of which there are many with illustrations by outstanding artists. At least one good collection of nursery rhymes such as *Marguerite de Angeli's Book of Nursery and Mother Goose Rhymes* (Doubleday, 1954) should be included. This beautifully illustrated book is probably most suitable for use by teachers with pupils. A selection from this book for the very young child is entitled *A Pocket Full of Posies* (Doubleday, 1961), also with illustrations by de Angeli. Some of the less expensive collections illustrated by Gustaf Tenggren, Feodor Rojankovsky, and others should also be included for the children to enjoy. Copies of Aesop's *Fables* and *Arabian Nights* in attractive format seem important for any school library. Elementary school libraries will need to include good collections of fairy tales, such as those collected by Andrew Lang and the Grimm brothers as well as those told by Hans Christian Andersen, though these, being modern fairy tales, are classified as fiction. One of the best collections of the Grimm tales is *Tales from Grimm*, translated and illustrated by Wanda Gág (Coward-McCann, 1936). A very recent rendition of another group of old tales is the *Norwegian Folk Tales*, collected by Peter Christen Asbjørnsen and Jørgen E. Moe and translated by Pat Shaw Iversen and Carl Norman (Viking, 1961).

It would seem too bad if children missed entirely the legends of Robin Hood and King Arthur in England and their counterparts in other countries. Boys of upper elementary school and junior high school are usually interested in these heroes when introduced to them. A new book, *Hero Tales from Many Lands* (Abingdon, 1961), compiled by Alice Isabel Hazeltine from thirty collections, some of which are out of print, should be useful for the purpose of introduction.

One type of stories which modern children generally seem to enjoy is the tall tale characteristic of a young and growing America surrounding such real heroes as Daniel Boone, Davy Crockett, and Johnny Appleseed, or the more recent legendary ones like Paul Bunyan, Pecos Bill, and John Henry. One of the best collections of tall tales is Anne Malcolmson's *Yankee Doodle's Cousins* (Houghton, 1941).

Richard Chase has made collections, which children generally enjoy, of folk tales brought from European countries and preserved in the southern mountains. Examples of these are *Jack Tales* (Houghton, 1943) and *Grandfather Tales* (Houghton, 1948). He has also compiled *The Complete Tales of Uncle Remus* by Joel Chandler Harris (Houghton, 1955), which to the lasting regret of those brought up on them are read less and less because of the difficult dialect. This book has the original illustrations by A. B. Frost, without which no Uncle Remus book is complete.

High school English classes often study folklore as a type of literature. For this, teachers find useful the books edited by Benjamin Albert Botkin, especially *Treasury of American Folklore; Stories, Ballads, and Traditions of the People* (Crown, 1944). If the study includes other countries, *Harvest of World Folk Tales,* edited by Milton Allan Rugoff (Viking, 1949), including two hundred tales from nineteen areas, will prove useful. Book selection aids offer a wide selection of folk tales from many countries of the world.

Citation of a few outstanding writers in the 300's with representative titles, again illustrating the wide variety of materials in the field, may prove helpful. Katherine Binney Shippen has written *Great Heritage* (Viking, 1947), which traces, with a chapter on each different product, the resources of the United States from its settlement to the present; *Miracle in Motion; the Story of America's Industry* (Harper, 1955); *Passage to America; the Story of the Great Migrations* (Harper, 1950); and *Pool of Knowledge; How the United Nations Share Their Skills* (Harper, 1954). The Shippen books all bear catchy titles, are on subjects about which there is not a wealth of material, and are interestingly written. Aimed at the junior high school level, they are not so difficult that good readers in the upper elementary grades cannot use them, yet they are on subjects of interest also to senior high school pupils.

John Joseph Floherty, whose books on many subjects are generally very successful, especially with boys, has contributed among others in the 300's such books as *Men Against Distance; the Story of Communications* (1954), *Money-Go-Round; the Strange Story of Money* (1944), *Our FBI; an Inside Story* (1951), and *Troopers All; Stories of State Police* (1954)—all published by Lippincott. More recent is *Youth and the FBI* (Lippincott, 1960), written with Mike McGrady about the FBI's activities in combating juvenile delinquency, and the second revised edition (1960) of *Aviation from the Ground Up* (classified in the 600's). Floherty's books are popular with boys reading on their own, as well as useful for correlating with curriculum studies.

A writer of similar books for a slightly younger group, Carroll Burleigh Colby, has contributed a variety of titles published by Coward-McCann, of which the following are examples: *Frogmen* (1954), *Ships of Our Navy* (1953), *Submarine* (1953), *FBI* (1954), *Park Ranger* (1955), and *Tall Timber* (1955). Many of the Colby books are largely pictorial and are useful for older pupils who are retarded in reading. Books by both Colby and Floherty may be used for interest in careers.

Naomi Buchheimer, with her *Let's Take a Trip to a Fire House* (1956), *Let's Go to a Post Office* (1957), *Let's Go to the Library* (1957) and several others, all Putnam publications, meets a need for reading material on subjects studied in schools which pupils of the second and third grades can read. These books should also be useful to teachers arranging excursions to widen the pupils' horizons.

Walter Buehr is a comparatively new writer who produces books with his own illustrations on some subjects not treated by other authors for the in-between readers, grades four to seven. Though Buehr writes also in the 500's and 600's, a few sample titles in the 300's are *Treasure; the Story of Money and Its Safeguarding* (Putnam, 1955); *Meat from Ranch to Table* (Morrow, 1956); and *Trucks and Trucking* (Putnam, 1957). The last-named book contains a glossary of the professional jargon of truck drivers that would intrigue any boy who has watched big trucks rolling along the countryside and envisioned himself at the steering wheel.

In the field of the 300's, which presents a wide variety of materials and includes some controversial subjects, the librarian and teachers should cooperate closely to provide the best books available. Standard book selection aids will be depended on for basic materials, with regular supplements and revisions to keep materials up to date. Current book-reviewing periodicals should be checked for new materials. Professional magazines which feature book reviews should be consulted regularly. Whenever possible, materials on controversial topics should be examined before purchase. Teachers should read materials before they are assigned for class use so as to prepare for questions which may arise.

Words and Their Use: 400 Classification

No school library will need a large collection of books in the 400's, and of the small number needed many will be classified as reference books to be used only in the library.

Among books classified as 400's will be various dictionaries of the English language and at least one dictionary for each foreign language taught in the school, as discussed in a previous chapter on reference books (Chapter 4). On the high school level, a few good books of English grammar should prove useful. Some books on remedial reading, probably in the professional collection, will be welcomed by the teachers. Other subjects for which books may be needed are the origin of words, history and development of alphabets, antonyms and synonyms, versification, and vocabulary building.

A few outstanding writers in this field are Mario Andrew Pei, philologist and author of *All About Language* (Lippincott, 1954) and *Language for Everybody; What It Is and How to Master It* (Devin-Adair, 1956); Charles Earle Funk, who has compiled several books dealing wtih origins of curious expressions, including *Heavens to Betsy! And Other Curious Sayings* (Harper, 1955), *Hog on Ice, and Other Curious Expressions* (Harper, 1948), and *Thereby Hangs a Tale; Stories of Curious Word Origins* (Harper, 1950), which prove interesting to high school pupils; and Wilfred John Funk, author of *Word Origins and Their Romantic Stories* (W. Funk, 1950).

For elementary pupils, Antonio Frasconi's *See and Say, Guarda e Parla, Mira y Habla, Regarde et Parle* (Harcourt, 1955), a picture book in four languages, should prove interesting to children and useful in arousing interest in other languages. A more recent book, Sesyle Joslin's *There Is a Dragon in My Bed* (Harcourt, 1961) is a French-English picture book which might serve a similar purpose. Some school libraries may also be interested in translations of children's books into other languages. Examples are renditions of *The Five Brothers* by Claire Huchet Bishop in French (Coward-McCann, 1960) and of *Curious George* by H. A. Rey, translated into Spanish by Pedro Villa Fernandez (Houghton, 1961). If elementary schools follow the trend of teaching foreign languages, a dictionary for each language taught will be needed, as suggested in the chapter on reference books.

Samuel and Beryl Williams Epstein have written for a slightly older group *The First Book of Words* (F. Watts, 1954), giving the history of the English language, telling how words came to be and how they have changed to meet the needs of the times.

On either level, the use of books in the 400's will be determined by classroom procedure and the teacher's assignments, since few books in this category are of general interest for reading.

○

CHAPTER 7

SCIENCE AND TECHNOLOGY

BOOKS IN THE FIELD OF PURE SCIENCE: 500 CLASSIFICATION

Ever since the launching of the first Sputnik in October 1957, there has been increased interest in books on science for the school library. This interest is reflected in the wealth of material suitable for children and young people—books on a wide variety of scientific topics; periodical articles, often with lists of suggested science books; and science books added to school library collections following increased demands of the expanding curriculum.

As one surveys books listed in the book selection aids, it is difficult to find any subject division in science on which some material will not be needed in any school library. Briefly these divisions are: Mathematics; Astronomy, with subdivisions of sun, moon, stars, planets; Physics, including a fairly new section on atomic energy; Chemistry and Allied Sciences; Earth Sciences, embracing rocks and minerals, earthquakes and volcanoes, and weather; Paleontology with its study of fossils and prehistoric animals, fascinating to all children; Anthropology and Biology, of which archeology and anthropology are subtopics; Botanical Sciences, divided as to types of plants; and Zoological Sciences, with subdivisions of birds, insects, fish, reptiles, mammals, etc. As can be noted, the 500 classification is an interrelated group of subjects, most of which are of interest to all boys and many girls.

The need for science materials in school libraries is present on the elementary level as well as in junior and senior high schools. Many of the subjects selected for unit study by elementary teachers and pupils are in the field of science and librarians are called upon to supply materials to use with them. On the high school level, more than usual emphasis is being placed on teaching science and a growing number of pupils are enrolled in science classes. To meet increased science needs, school librarians are searching for the best materials in the science field.

Selection in science for the school library presents some problems not encountered in other fields, certainly not so frequently. Material should be up to date in all fields, but in science, where changes take place so frequently, some books go out of date soon after they become a part of the school library collection. The school librarian on a limited budget finds it difficult to supply scientific materials that continue to be fresh, accurate, and up to date. He must also be constantly at work evaluating books in the collection and weeding out those no longer useful.

Fortunately there is a good backlog of science materials written by outstanding writers which remain usable over a considerable period of time. Many such books contain topics in which change is not so frequent. A few examples are: *Strange Animals I Have Known* by Raymond Lee Ditmars (Harcourt, 1931), in which the author recounts his interesting experiences in collecting specimens for the New York Zoological Park; *Stars for Sam* (Harcourt, 1931), now in a revised edition edited by Paul F. Brandwein (Harcourt, 1960), and other books by William Maxwell Reed which children still read with pleasure and profit; Harriet E. Huntington's *Let's Go Outdoors* (Doubleday, 1939), a book of nature study with photographs for the younger readers; and *The Land We Live On* (Doubleday, 1944) by Carroll Lane Fenton and Mildred Adams Fenton, which shows how soil is made, changed, wasted, or destroyed, and how it may be restored.

Other science books of lasting value are revised from time to time. Examples of this type are: *How Big Is Big? From Stars to Atoms* by Herman and Nina Schneider (W. R. Scott, 1950), a new edition of a 1946 book, and *Handbook of Nature-Study* by Anna Botsford Comstock (Comstock Publishing, 1939), now in its twenty-fourth edition. First published in 1911, this book contains some material on virtually all phases of nature study and is useful with high school pupils and for teachers of science at any level.

Somewhat comparable to the Comstock book are two more recent books by Bertha Morris Parker, *The Golden Treasury of Natural History* (Simon & Schuster, 1952) and *The Golden Book of Science* (Simon, & Schuster, 1956). Because of the nature of the material in these books, especially the colored pictures, they should prove useful in elementary and junior high school libraries. Bertha Morris Parker, with several others, is author of some eighty titles in the Basic Science Education Series published by Row, Peterson for grades one through nine. Each of these pamphlets consists of about forty pages of interesting text with colored pictures on one of a wide variety of scientific topics. Among the 1959 titles are *How Animals Get Food,* for elementary grades, and *The Everyday Atom,* for junior high schools.

Another series of pamphlets in the 500's is the Webster Classroom Science Library published by the Webster Publishing Company. The text is prepared by Kay Ware and other writers and is accompanied by many clear illustrations in black and white. Two representative titles, both published in 1957, are *Let's Read About Flowers* and *Let's Read About Trees.* These pamphlets are also for younger readers.

In addition to those already mentioned, a few other outstanding writers in science may be listed. For a number of years, Roy Chapman Andrews wrote on the high school level and several of his books, including *Meet Your Ancestors; a Biography of Primitive Man* (Viking, 1945), are still on standard lists. More recently he has contributed several volumes in the Allabout Books series, for example *All About Dinosaurs* (Random House, 1953) for junior high school and upper elementary pupils. Nelson Frederick Beeler's "Experiments" books are helpful wherever science is taught. Ira Maximilian Freeman and Mae Blacker Freeman, a husband and wife team, have a series of "Fun with" books, most of them in science. John Bryan Lewellen, whose books are also in the 300's and 600's, has two notable books in the 500's: *The Mighty Atom* (Knopf, 1955) for grades three to six and *You and Atomic Energy and Its Wonderful Uses* (Childrens Press, 1949) for grades five to nine. His *Understanding Electronics: From Vacuum Tube to Thinking Machine* (Crowell, 1957) meets a need of both junior and senior high school pupils.

Other writers are Olive Lydia Earle and Roger Tory Peterson on the subject of birds, and Edwin Way Teale who usually writes about insects. Peterson is also editor of the Peterson Field Guide Series sponsored by the National Wildlife Federation and the National Audubon Society. An example of the books in this series is *Field Guide to the Mammals* (Houghton, 1952) by William Henry Burt.

Anne Terry White has books on a variety of subjects, most often about prehistoric times. Outstanding titles are *First Men in the World* (Random House, 1953) and *Prehistoric America* (Random House, 1951), both in the Landmark Books series. Several other books by Mrs. White similar to these are classified in the 900's and discussed in Chapter 9. However, in the 500's she has a book each on the subjects of stars, rivers, and rocks. A more recent book in this area is *The Fossil Book; a Record of Prehistoric Life* (Doubleday, 1958) by Carroll Lane Fenton and Mildred Adams Fenton. A fascinating book which surveys the plant and animal fossils of the past two million years, with hundreds of photographs, drawings and full-page colored illustrations, it is expensive but worth the high price. This book will probably be most useful in the reference collection.

In the field of electricity, though both have written on a variety of topics in the 500's and 600's, the names of Raymond Francis Yates and Alfred Powell Morgan are outstanding on the high school level. Morgan's *Adventures in Electrochemistry* (Scribner, 1959) is the revised edition of *Things a Boy Can Do with Electrochemistry* (1940).

However, the majority of books on science, especially those on the elementary level, have been writen by a younger group of writers and published largely since 1950. There are books on almost every topic in the 500's from the older one of animals to the more recent topic of atomic energy. Teachers and librarians, becoming acquainted for the first time with books for children and young people, are astounded at the number available in science. These new books are fresh, interesting, and attractive in format, and usually have good illustrations. Teachers find Jane Werner Watson's *World of Science; Scientists at Work Today in Many Challenging Fields* (Simon & Schuster, 1958) very good as an overview of science for elementary pupils. Examples of two recent books on one phase of science are *Western Butterflies* by Arthur C. Smith (Lippincott, 1961) and *Caterpillars* by Dorothy Sterling (Doubleday, 1961). Both books are illustrated in color and in black and white.

While space forbids listing many writers, a few more should be mentioned. Irving Adler, who also uses the pseudonym of Robert Irving, has written *Fire in Your Life* (Day, 1955) and *Weather in Your Life* (Day, 1959). Other titles are *Hurricanes and Twisters* (Knopf, 1955) and *The Sun and Its Family* (Day, 1958). Adler's books are usually illustrated by Ruth and Peggy Adler.

Glenn Orlando Blough writes interesting books in the field of science for younger readers. He devises catchy titles that appeal to children, such as *Wait for the Sunshine; the Story of Seasons and Growing Things* (McGraw, 1954) and *Who Lives in This House? A Story of Animal Families* (McGraw, 1957), and writes so simply that children in the first three grades get a taste of science.

Samuel Epstein and Beryl Williams Epstein have written, among other books, *The First Book of Electricity* (F. Watts, 1953) and *All About the Desert* (Random House, 1957). Roy A. Gallant has a long list of "Exploring" books, as *Exploring the Moon* (Garden City Books, 1955) and *Exploring the Weather* (Garden City Books, 1957) for upper elementary and junior high school pupils. These books are large in size and illustrated by different artists in black and white and in color. Like all similar books bound in boards and covered with paper, they should be ordered prebound. George Frederick Mason writes exclusively about animals. However, instead of dealing with some species of animals, as is the common pattern, each of his several books is about some phase of animal life, such as *Animal Tails* (Morrow, 1958). Mason illustrates his own books with black and white drawings which are clear and realistic. In the case of *Animal Tracks* (Morrow, 1943), for instance, the tracks are often drawn to correct size so that any child could easily identify tracks in woods and field.

Anna Pistorius writes a series of atractive books for small children, titles of which are in the form of a question: *What Tree Is It?* (Follett, 1953) and *What Dinosaur Is It?* (Follett, 1959). Each book describes and identifies a number of plants or animals, as the case may be, with large colored pictures and very brief text. The information is in the form of a quiz with answers at the end, so that each book is good for identification purposes. A similar series for the beginning reader is published by Benefic Press. *What Is a Fish?* (1958) and *What Is a Plant?* (1960) by Gene Darby are examples, though there is a long list from first grade through intermediate level on such topics as rockets and the solar system. Illa Podendorf has a number of books in the True Book Series, for example *The True Book of Insects* and *The True Book of Science Experiments* (Childrens Press, 1954). The latter book reflects the author's experiences as an elementary school teacher and will be useful to teachers also.

Herman and Nina Schneider might be mentioned also in the 600's, since they write in the field of applied science as well as pure science, with an occasional book on other subjects. Their books, on a variety of topics, range all the way from an easy book to one for junior high school readers and are read and enjoyed by children on each level. In addition to their above-mentioned *How Big Is Big?* for grades three to six, *Rocks, Rivers & the Changing Earth; a First Book about Geology* (W. R. Scott, 1951) will serve as an example of their books, this one for older readers, grades six to nine.

Millicent Ellis Selsam has written "Play with" books, such as *Play with Seeds* (Morrow, 1957), and also "See through" books, such as *See Through the Sea* (Harper, 1955), written with Betty Morrow, besides other books not part of any series. Mrs. Selsam's books are practical in that wherever possible she tells how things in nature contribute to man's welfare and comfort, as well as progress. Her books often include simple experiments which pupils can conduct with seeds, plants, and other things in nature. Irma Eleanor Schmidt Webber's science books are useful for the middle elementary grades, two to four and three to five. *Thanks to Trees;*

the Story of Their Use & Conservation (W. R. Scott, 1952) is a representative title, as is *Travelers All; the Story of How Plants Go Places* (W. R. Scott, 1944). The full-page illustrations in color by the author add a great deal to the simple text.

The list of books by Herbert Spencer Zim is perhaps the longest of any author in either *Children's Catalog* or *Standard Catalog for High School Libraries*. Most of his books are in the 500's, though a number are in the 600's. One wonders how Zim is able to write so many books on such different topics and manage each time to be successful in interesting his readers. As if to emphasize the number and variety of Zim's books, the *Children's Catalog* under the topic "Mammals" (599) lists the following: *Big Cats* (1955), *Elephants* (1946), *Great Whales* (1951), and *Monkeys* (1955)—all published by Morrow. In addition it lists a book, *Mammals; a Guide to Familiar American Species*, by Herbert S. Zim and Donald F. Hoffmeister (Simon & Schuster, 1955) in the Golden Nature Guide series for older readers. Zim has written an excellent book on hamsters, the fascinating animal often used for classroom observation and experimentation—*Golden Hamsters* (Morrow, 1951).

A program which has given impetus to science study in schools is the Traveling High School Science Library, administered by the American Association for the Advancement of Science and financed by the National Science Foundation, an agency of the United States Government. This program began operations in 1955 with 66 cooperating schools and planned to reach a projected total of 1,700 high schools for the school year 1959-1960. Each traveling library consists of 200 carefully selected science books for loan to schools. Each participating school receives at one time 50 books which are exchanged after two months for a similar group from another high school in the general area. In four periods of two months each, a school will have an opportunity to use all 200 books.

The objectives of the program are: (1) to stimulate an interest in reading science books; (2) to broaden the science background of high school students; (3) to encourage the choice of a scientific career by students with interests and abilities in science and mathematics; and (4) to demonstrate appropriate acquisitions for the high school library.

There are specified criteria which guide the selection of schools to receive the Traveling High School Science Library. Odds are in favor of the average-size high school which has a library and librarian and which meets certain requirements in its program of teaching science. While all high school libraries obviously cannot participate in this program, a pamphlet, *Books of the Traveling High School Science Library,* compiled by Hilary J. Deason, Director of the Science Library Program of the American Association for the Advancement of Science, is available to all as an aid in the selection of science books.[1] Librarians are reminded that books in the traveling library are largely on the adult level and selection should be made with pupils of a particular school in mind.

A similar program for elementary schools, the Traveling Elementary School Science Library, went into operation in September 1959. This consists of 160 books of science and mathematics for the first six grades, 40 in each of four collections to be kept by any participating school for a period of two months. In 1959-1960 these books were circulated to 1,000 elementary schools, each of which, among other requisites, had to have a centralized library. The aims of this program, similar to those for high schools, are: (1) to enlarge the elementary school library; (2) to stimulate establishment of libraries where they do not exist; (3) to provide enrichment materials for gifted children; and (4) to improve the teaching of science.

Librarians are again reminded that many books in the traveling library are difficult for pupils with limited background in science and that selection should be determined by conditions in the participating school.

A further aid is *The Science Book List for Children,* compiled by Hilary J. Deason, with Ruth N. Foy of the Baldwin Whitehall Schools in Pittsburgh, Pennsylvania, as library consultant (American Association for the Advancement of Science and the National

[1] Order latest edition from the American Association for the Advancement of Science, 1515 Massachusetts Ave., N.W., Washington 5, D.C.

Science Foundation, 1960.)[2] This list was prepared "to help elementary schools and children's divisions of public libraries build up adequate collections of science books for their science minded readers."

In closing this discussion of science materials in the school library, attention of school librarians is called to the fact that certain books in science are available for purchase under Title III of the National Defense Education Act. Details will not be given here, but each school librarian should get in touch with his local supervisor, either of school libraries or of schools in general, or with the school library supervisor in the state Department of Education, to ascertain how the new Federal act may be implemented in the local program for school library service.

APPLIED SCIENCE OR USEFUL ARTS: 600 CLASSIFICATION

Some books in the 600's are on topics similar to those in the 300's, while others are more like those of the 500's. In schools such books are used interchangeably when a class pursues a topic represented in any two, or perhaps in all three, classifications. In the social sciences, for example, there is overlapping when books deal with such subjects as communication, conservation, or transportation. In science, several topics are involved in the 600's as well as 500's. For example, books on wild animals, their habits and behavior, are classified in 591, while those on domestic animals, including pets or potential pets, such as Zim's book *Golden Hamsters*, already mentioned, are in 636. Books about chemistry as a science are classified as 540, while books about chemistry in industries are in 660. In choosing books in the 600's, the school librarian must therefore keep in mind offerings also in the 300's and 500's so that they will complement rather than duplicate each other.

Some years ago school libraries would not have needed many books in the 600's. Indeed, not a great many books were available in this field—very few on the elementary level. There were books on agriculture, airplanes, domestic animals, fire prevention and

---

[2] This list, like the pamphlet noted above, may be ordered from the American Association for the Advancement of Science.

protection, home economics, hygiene, inventions and inventors, and physiology, still useful in school library collections. However, with the present unprecedented emphasis on things mechanical, the 600's now include books on such technical topics as aeronautics, engineering (both electrical and mechanical), motor vehicles, radio, submarines, and television.

Another comparatively recent innovation in modern offerings in the 600's is the inclusion of books dealing with reproduction, either intended for the pupils to read themselves or for use by teachers and parents in giving sex instruction to pupils. While schools differ in the use of such materials, school libraries generally include such books as *Being Born,* in a revised and enlarged edition by Frances Bruce Strain (Appleton, 1954); the third edition of Karl De Schweinitz's *Growing Up* (Macmillan, 1953); and *The Story of a Baby* (Viking, 1939), a picture book for very young readers, by Marie Hall Ets. In selecting material in this category, the school librarian should consult with the teachers, and perhaps with parent groups, as to what is needed and the use to be made of it in the school library.

A topic greatly expanded is aeronautics, especially in the area of interplanetary voyages, artificial satellites, rockets, jets, missiles, and whatever else the boys have in mind when they ask eagerly what the school library has on space travel. On the high school level, the topic motor vehicle engineering has also been expanded to include books on how to drive a car safely and how to keep one in good running condition. For the girls, as part of the modern collection on child care, usually considered in home economics classes, there are recent books on baby sitting. For both boys and girls a surprising number of books on medicine are available, dealing with strides made in the prevention of diseases and the development of new remedies such as the antibiotics.

In addition to the authors who write in both the 500's and 600's, some of whom have already been mentioned, there are also some writers who contribute books primarily in the field of applied science. Jeanne Bendick has written several of the "First Books" for younger readers in the 600's. Examples are *The First Book of Airplanes* (F. Watts, 1958); *The First Book of Space Travel,* now revised and rewritten (F. Watts, 1960), and *The First Book of Supermarkets* (F. Watts, 1954), about which subject very little else has been published. She has also written a new fourth edition of *Electronics for Young People* (McGraw, 1960), first published by McGraw in 1944 as *Electronics for Boys and Girls*, which has proved useful through the years. Another of her books, in collaboration with Robert Bendick, is the third revised edition of *Television Works Like This* (McGraw, 1959), replacing editions of the same title first published in 1949. In addition to her own books, Jeanne Bendick has illustrated books by Glenn O. Blough, Mary Elting, the Schneiders, and other writers in science and applied science. A fairly recent book in the field of electronics is *Using Electronics; a Book of Things to Make* (Crowell, 1958) by Harry Zarchy, who has also written a number of books about hobbies, classified in the 700's.

Franklyn Mansfield Branley, who is joint author with Nelson Frederick Beeler of some of the "Experiments" books in science, has written on his own *Experiments in the Principles of Space Travel* (Crowell, 1955), *Exploring by Satellite* and *Solar Energy*, both published by Crowell in 1957 for the junior high level. His *A Book of Moon Rockets for You,* with illustrations by Leonard Kessler (Crowell, 1959), is one of several books of science for the picture-book age. William Harry Crouse's *Understanding Science,* first published in 1948, is now in a new, revised edition (McGraw, 1956) and covers a wide variety of topics. Crouse has also written *Automotive Engines; Construction, Operation, and Maintenance* (McGraw, 1959), now in its second edition, and the fourth edition of *Automotive Mechanics* (McGraw, 1960).

Burr Watkins Leyson, whose name has long been associated with books on aeronautics, is also the author of *More Modern Wonders, and How They Work* (Dutton, 1955) and *More Marvels of Industrial Science* (Dutton, 1958), both revised editions of earlier titles. Fletcher Pratt was the author of *All About Rockets and Jets* (Random House, 1955). With Jack Coggins he wrote *Rockets, Satellites and Space Travel,* now in a revised edition (Random House, 1958), and *By Space Ship to the Moon,* now also in a revised edition (Random House, 1958). The former, first published in 1951 under the title *Rockets, Jets, Guided Missiles and Space Ships,* was edited by Willy Ley, one of several outstanding technical experts and scientists who have contributed books in the 600's for high school readers. Other such writers are Isaac Asimov, Wernher von Braun, Arthur Charles Clarke, and Lester Del Rey. These have also made some contribution to the field of science fiction.

All the books in the 600's are not on space travel and of interest chiefly to boys. There are also books that appeal to the girls, principally in the 640's under the general heading Home Economics, on such subjects as foods, entertaining, clothing, fashions, and personal appearance. Such books are used often with books on personality in the 100's and books on etiquette in 395. Outside of class, girls with personal problems read them on their own.

In the line of foods and cookery, there are such names as Mary Davies Swartz Rose, whose *Foundations of Nutrition,* has been on school library shelves since it was first published in 1927. Now in its fifth edition (Macmillan, 1956), it has been reorganized and largely rewritten by Clara Mae Taylor and Grace Macleod. Fannie Merritt Farmer is famous for the *Boston Cooking-School Cook Book,* the tenth edition of which is a complete revision by Wilma Lord Perkins (Little, 1959) entitled the *All New Fannie Farmer Boston Cooking School Cookbook.* Mrs. Perkins is also the author of *Fannie Farmer Junior Cook Book* in a revised edition (Little, 1957). Of the two cookbooks by Irma S. Rombauer, *The Joy of Cooking* (Bobbs, 1951), written with the collaboration of her daughter, Marion Rombauer Becker, seems preferable.

Two authors of books about sewing are Byrta Carson, author of *How You Look and Dress; a First Course in Clothing* (McGraw, 1959), in its third edition, and Mildred Graves Ryan, author of *Dress Smartly* and *Sew Smartly,* both published by Scribner in 1956. A somewhat different book is *Toys to Sew* by Charlotte L. Davis and Jessie Robinson (Lippincott, 1961). With simple directions and clear illustrations, it tells how to make puppets as well as rag dolls and stuffed animals.

As will be seen from this brief discussion of subjects, with representative authors and titles, books available for selection in the 600's are of a practical nature, some of them in the how-to-do-it category. Since many of the topics are allied to what men do for a living—agriculture, engineering, medicine, to name only three —these books are often useful in study of certain careers or in any program of vocational guidance. While most materials in the 600's are called for in school libraries in connection with classroom activities, some subjects, for example space travel and allied topics, are currently very popular for general reading. Selection of books in the 600's, as mentioned earlier, should be considered in light of certain sections of the 300's and 500's where there are similar materials.

CHAPTER 8

o

THE ARTS AND LITERATURE

ART, MUSIC, AND SPORTS: 700 CLASSIFICATION

Books from the 700 classification included in school library collections will depend largely on the curriculum and its demands for materials in the fine arts. However, at least three broad areas (art, music, and sports) will probably be represented in any school library. In the realm of sports particularly, the pupils read on their own and there is great demand especially from boys for books about athletic games: how they are played, what the rules are, and how a player may improve his game. With midget teams and little leagues springing up all over the country, the source of demand for sports books gets younger all the while. Pupils also ask for books about hobbies of various kinds, some of which are classified in the 700's.

An old stand-by in art history is *Art Through the Ages* by Helen Gardner (Harcourt, 1959). This book was published first in 1926 and is now in its fourth edition, revised under the editorship of Sumner McKnight Crosby by the Department of History of Art at Yale University. It offers the reader a basic understanding of the principal forms of art throughout the ages and, because of its wide scope, is a book which the school librarian may wish to keep in the reference collection and duplicate for circulation. Another book which pupils will probably enjoy more on their own is Thomas Craven's *Rainbow Book of Art* (World Publishing, 1956), which contains hundreds of well-chosen reproductions, many in full color. Craven has also edited *Treasury of Art Masterpieces; from the Renaissance to the Present Day,* now in a revised and enlarged edition (Simon & Schuster, 1952) which high school libraries with demand for art history books might consider. A book simple enough for upper elementary pupils is *Famous Paintings; an Introduction to Art for Young People,* by Alice

Elizabeth Chase (Platt, 1951). This book includes 172 examples of pictures produced in the last five thousand years, divided by subjects of interest to children. Elementary school libraries will probably want a copy of another old stand-by, now in a revised and enlarged edition, *Child's History of Art* (Appleton, 1951), by Virgil Mores Hillyer and Edward Greene Huey, which covers architecture and sculpture, as well as painting.

Helpful for teachers, especially on the elementary level, is a book, *Pioneer Art in America,* by Carolyn Sherwin Bailey (Viking, 1944). This book covers, among many other topics, American craftsmen who have worked in various media of the decorative arts. Such material will probably be used with classes in the social studies. A practical book is *Creative Hands; an Introduction to Craft Techniques,* by Doris E. Cox and Barbara Warren, now in a second edition (Wiley, 1951). Several of the "Made in" books deal with crafts of different countries and are classified in 745. An outstanding example is *Made in Mexico* (Knopf, 1952) by Patricia Fent Ross. Like others of the series, this book explains how many things are made in Mexico, together with interesting customs connected with their use. However, this book also has chapters on such things as Mexican music and the dance, literature, and science, not actually involved with handicrafts.

Many books in fine arts link up with the widespread interest in hobbies among school pupils, especially about junior high school age. Such a book is *Catalogue of the World's Most Popular Coins* (Sterling, 1956) by Fred Reinfeld. This book is useful both for identifying coins and for introducing the reader to the art of collecting. It includes information about coins that are easy to locate as well as those that are more elusive. This is likewise a book often recommended for reference use. Reinfeld is joint author with David Alfred Boehm, the latter using the pen name Robert V. Masters, of a revised edition of *Coinometry* (Sterling, 1958), which traces the history of money in America. The book is well illustrated with photographs which make it useful also for purposes of identification.

There are a number of books whose titles begin "Fun with," such as *Fun with Shells* (Lippincott, 1958) by Joseph Leeming, who has produced similar books about clay, string, wood, and other materials, and *Fun with a Pencil* by Andrew Loomis (Viking, 1939). For pupils interested in learning to draw, Amy Hogeboom's books, such as *Cats and How to Draw Them* (Vanguard, 1949) and *Dogs and How to Draw Them* (Vanguard, 1944), prove intriguing. She presents animals of several breeds in various poses, each with a photograph and simple line drawing to show how the animal may be sketched.

Harry Zarchy has a long list of books dealing with hobbies, especially with how to make things, all illustrated by the author. A good example is *Let's Make a Lot of Things; Crafts for Home, School, and Camp* (Knopf, 1948). Other books by Zarchy are *Ceramics* (Knopf, 1954), and *Jewelry Making and Enameling* (Knopf, 1959). Zarchy has also written under the pseudonym of Roger Lewis such books as *Sculpture; Clay, Soap, & Other Materials* (Knopf, 1952) and *Weaving,* (Knopf, 1953). Under either name, his books are practical and helpful, qualities appreciated by readers wanting information about hobbies. Handicraft books are usually designated as suitable for grades six to nine, but are not actually confined to any one level of appeal or use in a school library.

There are some very good books on photography for amateur enthusiasts, who are numerous, now that candid cameras and Polaroids with on-the-spot development have made the subject increasingly popular. An old stand-by is *How To Make Good Pictures,* published by the Eastman Kodak Company, Rochester, New York, and distributed by Random House. This book is revised frequently, so the school librarian will want the latest edition. The subtitle varies, the one for the thirtieth edition (1957) being "an entertaining, authoritative handbook for everyone who takes pictures." The contents cover just about everything the amateur would need to know. For those who attempt home movies, Eastman has a similar publication entitled *How to Make Good Home Movies,* first published in 1938 but with frequent revisions to keep the material up to date. Both books are nontechnical and very practical, and high school pupils find them helpful.

Another book popular with young people, probably because of its title, is *Photography for Teen-Agers,* now in its second edition, by Lucile Robertson Marshall (Prentice-Hall, 1957). It is a complete handbook, covering every phase of the subject, and contains a chapter on how to make the hobby earn money for the amateur photographer. A book which children in the upper elementary grades can use is *Fun with Your Camera* by Mae Blacker Freeman and Ira Maximilian Freeman (Random House, 1955), which includes many suggestions for avoiding errors common among beginners in photography.

How Music Grew; from Prehistoric Times to the Present Day by Marion Bauer and Ethel Peyser will be found in many school libraries. First published by Putnam in 1925, it was completely revised in 1939. This is another book which often proves useful in the reference collection. These same authors have written two other books, *Music Through the Ages* (Putnam, 1946) and *Twentieth Century Music* (Putnam, 1947), both of these new editions, completely revised. The former contains biographical sketches of important musicians as the various types of music are considered. The latter is a guide to modern music for those who listen to it in concert halls or over the air.

A history of music in this country is *Our American Music; Three Hundred Years of It* by John Tasker Howard. The third edition, revised and reset (Crowell, 1954), has supplementary chapters by James Lyons and traces the development of various types of American music from early New England days to the present. John Tasker Howard, in collaboration with George Kent Bellows, has also written *Short History of Music in America* (Crowell, 1957), which includes all types of music from all periods of history.

A book which may be correlated with American history is *History Sings; Backgrounds of American Music* by Hazel Gertrude Kinscella (University Publishing, 1957). Teachers like this book because it gives a background of American music as it developed in various periods of American history, which makes it useful with history classes. This is a new edition of a book first published in 1940. It includes, by way of example, brief information about the song "Cielito Lindo" popular during the pioneer days of California and revived fairly recently. There is a section of "Lonesome Tunes," still preserved in the mountains of Kentucky, Tennessee, and Virginia. Discussed also is the background of "Carry Me Back to Old Virginny" and other post-Civil War songs by James A. Bland.

Among books on opera for young readers, probably the best is the newly revised edition of *Victor Book of Operas* by Louis Biancolli and Robert Bagar (Simon & Schuster, 1953). This book was first published in 1912 as *Victor Book of the Opera*. Several new operas have been added in the later edition and some of the older operas recently revived are likewise included. Young people like the act-by-act stories of standard operas which they hear. The book also includes a list of records available for each opera discussed and for some not included.

With an increased nation-wide interest in folklore, including folk music, material about folk songs should be in school libraries. Perhaps the best collections for high school use are *American Ballads and Folk Songs,* collected and compiled by John Avery Lomax and his son, Alan (Macmillan, 1934), and Carl Sandburg's *American Songbag* (Harcourt, 1927). In the former the songs are divided by types, such as "Working on the Railroad," "Break Downs and Play Parties," and "Spirituals" of both the white and Negro races, while the Sandburg book, with songs from all parts of America, forms a veritable folk-song history of the country. Carl Lamson Carmer has compiled *America Sings; Stories and Songs of Our Country's Growing* (Knopf, 1942), which is useful with upper elementary and junior high school pupils. Opal Wheeler's *Sing for America* (Dutton, 1944), a book of folk songs for younger children with excellent colored illustrations by Gustaf Tenggren, is now out of print but is useful in libraries which have a copy or can secure one. A story explaining the origin of each folk song is helpful in making children interested in folk music.

For the very young, there is *Singing Time; Songs for Nursery & School* by Satis Narrona Barton Coleman and Alice G. Thorne (Day, 1929), also with very nice illustrations, and *The New Singing Time; a Book of Songs for Little Children* (Day, 1950) by Mrs. Coleman alone.

If there is an orchestra group in the school, or even in the community, there will be interest among some pupils in orchestras and orchestral music. On the upper elementary and junior high school levels, there are two excellent choices: *Tune-Up; the Instruments of the Orchestra and Their Players* by Harriet E. Huntington (Doubleday, 1942), and Marion Lacey's *Picture Book of Musical Instruments* (Lothrop, 1942). Each of these books pictures various types of instruments and gives their origin, construction, and contribution to the symphony orchestra. Probably the best book for the high school level is *From These Comes Music; Instruments of the Band and Orchestra* by Hope Stoddard (Crowell, 1952). Another book in this field, published in 1950 by Houghton, is *This Is an Orchestra* by Elsa Z. Posell. Both books describe the various instruments, their positions in the orchestra, and their contributions to the music. The latter book is more suitable for use with junior high school pupils but can be used also in elementary school libraries.

The subject of Recreation (790) has one of the largest groups of books for young people in the field of fine arts. Among others, it includes such subjects as: games, movies, puppets, circuses, rodeos, the theater, ballet, parties, puzzles and riddles, magic, chess, and card games. Chess is reported popular even with some elementary school pupils, probably because of increased interest in mathematics. A recent book, *Chess for Young People* by Fred Reinfeld (Holt, 1961), should interest high school pupils. The author, whose books about coins have been discussed above, is a past chess master. Most important of all in school libraries are athletics and sports, including not only the traditional ones of basketball, baseball, football, track, etc., but also the comparatively new sport of skin diving. Archery seems to be enjoying quite a fad now, especially among pupils of junior high school age who attend summer camps. Books on hunting, including adventurous books about big game hunting such as those by James Edward Corbett and Theodore J. Waldeck, seem not to be so popular as some years ago.

Only a few of the more important titles in the 790's can be singled out for mention. Though it is old, there is still probably not a better general book than *Games,* by Jessie Hubbell Bancroft (Macmillan, 1937). This is the revised and enlarged edition of a 1909 book published under the title *Games for the Playground, Home, School and Gymnasium.* Primarily for use by teachers, it is used also by pupils as they plan get-togethers of various kinds. The book contains over 400 games from many countries, with music, diagrams, and pictures wherever needed. *Games of Many Nations,* by E. O. Harbin (Abingdon, 1954), may prove of help to teachers who consider amusements and sports part of the culture of various people. The third edition of *The Story of the Olympic Games, 776 B.C.—1960 A.D.,* by John Kieran and Arthur Daley (Lippincott, 1961), proves a useful addition to the high school collection, as pupils seeing games on television and reading about them in the newspapers often want additional information about the Olympics.

The high school library will probably have the *Encyclopedia of Sports* by Frank Grant Menke (A. S. Barnes, 1953), a new and revised edition of the 1947 *New Encyclopedia of Sports.* This book presents historical facts about indoor and outdoor sports and games, rules, records, lists of champions, attendance totals, salaries, etc.

Every school library will need books on basketball, baseball, and football. An assortment of titles on each of these games is available, some of them written or edited by outstanding players and coaches. Choice of such books most helpful for a given school library is likely to be made with the cooperation of the coach or perhaps a committee of school athletes.

For elementary children, several of the "First Book" series are on athletics and sports. Examples are *The First Book of Baseball* by Mary Elting, written under the pseudonym of Benjamin Brewster, with pictures by Jeanne Bendick, now in a revised edition

(F. Watts, 1958), and *The First Book of Basketball* by Don Schiffer (F. Watts, 1959). Other examples of this series in the 700's are *The First Book of the Ballet* by Noel Streatfeild (F. Watts, 1953) and *The First Book of Jazz,* by Langston Hughes (F. Watts, 1955), but those are addressed to junior high school pupils rather than to pupils in elementary schools.

For boys interested in guns and similar weapons, two books by Carroll Burleigh Colby may be useful. They are *First Bow and Arrow; How To Use It Skillfully for Outdoor Fun* (Coward-McCann, 1955) and *First Rifle; How to Shoot It Straight and Use It Safely* (Coward-McCann, 1954), both for readers of grades five to about eight. As in the author's other books, the material is presented simply but clearly and further elucidated by realistic pen and ink drawings.

LITERATURE—DRAMA, ESSAYS, POETRY, AND SHORT STORIES: 800 CLASSIFICATION

Elementary Schools

Because needs in the 800's are so different in elementary schools from those in high schools, materials on the two levels are here being considered separately. Other than poetry, the 800's do not offer an extensive field of reading for pupils in the elementary grades. Essays are not considered at all and drama is not studied on the elementary level. When groups of children wish to present a play for a school program, they will most likely write it themselves, probably using material derived from some classroom situation. Short stories are not usually among the reading interests of young children. The nearest thing to short stories consists of excerpts from favorite books of fiction or simple stories gathered into a collection. An index useful in locating hard-to-find stories for children is *Subject and Title Index to Short Stories for Children* (A.L.A., 1955), which elementary school librarians may wish to consider.

There are available numerous anthologies of children's literature, either poetry or prose selections, sometimes a combination of the two. These are probably most useful to teachers who like to have at hand "pick-up-reading" for any extra time in school or for some special occasion. An anthology of entertaining stories and poems, *The Arbuthnot Anthology of Children's Literature,* compiled by May Hill Arbuthnot, is three volumes in one (Scott, 1961). The individual titles are *Time for Poetry, Time for Fairy Tales, Old and New;* and *Time for True Tales and Almost True.* These may be purchased as separates, a revised edition of each having been published by Scott in 1961. *Anthology of Children's Literature,* edited by Edna Johnson, Evelyn R. Sickels, and Frances Eichenberg, now in its third edition (Houghton, 1959), is outstanding both for its comprehensive coverage and quality of selections.

Poetry. There is a real need on the elementary level for poetry, both in single volumes by outstanding poets and in collections of poems by many writers. To locate poems in scattered sources the library will need *Index to Children's Poetry,* compiled by John Edward Brewton and Sara Westbrook Brewton (Wilson, 1942), and its *First Supplement* (1954). This is a title, subject, author, and first-line index to poetry in collections, which proves useful in school libraries. There is also the *Subject Index to Poetry for Children and Young People,* compiled by Violet Sell and others (A.L.A., 1957), which indexes 157 poetry collections under many subjects useful in elementary schools. Small libraries may consider these indexes rather expensive for their limited collections of poetry, and they will probably be kept in the reference collections.

The Brewtons (see above) have also compiled a good collection of poetry entitled *Bridled with Rainbows; Poems about Many Things of Earth and Sky* (Macmillan, 1949), and another, *Gaily We Parade; a Collection of Poems about People, Here, There and Everywhere* (Macmillan, 1940). An old, but still very good, general collection of poetry for boys and girls is Mildred P. Harrington's *Ring-a-Round* (Macmillan, 1930). The compiler, a former children's librarian who knows and loves children's poetry, made these selections for her own nieces and nephews, and the book contains many favorite poems of all children. It is appropriately illustrated by Corydon Bell. More recently, Helen Josephine

Ferris, long-time editor of Junior Literary Guild, has edited *Favorite Poems, Old and New* (Doubleday, 1957), an excellent book which contains more than 700 poems divided into eighteen sections according to children's interests, such as "Animals," "Fairies," "Transportation." The illustrations in this collection are by Leonard Weisgard.

Sung Under the Silver Umbrella contains about two hundred poems selected by the Literature Committee of the Association for Childhood Education International (Macmillan, 1935). Some are by older poets, often not represented in the more recent anthologies, while some are by contemporary poets.

Very Young Verses (Houghton, 1945), compiled by two nursery school teachers, Barbara Peck Geismer and Antoinette Brown Suter, is a collection of poetry useful with young children for almost any occasion. Blanche Jennings Thompson has compiled a very helpful collection of poetry which teachers generally like under the title *Silver Pennies* (Macmillan, 1925). A sequel, *More Silver Pennies*, with the same compiler and publisher (1938), proves not so good as *Silver Pennies*.

Another collection mostly of poetry which teachers like, especially for use with classwork, is *My American Heritage; A Collection of Songs, Poems, Speeches, Sayings, and Other Writings Dear to Our Hearts*, compiled by Ralph B. Henry and Lucille Pannell (Rand McNally, 1949), which suggests something for almost any occasion.

Lastly, reference must be made to several collections of poetry, all acceptable in school libraries, edited by Louis Untermeyer. A favorite among his collections for upper elementary pupils is *Stars To Steer By* (Harcourt, 1941), which includes 150 poems arranged under a variety of headings such as "Bridge of Books," "The Merry Heart," and "With Many Voices."

While the poetry section of any library will undoubtedly start with anthologies containing poems by many poets, it will later expand to include individual volumes of poetry by some of the children's favorites. It is not possible to name all writers of poetry for younger children, but some whose poetry should be available to elementary pupils are: Dorothy Aldis, Harry Behn, Walter de la Mare, Eleanor Farjeon, Eugene Field, Robert Frost, Rose Fyleman, Edward Lear, A. A. Milne, Elizabeth MacKinstry, Christopher Morley, Elizabeth Madox Roberts, Christina Rossetti, Carl Sandburg, Robert Louis Stevenson, Sara Teasdale, and Nancy Byrd Turner.

It would seem a pity, for instance, for any child passing through the early elementary grades to miss Alan Alexander Milne's poems in *When We Were Very Young* (1924) and *Now We Are Six* (1927, reprinted in 1950), both published by Dutton with charming black and white drawings by Ernest H. Shepard. Librarians may also be interested in the recent edition (Dutton, 1961) of Milne's classics in a larger format. Knopf has a 1961 edition of Walter de la Mare's *Peacock Pie* with illustrations by Barbara Cooney, who won the Caldecott Medal in 1959 for *Chanticleer and the Fox,* adapted from Chaucer.

Junior and Senior High Schools

Reference Books. Because high school classes do work in various phases of literature, any library serving them will have need of books to be used as reference. *Reader's Encyclopedia; an Encyclopedia of World Literature and the Arts, with Supplement* (Crowell, 1955), edited by William Rose Benét will prove helpful in any high school library. First published in 1948, the book is arranged alphabetically and contains 19,088 articles covering many phases of literature and allied topics. Some high school libraries may wish to include also John Albert Macy's *Story of the World's Literature* (Liveright, 1950), a history of literature that includes the principal literatures of the world but is devoted largely to English and American literature.

Familiar Quotations; a Collection of Passages, Phrases and Proverbs Traced to Their Sources in Ancient and Modern Literature, by John Bartlett, will be needed in any high school library. It is now in its thirteenth edition, completely revised (Little, 1955). Another good index to quotations is *Home Book of Quotations, Classical and Modern,* selected and arranged by Burton Egbert

Stevenson (Dodd, 1959), which is in its ninth edition. This is a comprehensive collection of almost 75,000 quotations by nearly 5,000 authors arranged alphabetically by subject, a feature which makes it useful in schools.

Since its original publication in 1904, *Granger's Index to Poetry*, by Edith Granger, has been an indispensable aid to librarians. The fifth edition, newly revised under the editorship of William F. Bernhardt, indexes 574 volumes of poetry anthologies published through June 30, 1960 (Columbia University Press, 1962).

Poetry. In high schools, because classes often study literature by countries, librarians may wish to separate American poetry from British poetry, as is done in the *Standard Catalog for High School Libraries*. Many libraries, however, classify all literature in the English language in the 820's, so that all poetry would be in 821.

Among American poets whose poems should be available to high school pupils are Stephen Vincent Benét, Rosemary Benét, Countee Cullen, Emily Dickinson, Paul Laurence Dunbar, Robert Frost, Langston Hughes, James Weldon Johnson, Vachel Lindsay, Henry Wadsworth Longfellow, Amy Lowell, Edna St. Vincent Millay, James Whitcomb Riley, Edwin Arlington Robinson, Carl Sandburg, Sara Teasdale, Mark Van Doren, John Greenleaf Whittier, and Walt Whitman.

Some of the outstanding British poets whose works should be in high school libraries are Elizabeth Barrett Browning, Robert Browning, Robert Burns, Rudyard Kipling, John Masefield, John Milton, Alfred Noyes, William Shakespeare, Percy Bysshe Shelley, Alfred Tennyson, and William Wordsworth.

Works of these poets are available in separate volumes and in many splendid collections. An outstanding anthology is *An Inheritance of Poetry*, collected and arranged by Gladys L. Adshead and Annis Duff (Houghton, 1948). This is a collection of American and British poetry from many sources chosen especially for older boys and girls. An old stand-by is the *Oxford Book of English Verse, 1250-1918,* chosen and edited by Sir Arthur Quiller-Couch, the latest edition of which was published in 1959 (Oxford). Burton Egbert Stevenson's *Home Book of Verse for Young Folks,* in its revised and enlarged edition (Holt, 1929), is especially suitable for use with high school readers, as its title implies. *This Singing World; an Anthology of Modern Poetry for Young People,* collected and edited by Louis Untermeyer (Harcourt, 1923), is another example of poetry for adolescents. This same compiler has edited *Modern British Poetry* (Harcourt, 1950), a chronological arrangement of selections of poetry from Thomas Hardy to Dylan Thomas and Spender which some larger high schools may find useful. This book was first published in 1920. A companion volume to the above is *Modern American Poetry,* also edited by Untermeyer (Harcourt, 1950); it was first published in 1929. The chronological arrangement makes the volume useful when poetry is studied by periods, and the biographical and critical sketches preceding each poet's work prove a valuable feature.

Another collection with an American flavor is the revised and enlarged edition of *Cowboy Songs and Other Frontier Ballads* compiled by John Avery Lomax and his son, Alan (Macmillan, 1938). These songs were collected from western mining camps and cattle ranches and appeal especially to boys.

Poems of American History, in a revised edition compiled by Burton Egbert Stevenson (Houghton, 1922), contains about eight hundred poems classified historically from the time of the discovery of America to the twentieth century. There is an explanation of the setting before each poem, which proves helpful to students.

Golden Slippers; an Anthology of Negro Poetry for Young Readers, compiled by Arna Wendell Bontemps (Harper, 1941), is one of the best volumes to introduce high school pupils to Negro poetry and poets. Senior high school libraries wanting more than an introduction might choose either *Poetry of the Negro, 1746-1949,* edited by Bontemps and Langston Hughes (Doubleday, 1949), or the revised edition of the *Book of American Negro Poetry* of which James Weldon Johnson was the editor (Harcourt,

1931). The former is probably preferable, not only because of the later date, but also because the selections are somewhat more suitable for high school readers.

In 1927 Doubleday published *The Winged Horse; the Story of the Poets and Their Poetry* by Joseph Auslander and Frank Ernest Hill, a book which has proved invaluable in high school libraries. As the title implies, it is a history and criticism of poetry from the earliest times to the twentieth century. The book is written in narrative form which interests high school readers. In 1929 Doubleday published *The Winged Horse Anthology* compiled by Auslander and Hill, containing all the poems mentioned in *The Winged Horse,* which it complemented and which senior high school libraries particularly have found useful.

Drama. Drama is of interest more in senior than in junior high schools. Speech classes use a great deal of material in drama, and advanced English classes usually have a unit on drama. In either case, plays are studied in the classroom or read aloud, with pupils serving as characters. Pupils often present public performances of plays and a few teachers attempt playwriting on the high school level. Some pupils, usually girls, choose plays as a form of recreational reading.

Some of the American dramatists whose plays should be available to high school pupils include: Maxwell Anderson, Mary Coyle Chase, Eugene Gladstone O'Neill, George Simon Kaufman and Moss Hart, Oscar Hammerstein, Robert Emmet Sherwood, and Thornton Niven Wilder. A few plays by Arthur Miller, especially *Death of a Salesman,* and by Tennessee Williams, notably *Glass Menagerie,* and by other modern playwrights are found in collections of plays for high schools.

Among the best collections of American plays for high schools are those compiled and edited by John Gassner, who has written *Masters of the Drama,* now in its third edition revised and enlarged (Dover, 1954). This is a history of the drama in the major countries of the world with special attention given to America and England, a survey through the ages from the Greeks to Arthur Miller. The third edition adds two chapters on the drama since the Second World War. Gassner's series of collections, each entitled *Best Plays of the Modern American Theatre*, continues to prove useful in high school collections. The fourth of these covers the years 1951-1957 (Crown 1958). Another collection which he has edited is *Twenty Best European Plays on the American Stage* (Crown, 1957).

A comprehensive collection which may be needed in large libraries is *Representative American Plays; from 1767 to the Present Day* (Appleton, 1953), edited by Arthur Hobson Quinn and first published in 1917. The seventh edition contains thirty-one plays illustrating the development of the American drama. It begins with *The Prince of Parthia* by Thomas Godfrey, the first play written in America and performed in America by a professional company of actors (1767). A tragedy in blank verse, the play will probably no longer be read by the average high school pupil. The collection ends with *South Pacific,* by Oscar Hammerstein and Joshua Logan, adapted from James Albert Michener's *Tales of the South Pacific.*

Some high school libraries may wish to include an annual collection of plays, such as the "Best Plays" series published by Dodd, to acquaint pupils with current plays. This series has been edited by Louis Kronenberger since 1952. Attention should be called to the fact that this annual volume does not give in full the text of any play.

A few modern plays which appeal especially to high school pupils are *Diary of Anne Frank*, the Pulitzer Prize play for 1956, dramatized by Frances Goodrich and Albert Hackett and based on Anne Frank's *Diary of a Young Girl*, which is classified in 949.2; *Teahouse of the August Moon*, a play which won the Pulitzer Prize for 1954, adapted by John Patrick (pseudonym of John Patrick Goggan) from the novel of the same title by Vern Sneider; and *The King and I*, by Oscar Hammerstein, based on the book *Anna and the King of Siam* by Margaret Landon and first presented in 1951.

British playwrights whose works are usually available in high school libraries are Sir James Barrie, John Drinkwater, Lord

Dunsany, John Galsworthy, Oliver Goldsmith, Lady Gregory, George Bernard Shaw, Richard Brinsley Butler Sheridan, William Shakespeare, and William Butler Yeats. To these should be added the Irish playwright John Millington Synge, whose *Riders to the Sea* and *The Playboy of the Western World* are often included in collections of plays for high schools.

In addition to the actual plays of Shakespeare, there are several good books which supply useful material for a study of his plays and the times in which they were written. Marchette Gaylord Chute has written *Introduction to Shakespeare* (Dutton, 1951) and *Shakespeare of London* (Dutton, 1949). These books throw light on Shakespeare as a man and a playwright, the times in which he lived and worked, the actors and their costumes, and the theater in which Shakespeare's plays were presented. Another somewhat similar book is *Shakespeare and the Players,* by Cyril Walter Hodges (Coward-McCann, 1949), which records the development of the theater in the Elizabethan era.

Junior high school libraries will surely want a copy of *Tales from Shakespeare,* by Charles and Mary Lamb, a retelling of a classic which has become a classic in its own right. (The problem of retold classics will be discussed in Part III.) This is available in numerous editions, including a fairly new one in the Children's Illustrated Classics series (Dutton, 1957) with eight plates in color and line drawings by Arthur Rackham. Lamb's *Tales* has introduced Shakespeare's plays to many generations of readers. A similar book on the senior high school level is *Stories from Shakespeare* (World Publishing, 1956) by Marchette Chute (see above). This book gives résumés of the thirty-six plays of Shakespeare's First Folio, and is designed as an introduction to the plays themselves. While less space is devoted to each play, Miss Chute's book holds more to the dramatic form than does Lamb's *Tales* since it includes excerpts from the plays.

Useful in any study of the theater of Shakespeare's time is an older book, *Shakespeare's Theater* by Ashley Horace Thorndike (Macmillan, 1916). The high school library may also wish to consider Sheldon Warren Cheney's *The Theatre; Three Thousand*

Years of Drama, Acting and Stagecraft (Longmans, 1959). This is a revised and enlarged edition of a book first published in 1929 and contains a section on, among many other topics, Shakespeare's theater. Highly recommended for junior high school pupils is a briefer and more simply written book, *The Theatre* by Helen and R. V. B. Leacroft in the Informative Reference Series (Roy Publishers, 1961). This book contains a list of further readings for those interested in the subject. Books about the theater are classified in 792, though often used in connection with the study of drama.

High school libraries should make no effort to supply multiple copies of plays for classroom reading, requiring instead that all pupils taking parts have copies. These should be supplied from other funds in inexpensive editions, paperbacks whenever available. Another problem is presented when pupils wish to use library copies of a play to be presented for class or other school program. This practice results usually in prolonged loans which limit the use of other plays in the anthology and may lead to mutilation of the book as the play is cut and marked. Such material should be duplicated for use by the players, the book remaining in the library. Copies of nonroyalty plays which pupils may perform are not a legitimate part of a high school library collection.

Short Stories. No special problems are involved in the selection of short stories for high school collections. There are a great many short stories available, both in volumes by individual writers and in anthologies representing the work of many authors on a wide variety of themes. Young people read short stories for classes studying the short story. Some pupils also read short stories purely for recreation as a fairly steady diet. Short stories often serve as an introduction to longer books of fiction. They are discussed here, rather than with Fiction in Chapter 10, because most high schools study the short story as a form of literature in itself.

Every high school library will have in its collection entire volumes of short stories by outstanding short story writers: Joseph Conrad, Sir Arthur Conan Doyle, Bret Harte, Nathaniel Hawthorne, O. Henry (pseudonym of William Sydney Porter), Washington Irving, Rudyard Kipling, Edgar Allan Poe, and others.

In addition, there will be anthologies with selections from the works of the above writers and many others, some of whom are currently writing for magazines.

There are compilations of teen-age stories, often previously published in such magazines as *American Girl, Boys' Life,* and *Seventeen. Under Twenty,* edited by May Lamberton Becker (Harcourt, 1932), is an example of titles of older collections of teen-age stories. School librarians will also be alert to choose more recent collections, such as those of stories from *Seventeen,* which are popular with adolescents.

For girls there are collections with romantic themes. A good older example is *Love Comes Riding; Stories of Romance and Adventure for Girls,* compiled by Helen Josephine Ferris (Harcourt, 1929). Miss Ferris has a more recent similar collection entitled *Girls, Girls, Girls; Stories of Love, Courage and Quest for Happiness* in the Terrific Triple Title series published by Franklin Watts (1957).

Boys enjoy science fiction in short story form as well as in full-length novels. Groff Conklin has compiled several books of science fiction short stories, *Invaders of Earth* (Vanguard, 1952) for example. These include older stories by Sir Arthur Conan Doyle and Edgar Allan Poe, and some by more recent writers such as Isaac Asimov, Arthur Charles Clarke (who are both scientists), and Robert Anson Heinlein. Experienced school librarians discover that science fiction short stories need to be read by teachers and librarians because their fantastic involvement is not always confined to science.

Collections of mystery and detective stories are probably best represented by compilations by Howard Haycraft, a devotee of and authority on the mystery story. An early collection is the *Boys' Book of Great Detective Stories* (Harper, 1938), followed in 1940 by the *Boys' Second Book of Great Detective Stories.* High school libraries needing additional mystery stories may be interested in *Treasury of Great Mysteries,* in two volumes compiled by Howard Haycraft and John Beecroft (Simon & Schuster, 1957), and their more recent *Ten Great Mysteries* (Doubleday, 1959).

One of the best collections for high schools, seldom included in book selection aids, is *Mystery and the Detective* (Appleton, 1938) compiled and edited by Blanche Colton Williams, long-time teacher of high school English, who at the time of its publication was head of the English Department of Hunter College in New York City. This book is one of the few sources for "Buttons" by E. M. Winch, one of the best mystery stories for young people. It also includes "Miss Hinch," by Henry Sydnor Harrison, another favorite with high school readers.

Humorous short stories for young people are represented in *Best American Humorous Short Stories*, edited by R. N. Linscott (Random House, 1945). Margaret Clara Scoggin, director of work with young people at the New York Public Library and editor of "Outlook Tower" in the *Horn Book*, has compiled *Chucklebait; Funny Stories for Everyone* (Knopf, 1945) and *More Chucklebait; Funny Stories for Everyone* (Knopf, 1949). *I Couldn't Help Laughing*, with the stories selected and introduced by Ogden Nash (Lippincott, 1957), contains some humorous short stories not found in other sources. Phyllis Reid Fenner, who has compiled anthologies of stories on many subjects and who was responsible for the Terrific Triple Title series, has several collections of humorous stories, including *Fun, Fun, Fun; Stories of Mischief and Mirth, Fantasy and Farce, Whimsy and Nonsense* (F. Watts, 1953).

Benjamin Alexander Heydrick is responsible for the collection *Americans All* which has been revised by Blanche Jennings Thompson (Harcourt, 1941). May Lamberton Becker, in her *Golden Tales of Our America; Stories of Our Background and Tradition* (Dodd, 1929), began a series of "Golden Tales" involving the various regions of the United States. Her *Growing Up with America* (Lippincott, 1941) represents a selection of stories divided by periods of American history. While these collections contain valuable material, they are not generally popular with students and need to be introduced by teachers.

Some high school libraries may want to include the latest edition of the *Best American Short Stories*, edited by Martha Foley and David Burnett and published by Houghton, or the occasional collection of best stories chosen from these yearbooks. They may also want to include collections of prize-winning stories, such as the O. Henry Memorial Award story collections published by Hanover House.

Essays. The essay is apparently in decline in American high schools. Teachers usually confine consideration of the essay to that section of the literature textbook devoted to the subject with representative essays included. School librarians, having fewer calls for essays, do not add them in great numbers to high school collections.

Standard book selection aids suggest only the minimum number of books of essays. An older title which continues to be recommended is the third edition of *Essays, Old and New* (Harcourt, 1955) edited by Robert U. Jameson, bringing up to date Essie Chamberlain's anthology which was first published in 1926 and revised in 1934. This is a good collection with a wide selection of essays, an introduction on the essay, and biographical notes.

While *Standard Catalog for High School Libraries* still includes individual volumes by British essayists—Addison, Bacon, Carlyle, Lamb, Macaulay, and Stevenson—practically nothing is offered under the heading "American Essays."

Two divisions of literature closely allied with essays may be used to supplement, or substitute for, essays. They are "American Satire and Humor" and "American Miscellany." Some books by Robert Benchley, Clarence Day, Emily Kimbrough, Stephen Leacock, Ruth McKenney, Ogden Nash, Cornelia Otis Skinner, James Thurber, E. B. White, and others are in most high school libraries and are generally liked by young people.

Two good collections of such material are *Home Book of Laughter,* edited by May Lamberton Becker (Dodd, 1948), and *Humor of America* (Appleton, 1945) edited by Max John Herzberg and Leon Mones. Herzberg, a former high school English teacher, has compiled other anthologies for use by high schools.

Essays, it is true, have never been a favorite type of reading for young people. They are often likely to be too subjective and most often are musings based on adult experiences. Essays tend to lack most of the factors which young people demand in their reading. And, of course, there is competition with other types of reading or with other media of communication for the time of the high school pupils. Perhaps teachers must bear partial blame for trying to make pupils interpret essays, instead of merely enjoying them. Emphasis may also have been laid on traditional essays rather than the more recent ones which might have greater appeal.

Some of the older school libraries have adequate collections of essays. Many high schools, despite the apparent trend, continue to teach essays as a type of literature. Some English teachers, largely because of their own interest in and enthusiasm for essays, are quite successful in getting pupils to read essays—even to write them. To emphasize the up-to-dateness of essays, these teachers often use editorials in the morning paper as a starting point and go from there to more formal essays.

School librarians will be guided by the demand for essays in individual schools and add to the library collection according to the demand. Obviously it is not good policy to purchase any material which will not be used. Older editions of book selection aids include collections of essays which do not become dated as do many other types of materials.

PEOPLE, PLACES, AND TIMES
900 CLASSIFICATION

BIOGRAPHY

Biography is a very important type of reading matter in any school library. There is probably no subject field which cannot be linked with it in some way. Teachers correlate biography with various studies in the curriculum—history, literature, science, and others. Pupils read biography as readily as they do fiction, often in preference to it. There are values for the development of character and understanding to be found in biography, probably to a greater degree than in any other field. In reading biography, the young reader learns how others have reacted to problems which he faces. He meets people from other sections of his own country and from other countries of the world. Biography brings him into contact with people of other races and cultures, those with religious beliefs and political ideologies different from his own. The fact that these people are real, often still living, makes them somehow more convincing than characters in fiction, however true to life. Interest in careers may be initiated or fanned into reality when a pupil reads the interesting biography of a person who has achieved success in his chosen career. Biography also offers reading for other personal interests. This is especially true of books about people outstanding in the field of sports, popular with pupils at all levels.

Biographical works are divided into two types: collective biography, comprising works which relate the lives of more than one person; and individual biography, works confined to the life of one individual, written either by himself or by another person. Collective biography is generally classified as 920. Individual biography is classified as 92 in the Wilson catalogs, 921 in the "Basic Book Collections," and B in many library collections.

Biography does not enter the reading life of a child much before the fourth grade. Before that time he has, of course, listened to or read for himself brief stories of real people, but the average pupil entering fourth grade has probably not read an account of the entire life of any person. Most of the biographies listed in *Children's Catalog* are graded six or seven to nine. Many of these are also included in *Standard Catalog for High School Libraries*. However, the number of interesting biographies written for younger children is increasing. Outstanding among these are well-illustrated biographies for grades three to five by Ingri Mortenson d'Aulaire and Edgar Parin d'Aulaire. Published by Doubleday, they are simply written and amplified by colored lithographs. *Abraham Lincoln* (1957, first published in 1939) won the Caldecott Medal in 1940. A more recent example is *Columbus* (1955). Other examples of biographies simple enough for very young readers are *Little Brother of the Wilderness; the Story of Johnny Appleseed* by Meridel Le Sueur (Knopf, 1947), and two books by Enid La Monte Meadowcroft, *On Indian Trails with Daniel Boone* (Crowell, 1947) and *Holding the Fort with Daniel Boone* (Crowell, 1958). As more biographies become available on their level, children under grade four will undoubtedly read them.

Many children are probably introduced to biography through the Childhood of Famous Americans series which they read because the books have simple and rather fast-moving stories, not because they are biographies. Some of this series may be read by third grade pupils. Only a few of these titles are included in the *Children's Catalog*, but the publisher's list is a rather long one. They are published by Bobbs-Merrill and, as the series title indicates, are limited, except for a brief statement at the end of each book, to the childhood of the biographee. Regardless of the author, these biographies are written very much to a pattern, are graded four to six, and until recently have been identical in format with approximately the same number of pages and the same type of silhouette illustrations.

Many school librarians and teachers deplore the fact that this series does not give more actual facts about a famous person's adult life. While childhood is important in the development of any person, children need to know more about a person's contribution to his country or to the world at large. Besides, very little is known about the childhood of many important personages and a biography about their childhood becomes more nearly fiction. When well written, it does make the times in which the biographee grew up live for children. Moreover, books in the Childhood of Famous Americans series are useful to help introduce children to biography and to stimulate older pupils whose reading level is low. A problem is presented, however, when the better readers continue to read them after they are fully capable of reading more mature biographies which give a complete life story.

COLLECTIVE BIOGRAPHY

Collective biography offers a variety of materials useful when only a brief life sketch is needed. The volume may be about a single family, as *The Young Brontës* by Mary Louise Jarden (Viking, 1938) or *The Peabody Sisters of Salem* (Little, 1950) by Louise Hall Tharp. On the other hand, a collection may contain a large number of brief biographies as in *Makers of the Modern World* by Louis Untermeyer (Simon and Schuster, 1955), which, according to the subtitle, covers "the lives of ninety-two writers, artists, scientists, statesmen, inventors, philosophers, composers, and other creators who formed the pattern of our century."

Collections may include lives of outstanding Americans, such as *Story of the Presidents of the United States of America* by Maud and Miska Petersham (Macmillan, 1953) for grades four to seven, or, for high school readers, *The Presidents in American History* by Charles Austin Beard. In the revised edition (Messner, 1957) the material has been brought forward by the author's son, William Beard, to include the administrations of Truman and Eisenhower.

There are also collections of biographies of people of many countries or races. An example is *Our Foreign-Born Citizens* by Annie E. S. Beard, now in a new revised edition by William A. Fahey (Crowell, 1955). *We Have Tomorrow,* by Arna Wendell

Bontemps (Houghton, 1945), has stories of twelve Negroes who have distinguished themselves in some art or profession. For older readers there is a similar book, *Great American Negroes* by Ben Albert Richardson, now revised by William A. Fahey (Crowell, 1956).

Collective biography may emphasize a trait or virtue, as in *Armed with Courage,* by May Yonge McNeer and Lynd Ward (Abingdon, 1957), containing stories of seven men and women whose lives exemplify physical and spiritual courage. Other examples are *Ten Brave Men; Makers of the American Way* (1951) and *Ten Brave Women* (1953), both by Sonia Daugherty with drawings by her husband, James Daugherty, and published by Lippincott.

Sometimes collections have historical significance, as in *Calico and Crinoline; True Stories of American Women, 1608-1865* (Viking, 1935), by Eleanor Maria Sickels, and *Children of the Handicrafts,* by Carolyn Sherwin Bailey (Viking, 1935), which gives the stories of the childhood of seventeen early American craftsmen, most of whom became famous.

A number of collections of biographies have titles beginning with "Famous," as *Famous Composers, Famous Explorers, Famous Men of Science.* Many of these belong to the series Famous Biographies for Young People acquired about ten years ago by Dodd, Mead from A. S. Barnes. Some two or three titles are added every year, and the total is about thirty. A recent example is Laura Benét's *Famous American Humorists* (Dodd, 1959). Books with somewhat similar titles are published by Crowell.

INDIVIDUAL BIOGRAPHY

In the selection of individual biography for a school library collection, emphasis is on the person about whom the biography is written. There may be need, for example, for a biography of Madame Curie because there is none in the collection. The search may be for *another* biography of Abraham Lincoln with perhaps a different emphasis or about a period of his life not otherwise covered by the present collection. A person of current interest may not be represented in the collection because a good biography for young people has not yet been written. School librarians who have been awaiting material on Amelia Earhart, for example, will be interested in *Amelia Earhart: First Lady of the Air* by Jerry Seibert (Houghton, 1960). There is also *Leonard Bernstein*, a recent biography of the young composer, conductor, lecturer, and author by David Ewen (Chilton, 1960). At the same time, the author of a biography is important, as in other books, and can make the difference between a book which young readers enjoy and suggest to others, and one which they allow to gather dust on the shelves.

A number of people are at present writing biography for children and young people. Some of these are noted writers in other fields as well. James Henry Daugherty, an outstanding writer and illustrator in the pioneer period of American history, has written several biographies, including *Daniel Boone* (Viking, 1939) which won the Newbery Medal in 1940. Beryl Williams Epstein and her husband, Samuel, authors of numerous books in the fields of science, useful arts, and geography on the elementary level, have written several books of biography for high school readers, including *Marconi, Pioneer of Radio* (Messner, 1943) under the pseudonym Douglas Coe. Katherine Binney Shippen, mentioned previously for her books in the social sciences and other fields, is the author of several biographies, one of which is *Leif Eriksson, First Voyager to America* (Harper, 1951). Armstrong Sperry, whose action-filled sea stories are read by the boys, has written biographies of such famous mariners as Captain Cook, John Paul Jones, and Christopher Columbus.

Only a few well-known biographical writers can be mentioned here. Noteworthy among those is Clara Ingram Judson, who has written a number of biographies of famous Americans for grades six to eight or nine. Typical of her titles are *City Neighbor; the Story of Jane Addams* (Scribner, 1951) and *Andrew Jackson, Frontier Statesman* (Follett, 1954). The d'Aulaires specialize in biographies of outstanding Americans with lovely lithographic illustrations for grades three to five, as has already been mentioned. Nina Brown Baker has written several interesting biographies of

South American heroes, including *He Wouldn't Be King; the Story of Simon Bolivar* (Vanguard, 1941). Sybil Deucher writes alone and in collaboration with Opal Wheeler; both are interested in lives of celebrated musicians and have written biographies of a number of these. Typical titles are *Mozart, the Wonder Boy* (Dutton, 1941), in a new, enlarged edition, and *Edward MacDowell and His Cabin in the Pines* (Dutton, 1940). David Ewen specializes in biographies of composers—individual biography as well as collective. Claire Lee Purdy also prefers musicians, one of her biographies being *He Heard America Sing; the Story of Stephen Foster* (Messner, 1940). Jeanette Eaton prefers renowned Americans and her *Leader by Destiny: George Washington, Man and Patriot* (Harcourt, 1938) is still probably the best biography of Washington for high school students. She has also done a briefer and more simple biography, *Washington, the Nation's First Hero* (Morrow, 1951) for elementary school readers. Shirley Graham writes biographies of distinguished Negroes, including Booker T. Washington, George Washington Carver, and Phyllis Wheatley. May Yonge McNeer has written the biographies of at least two religious reformers, *Martin Luther* (Abingdon, 1953) and *John Wesley* (Abingdon, 1951) in collaboration with her husband, Lynd Ward, who also did the illustrations, some of them double-page pictures in rich colors. Elizabeth Blake Ripley has done a series of biographies of prominent artists for pupils of junior high school level. Doris Shannon Garst has to her credit a long list of biographies of persons connected with the westward movement in American history, including those of several outstanding Indians.

If one is interested in biographies of literary figures, there are several by Laura Benét, the first being *The Boy Shelley* (Dodd, 1937). *Invincible Louisa* (Little, 1933), the story of the author of *Little Women*, won for Cornelia Lynde Meigs the Newbery Medal, the first biography to win this medal. There is *Romantic Rebel; the Story of Nathaniel Hawthorne* (Appleton, 1932) written by his own granddaughter, Hildegarde Hawthorne. More recently Jeanette Eaton has added *America's Own Mark Twain* (Morrow,

1958), one of several biographies of Samuel Clemens. A recent biography of an author about whom little is available for young people is *Stephen Crane; the Story of an American Writer* (Crowell, 1961) by Ruth Franchere. Boys and girls usually like to read a biography of an author whose books they enjoy.

In studying inventions and their inventors, pupils will find such biographies as *Young Man in a Hurry; the Story of Cyrus W. Field* (Harper, 1958) by Jean Lee Latham, who is a Newbery Medal winner, and *Benjamin Franklin* by Clara Ingram Judson (Follett, 1957), each for grades six to eight or higher. A helpful feature of *Benjamin Franklin* is a list at the end of the book of his discoveries, inventions, and other accomplishments. Among biographies of the pioneers, several of Daniel Boone are available. *Daniel Boone* (Viking, 1939) by Daugherty for junior high school readers has already been mentioned. *Daniel Boone, Wilderness Scout* by Stewart Edward White is still probably the best biography of Boone for high school pupils. First published in 1922, this book was reprinted by Doubleday in a Young Moderns edition in 1946.

Interested readers will find quite a few individual biographies of Negroes. Two that should be mentioned here are *Trumpeter's Tale; the Story of Young Louis Armstrong*, by Jeanette Eaton (Morrow, 1955) and *Mary McLeod Bethune*, an account of the woman who accomplished so much for the education of her own race in the South, by Emma Gelders Sterne (Knopf, 1957).

Biographies of persons who have succeeded in spite of handicaps appeal to young people. The best example is, of course, *The Story of My Life* by Helen Keller (Doubleday, 1954), first published in 1903. *The Helen Keller Story* by Catherine Owens Peare (Crowell, 1959) is one of several recent biographies of Miss Keller. Any biography of Franklin Delano Roosevelt would cover his struggle to come back after a bout with polio which left him handicapped. While there are few satisfactory biographies of F. D. R. for young readers, high school pupils will read John Gunther's *Roosevelt in Retrospect; a Profile in History* (Harper, 1950). Louise Maxwell Baker in *Out on a Limb* (McGraw, 1946) tells how she made a good life for herself despite the loss of a leg in childhood. Boys, especially those interested in war experiences, as most are, read Paul Brickhill's *Reach for the Sky; the Story of Douglas Bader, Legless Ace of the Battle of Britain* (Norton, 1954). Boys who like sports read *It's Good To Be Alive* (Little, 1959), Roy Campanella's own story of his struggle to survive and make a new life for himself after he was crippled. In *My Left Foot* (Simon & Schuster, 1955), Christy Brown, an Irish lad, victim of cerebral palsy and almost totally paralyzed from birth, tells how, through his own efforts and those of his mother, he learned to write and paint creditably with his left foot, and how, with the cooperation of doctors and others, he learned to walk and talk and to use a typewriter for his writing. Another inspirational book is Ved Parkash Mehta's *Face to Face; an Autobiography* (Little, 1957), describing his blind childhood in a cultured home in India and his education in the United States.

In addition to the Childhood of Famous Americans series already mentioned, attention should also be called to the individual biographies in the Random House historical series, Landmark Books and World Landmark Books. Genevieve Stump Foster has a brief series of biographies published by Scribner, which is called the Initial Biography series because each book's cover features the initials of the biographee. She has so far written *Andrew Jackson* (1951), *Abraham Lincoln* (1950), *Theodore Roosevelt* (1954), and *George Washington* (1949) in this series. A somewhat similar series, though for slightly older readers, is Signature Books published by Grosset and Dunlap, the cover of each bearing the signature of the person about whom the book is written. Among several other publishers who issue biographies for children and young people, Messner is exceptional for both quantity and quality, especially on the junior high school level.

The above suggests that almost any need in school may be met by good biographies. Readers interested in biographies in connection with careers will find subjects in almost all fields represented: doctors, nurses, dancers, singers, actors, teachers, athletes, pioneers in aviation, those who have followed unusual careers. As in collective biography, the outstanding Presidents are represented in individual biography, a few by several books.

It may be helpful to list some of the characteristics of a biography desirable for young readers. A good biography causes the person about whom it is written to come alive. It should make the reader feel that he actually knows the subject—even one who lived years ago. He should know how the biographee looked, thought, and reacted. The reader should know not only the kind of person the biographee was but some things that made him so. A good biography not only informs the young reader as to the contribution made by the biographee to the stream of history, but inspires him to make a worthy contribution of his own.

A biography for very young readers needs to be simply written. The use of conversation to vary the pace of narration is a good device. Interesting incidents help to gain the reader's attention initially and to hold it throughout the book. Indeed biography should have the narrative interest of fiction. There should be action and adventure, wherever the biography lends itself to such treatment. Perhaps the most widely read biographies are about characters whose lives were intrinsically adventurous. This is especially true through the level of junior high school, after which more adult biographies are read and enjoyed.

Geography and Travel

One of the most interesting divisions of the 900's is 910, covering the general topic of geography and travel. This division includes atlases, gazetteers, maps, and accounts of voyages and travels of various kinds to many places. In fact, most places on the globe have now been covered by at least one book of travel, though once in a while a book appears on a new area. This is true also of books for children and young people. In 910 are all books of geography, with emphasis on social life and customs— how people live, what their occupations are, and what products they have that are needed by other peoples of the world.

Materials in geography and travel are used by elementary teachers and pupils in their social science units as they study individual countries, or, as is more likely, regions of the world under topics such as countries to the far north, desert lands, the Orient, etc. There is a need at present for material on various countries which can be used by pupils in grades two and three. On the high school level, books of travel are read largely for individual book reports, for the study of types of books, and for correlating with history classes, as well as for personal interest.

Probably no group of books boasts more alluring titles than those in the 910's. *Beyond the Purple Horizon, Camel-Bells of Baghdad, Land Below the Wind,* and *Royal Road to Romance* are some older examples that come quickly to mind. Among the more recent titles are *Edge of the Jungle, Epic of Everest, Within the Circle,* and *Rumble of a Distant Drum.* Many of the travel books are filled with stories of adventure and read like fiction or biography so that, when young readers are introduced to them, they read them on their own. Travel books are warm and personal. They give vicarious experience to those who may never travel otherwise. There is also no better group of books to increase knowledge of other people and to lay a firm foundation for international understanding.

Among the older books which have been included in standard book selection aids are *A Child's Geography of the World,* and *A Child's History of the World,* by Virgil Mores Hillyer, founder of the Calvert system of schools and general editor of a variety of materials used largely by Americans abroad teaching their own children. Published first by Appleton in the 1920's, both these books were issued in more modern format in 1951 after revision by Edward G. Huey.

A Day in Old Athens; a Picture of Athenian Life (first edition, Allyn, 1914, reprinted by Biblo and Tannen, 1960) and *A Day in Old Rome; a Picture of Roman Life* (first edition, Allyn, 1925, reprinted by Biblo and Tannen, 1959), by William Stearns Davis, are two older books that are used on the high school level in any study of ancient times. They cover daily life, costumes, government, religion, and similar topics in the Athens of 360 B.C. and in the Rome of 134 A.D. as seen through the eyes of an imaginary visitor. This author has also written *Life in Elizabethan Days; a Picture of a Typical English Community at the End of the Sixteenth Century* (Harper, 1930).

Everyday Things in Ancient Greece by Marjorie Courtney Quennell and Charles Henry Bourne Quennell, recently revised by Kathleen Freeman (Putnam, 1954), is also a stand-by; it combines into one volume three books about Greece published between 1930 and 1933. This is one of a series by the Quennells, all having either "Everyday Things" or "Everyday Life" in the titles, and all generally useful in classwork. *Roman Life,* by Mary Johnston (Scott, 1957), replaces *Private Life of the Romans,* by Harold Whetstone Johnston, first published in 1903 and revised by Mary Johnston in 1932, which has long proved useful in high school libraries. A more recent book, *Everyday Life in Ancient Times; Highlights of the Beginnings of Western Civilization in Mesopotamia, Egypt, Greece, and Rome* (National Geographic Society, 1958) contains 215 illustrations, 120 of which are paintings by H. M. Herget. This book, first published in 1951, was reprinted from the *National Geographic Magazine* and each chapter has a different author.

Anne Terry White's *Lost Worlds; Adventures in Archaeology* (Random House, 1941) should be considered for use in every school library. It is the thrilling story of the discovery of four lost civilizations, including an excellent description of King Tut's magnificent tomb. A more recent, and more inclusive book is her *All About Archaeology* (Random House, 1959) covering not only the ruins of Greece and the pyramids of Egypt, but also the ancient cities of the new world.

A book similar to several of those named above is *Everyday Things in American Life, 1607-1776* (Scribner, 1937) by William Chauncy Langdon. Langdon followed this in 1941 with another book covering the years 1776 to 1876. These well-illustrated books describe the life of early Americans, their customs, occupations, machinery, modes of transportation, and societies. Two informative older books by Alice Morse Earle are *Home Life in Colonial Days* (Macmillan, 1898) and *Child Life in Colonial Days* (Macmillan, 1899). A more recent book, filling somewhat the same need, is *Colonial Living,* written and illustrated by Edwin Tunis (World Publishing, 1957). It contains a great deal of material on the seventeenth and eighteenth centuries in America and is copiously illustrated. A companion volume by the same author is *Frontier Living* (1961), which treats almost all phases of frontier life as Americans moved to the West.

Through the years several writers have made careers of traveling and writing books recounting their journeys. The most outstanding example of such a writer today is John Gunther with his series of titles beginning "Inside," one of which is *Inside Russia Today* (Harper, 1958). *Inside Europe*, the first and perhaps the best book of this series, has not been revised since 1940. However, *Inside Europe Today* is an entirely new book, dealing with contemporary history with emphasis on political, social, and economic changes during the past twenty-five years. It was first published by Harper in 1961, and a revised edition appeared in early 1962. In some of his other books he has not maintained his original standard of accuracy. The length of his books also deters some high school pupils from choosing them.

More recently, Gunther has been working on a series of travel books for young readers. Published by Harper, this series is known as Meet the World Books. In 1958 he collaborated with Samuel and Beryl Williams Epstein, discussed earlier in this book, on *Meet South Africa*. A similar book with the same authors, *Meet North Africa*, was published in 1957. The most recent book in this series is *Meet the Congo and Its Neighbors* (1959) which Gunther wrote alone. In all three, Gunther adapted material included in his *Inside Africa* (Harper, 1955), classified as History.

In this connection, attention should be called to a fairly new book, *The Illustrated Book about Africa*, written by Felix Sutton with an introduction by Stuart Cloete (Grosset, 1959). This book for grades five to six should be useful for younger pupils because of its numerous large colored illustrations and its coverage of such topics as animals, birds, trees, and transportation. Agnes Edwards Rothery has written books of travel about several countries, the titles of which usually include the word "Roundabout." Examples are *Italian Roundabout* (Dodd, 1950) and *Iceland Roundabout* (Dodd, 1957), the latter first published in 1948.

Justice William Orville Douglas, an energetic traveler when he is not serving on the Supreme Court, has written several books that are useful in high school libraries. Among these are *Strange Lands and Friendly People* (Harper, 1951), an account of his visits to Persia, Greece, Israel, India, and the Arab and Moslem states; *Beyond the High Himalayas* (Doubleday, 1952); and *Russian Journey* (Doubleday, 1956). His more recent book, *Exploring the Himalaya,* a World Landmark Book published by Random House in 1958, is for younger readers, grades six to eight.

For younger readers also, Vernon Quinn has written several books about continents. Their titles begin with "Picture Map Geography" and the illustrations feature maps of resources, products, and the like. *Picture Map Geography of Canada and Alaska,* first published in 1944, was reissued by Lippincott in 1954. The new edition was revised to include material on Newfoundland but the section on Alaska is somewhat out of date since her recent acquisition of statehood. It is regrettable that the colored maps of the original edition are in black and white in the more recent one. Two new books on this area are *Alaska, the Forty-ninth State,* by Willis Lindquist (McGraw, 1959), and *Life in America: Alaska,* by Stuart R. Tompkins, in the Life in America Series (Fideler, 1960), published formerly as *Let's Read about Alaska* (1949).

Hester O'Neill has several books with titles beginning "The Picture Story" featuring pictures by Ursula Koering and published by McKay. Examples are *The Picture Story of Norway* (1951), *The Picture Story of Denmark* (1952), and *The Picture Story of Sweden* (1953).

Attilio Gatti and his wife, Ellen Morgan Waddill Gatti, are other writers of books of travel on the elementary level. Together they have produced *The New Africa* (Scribner, 1960), based on first-hand knowledge of Africa with its many present-day problems. Mr. Gatti alone has written *Here Is the Veld* (Scribner, 1948) and *Africa Is Adventure* (Messner, 1959). Another book by the same author, though not about his favorite continent, is *Mediterranean Spotlights* (Scribner, 1945). In the Gatti books the reader will find reliable information interestingly presented and outstanding photographs taken by the authors during their travels.

Attention should be called here to some of the excellent series of books on geography and travel for children and young people. A few have already been mentioned. Portraits of the Nations Series is published by Lippincott with such well-known writers as Eric Philbrook Kelly, Alan Paton, and Josephine Budd Vaughan represented. The titles of this series usually begin with "The Land and People of" or a variation of this. Selected for special mention are several by Lillian J. Bragdon, who takes a legendary character and tells about the country in which he lived. An example is *The Land of William Tell,* first published in 1938 by Stokes and revised in a 1953 edition published by Lippincott, containing thirty-five reproductions of photographs and a map. A recent addition to this series is *The Land and People of Finland* (1959) by Allena Champlin Best, who uses the pseudonym Erick Berry.

The Fideler Company series of Life in America Books is outstanding for the quantity and quality of the photographs in each book. An example is *Life in America: the South,* by Richard E. Banta, first published in 1951 and issued with revisions in 1955 and 1960. A similar Fideler series is exemplified by *Life in Europe: Sweden,* by Vincent H. and Ruth M. Malmström (1958). Another Fideler series, the Let's Read About Books, includes *Let's Read About South America* (1961) by R. E. Fideler and C. Kvande. Earlier Fideler had published another book on the same subject by Delia Goetz. Born and reared in Mexico, Miss Goetz has spent her life writing and working with materials about Latin America and her books are authoritative. Her *Neighbors to the South* (Harcourt, 1956) is still one of the best books on South America. This is a revised edition of a book first published in 1941.

More recently, Miss Goetz has written *Deserts* (Morrow, 1956), *Tropical Rain Forests* (Morrow, 1957), *Swamps* (Morrow, 1961), classified with books on science, and *The Arctic Tundra* (Morrow, 1958), all with illustrations by Louis Darling and all useful in school work.

There are now quite a few volumes in the World-in-Color Series edited by Doré Ogrizek and published by McGraw. Each book is composed of a series of articles, each written by a different person, on such subjects as the arts, drama and literature, and history. The illustrations are in color, as indicated in the title of the series. Examples are *France* (1959) and *Switzerland,* first published in 1951 but revised in 1955. The titles so far are confined largely to countries of Europe. The price per volume is high and will probably cause the average school librarian to examine his budget before deciding the books are essential.

The "Made in" books, while not a designated series, are often thought of as being one because of the similarity of titles. Several of these have already been mentioned in connection with the 700's because of their emphasis on the arts of various countries. Others stress features more nearly concerned with geography and travel, especially a country's contribution to world culture, and so are classified with the 910's.

Outstanding among these is *Made in China; the Story of China's Expression* by Grace Sydenstricker Yaukey, a sister of Pearl Buck who uses the pseudonym Cornelia Spencer. This was first published by Knopf in 1943. The 1952 edition contains new material concerning Free China. Mrs. Yaukey has a similar book, *Made in India; the Story of India's People and Their Gifts to the World* (Knopf, 1953), which is the revised edition of a book first published in 1946. These and other books in the series are used a great deal in schools and could be used more extensively if teachers knew of their availability.

Several interesting books of travel have been written by people about their own countries. A fairly old book of this type is Selma Ekrem's *Turkey, Old and New* (Scribner, 1947). In 1945, Harper published *Home to India* by Santha Rama Rau, a young Indian girl educated in England who returned to visit relatives whose language she could not speak. Later in *East of Home* (Harper, 1950) this same Indian girl gives an unusual picture of Asian affairs, with a personal account of visits and living in Japan, China, Indo-China, Siam, and Indonesia. Another very interesting book of this type is *Persia Is My Heart,* told by Najmeh Najafi to Helen Hinckley (Harper, 1953), which, in addition to picturing home life in Persia, offers explanations of the Moslem faith. Books of this category appeal particularly to girls of high school age who also enjoy *At Home in India* (Harcourt, 1956) by Cynthia Bowles. Her father, Chester Bowles, was United States Ambassador to India and she lived in India from 1951, when she was fifteen years old, until 1953.

Similar books are classified in biography if there is greater emphasis on the life of the author than on the social life of the country. School librarians are reminded to check both types of books when selecting for purchase or use in both the fields of biography and geography and travel.

Because they may not be mentioned elsewhere and should not be omitted, attention is called to books by Evelyn Schwartz Baird Stefánsson and her husband, Vilhjálmur Stefánsson, the noted Arctic explorer. Mr. Stefánsson's book *Friendly Arctic; the Story of Five Years in Polar Regions*, first published by Macmillan in 1921, was reissued in an enlarged edition in 1953. It deals with his third expedition, 1913-1918. Mrs. Stefánsson has written *Here Is Alaska*, now in a revised edition including information on Alaska's statehood and rapid development (Scribner, 1959), and *Within the Circle; Portrait of the Arctic* (Scribner, 1945). Another recent book is *Here Is the Far North* (Scribner, 1957), principally about Greenland and Iceland. School librarians will soon learn, if they do not already know, that photographs by Machetantz, some of whose work is used in Mrs. Stefánsson's books, are exceptionally good.

In conclusion, several criteria in selecting books on geography and travel should be emphasized. In the first place, it is essential that the author have lived or traveled extensively in the country of which he writes. One who has read two books on the subject or who has traveled for only a few weeks before writing a book has done no real service to young readers wanting to understand a foreign land. The author of books in the 910's should be able to write objectively, without prejudice in favor of or against the country in question. He should present a well-rounded picture of conditions, showing the life of the well-to-do people as well as the very poor. Ideally, the book should not stress the differences between foreign lands and the reader's country to the disadvantage of the former, but should emphasize how all peoples face the same problems and how they may work together in mutual understanding and to common advantage. The illustrative material in all books on geography and travel is important. Because such illustrations should be realistic, photographs are generally the most desirable. Recency in illustrations, as well as in the written material, is extremely important and school librarians should be alert to frequent revisions of books in this field.

HISTORY

Most of the material classified as history is used largely in connection with classwork in schools. Much of it, in fact, is of the textbook type and not likely to prove interesting to young readers. To be sure, there are some subjects, such as Indians, pioneer life, opening of the West, and anything dealing with cowboys, in which most elementary children are interested. Now that many schools present the history of ancient and medieval times in the sixth grade, there is need for books on Greece and Rome and on the days of feudalism, knights, and knighthood on a lower level than formerly when these were topics of interest only in junior high school. The junior high school readers are interested in books dealing with all types of historical adventure, continuing their interest in the West and in wars wherever they have been waged. On the high school level, there is a great deal of interest in war stories, those of the American Revolution or the Civil War, and more particularly personal accounts of world wars, especially World War II.

In world history, two books deserve special mention. *A Child's History of the World* by Virgil Mores Hillyer has been previously mentioned in the geography and travel section. First published in 1924, it has been revised with addition of new material by Edward G. Huey (Appleton, 1951). A fairly recent series of three books by Robert John Unstead is proving useful in the study of world history. The first is *Looking at History; Britain from Cavemen to the Present Day* (Macmillan, 1956). This book covers everything —food, dress, games, streets, tools, transportation—in the everyday life. It has sixteen color plates and almost one thousand other illustrations. The two books which follow are *People in History* (1957) and *Looking at Ancient History* (1960), also published by Macmillan.

Genevieve Stump Foster's series of Initial Biographies for grades four to six has already been mentioned in the section on biography. However, Mrs. Foster's earlier books are in the field of world history, written to discourage the teaching of history in separate segments. Her *George Washington's World* (Scribner, 1941) and *Abraham Lincoln's World* (Scribner, 1944), as well as others of this series, are different from most histories in that the author relates events in various parts of the world to incidents in the life of a familiar figure. Mrs. Foster also does illustrations which are not only distinctive but tie in appropriately with the text. While these books are filled with excellent material, especially when interpreted by a parent or teacher, many pupils of the age to use them, about grades six or seven to nine, lack sufficient background to follow the trends presented. The latest in this group is *The World of Captain John Smith, 1580-1631* (Scribner, 1959). The author has also written *Augustus Caesar's World; a Story of Ideas and Events from B.C. 44 to 14 A.D.* (Scribner, 1947), which will be discussed with books on ancient history.

As part of the celebration of the seventy-fifth anniversary of the founding of the American Library Association, Mrs. Foster was requested to write a book. Volume I of *Birthdays of Freedom* (Scribner, 1952), gives the story of the growth of the ideas of democracy from the time of early Egypt to the fall of Rome in 476 A.D. The second volume, published by Scribner in 1957, continues the narrative to July 4, 1776. Both volumes have decorative maps and double-page timetables showing events of the periods covered.

For somewhat older readers, Gertrude Hartman's books have stood the test of time. Her *World We Live in and How It Came To Be; a Pictured Outline of Man's Progress from the Earliest Days to the Present* (Macmillan, 1935) is one of the stand-bys in world history. In addition to the 1948 edition (Little) which is still available, there is now a second edition of *Builders of the Old World* (Heath, 1959) by Gertrude Hartman. This book discusses a great deal more than history, including such topics as geography, climate, resources, and phases of culture.

School librarians generally need information with illustrations about flags. Most standard encyclopedias have an excellent section of flags, reprints of which are sometimes available for use in the information file or for circulation to classrooms. A library needing a more exhaustive treatment will find the revised edition of *Flags of the World*, by H. Gresham Carr (Warne, 1961, first published in 1953), quite authoritative. It contains 340 flags in full color and over 400 text drawings in black and white. More than half the book, which is a British publication, treats flags of the British Commonwealth of Nations and the United States of America. For libraries unable to afford the more expensive book, Warne publishes a smaller book, *The Observer's Book of Flags* by Idrisyn Oliver Evans (1959) with 80 plates in color and 74 line drawings. In its compilation the editor had access to H. Gresham Carr's records for *Flags of the World*. Evans' book is one of a series of books of the field-guide type.

In ancient history, *Augustus Caesar's World; a Story of Ideas and Events from B.C. 44 to 14 A.D.*, by Genevieve Stump Foster (Scribner, 1947) has a wealth of material for pupils as young as sixth graders. An old but still very good book is Jennie Hall's *Buried Cities* (Macmillan, 1922) which discusses the early life in, and the eventual excavations of, Pompeii, Olympia, and Mycenae. The book is well illustrated with drawings and photographs which supplement the text. Dorothy Mills, from material used in teaching history at the Brearley School, has done a series of three books covering the eighth century B.C. through the fall of the Roman Empire. The first of these was *The Book of the Ancient World for Younger Readers; an Account of Our Common Heritage from the Dawn of Civilization to the Coming of the Greeks*, published by Putnam in 1923. This book was followed by *The Book of the Ancient Greeks; an Introduction to the History and Civilization of Greece from the Coming of the Greeks to the Conquest of Corinth by Rome in 146 B.C.* (Putnam, 1925) and *The Book of the Ancient Romans; an Introduction to the History and Civilization of Rome from the Traditional Date of the Founding of the City to its Fall in 476 A.D.* (Putnam, 1927). In the last book there is a large chronological chart which includes events discussed in all three books. The first of the three may be used in upper elementary and junior high schools; the others are useful also on the high school level. Another book on the elementary level, grades four to seven, is *The Gift of the River; a History of Ancient Egypt* (Crowell, 1937) by Enid LaMonte Meadowcroft, which readers find interesting. *Looking at Ancient History* (Macmillan, 1960) by Robert John Unstead was previously mentioned with a series of three histories by the same author.

Other Bible Lands by Bahija Lovejoy (Abingdon, 1961) will prove useful in school libraries which need this type of history. A chapter is devoted to each of eight countries: Arabia, Iraq, Egypt, Jordan, Syria, Lebanon, Turkey, and Iran. The book covers both history and areas of social sciences and the inclusion of a chart of Bible history makes it more useful.

A period of history that interests many readers is medieval times in Europe, covering the years from 476 to 1453 A.D. Three books on this period by authors already mentioned are pointed out for consideration. *Medieval Days and Ways* (Macmillan, 1937) by Gertrude Hartman, *The Middle Ages* by Dorothy Mills (Putnam, 1935), and William Stearns Davis' *Life on a Medieval Barony; a Picture of a Typical Feudal Community in the Thirteenth Century* (Harper, 1928).

An older book which should probably be considered for inclusion in any school library collection is *When Knights Were Bold* (Houghton, 1911), by Eva March Tappan, which pupils read on their own. Walter Buehr, mentioned earlier for his books on other subjects, has written *The Crusaders* (Putnam, 1959). While this book is useful because material on its period of history is none too plentiful for younger readers, it is limited in scope by its concentration on the First Crusade, having only a small section at the end devoted to the other crusades, especially the Children's Crusade. Buehr's earlier book, *Knights and Castles and Feudal Life* (Putnam, 1957), has a great deal of valuable, as well as interesting, information and can be used by younger readers than the Tappan book. In John Bryan Lewellen's *The True Book of*

Knights (Childrens Press, 1956), the treatment is somewhat super-
ficial. However, it does give information useful to a still younger
group, grades one to four, and may be used by older pupils who
are slow readers.

With the exception of material about the two world wars
and the history of America, there may not be too much demand
for books on modern history. However, some material on most
countries is listed in the standard book selection aids and may be
easily located. Two recent books about Hitler should prove useful
in any study of World War II or the present situation in Germany.
They are *The Rise and Fall of Adolf Hitler,* a World Landmark
Book by William L. Shirer (Random House, 1961), and *Hitler and
Nazism* (F. Watts, 1961) by Louis Leo Snyder.

There is very little material on Russia for children and young
people. For high schools, John Gunther's *Inside Russia Today*
(Harper, 1958), already mentioned in the discussion of geography
and travel, should prove useful. *The First Book of the Soviet Union*
by Louis Leo Snyder (F. Watts, 1959) seems promising for use
with junior high and upper elementary school pupils. Librarians
can expect a demand for historical material on countries which
appear in the headlines because of revolutions, internal strife,
changes in government, and the like. Recent examples are Cuba,
the Congo, and South Africa. This applies to material in Geography and Travel as well as History, since the two fields overlap.

High school pupils, especially boys facing service in the armed
forces, read books about personal experiences in World War II.
Some outstanding examples are such favorites as Dwight David
Eisenhower's *Crusade in Europe* (Doubleday, 1948), which gives
the complete story of World War II from the point of view of the
American and allied commander in Europe; *Hiroshima,* by John
Richard Hersey (Knopf, 1946), telling of the effects of the atomic
bomb on Japan; and *Three Came Home* (Little, 1947), by Agnes
Newton Keith, which is a sequel to her *Land Below the Wind*
(Little, 1939), the latter being classified as geography and travel.
More recent books of the same type are *Day of Infamy,* by
Walter Lord (Holt, 1957), covering the attack on Pearl Harbor
by the Japanese on December 7, 1941; *Bridge at Andau* by James

Albert Michener (Random House, 1957); and *The Battle of Midway* by Irving Werstein (Crowell, 1961), concerning a naval battle in the Pacific. The last one is for pupils of upper elementary grades rather than high school. A book which girls read, especially since the appearance of a popular movie based on it, is Anne Frank's *Diary of a Young Girl* (Doubleday, 1952), translated from the Dutch by B. M. Mooyaart-Doubleday. The Pulitzer Prize play based on this book is mentioned in the drama section of Chapter 8, above.

Sir Winston Churchill's series of histories, six volumes in all, beginning with *Gathering Storm* (Houghton, 1948) and ending with *Triumph and Tragedy* (Houghton, 1953) gives a comprehensive account of World War II. These volumes are used for classwork and interested pupils will read them alone. An abridgment of these six volumes, entitled *Memoirs of the Second World War* (Houghton, 1959), has been made by Denis Kelly. This book should be helpful in school libraries which feel they cannot afford or do not need the entire set. Katharine Savage's *The Story of the Second World War,* first published in England in 1957, has also been published in the United States (H. Z. Walck, 1958). Because there is such a scarcity of material on the world wars for the younger readers, two recent books by Louis Leo Snyder should prove helpful on the junior high school level. They are *The First Book of World War I* and *The First Book of World War II,* both published by Franklin Watts in 1958.

In the field of American history, books on Indians, their history, individual lives, tribes, customs, crafts, and other phases of their culture are in demand, despite some efforts to de-emphasize the study of Indians in schools. A few outstanding books have been selected for mention here, though there are others. Elizabeth Chesley Baity has written *Americans Before Columbus* (Viking, 1951), which covers the history of Indians from the time of their first migration from Asia to the discovery of America. This book is illustrated with photographs and with maps and drawings by Charles Buckles Falls. *The Book of Indian Crafts & Indian Lore* by Julian Harris Salomon (Harper, 1928) proves useful not only for classes but for clubs and camps doing work on the Indians.

Other writers of books about Indian crafts are Bernard Sterling
Mason and Walter Bernard Hunt. Robert Hofsinde, known also
by his Indian name, Gray-Wolf, has written many books on Indian
culture, two of which, *Indian Sign Language* (Morrow, 1956)
and *The Indian's Secret World* (Morrow, 1955), some school
libraries might need.

For younger readers, grades two to five, there is *In My
Mother's House* (Viking, 1951), a story of the day-to-day life of a
Pueblo Indian child in the Southwest, written by Ann Nolan
Clark when, teaching Indian children, she found little material
giving their viewpoint. A somewhat similar book for grades four
to five is *Dancing Cloud, the Navajo Boy* by Mary Marsh Buff
(Viking, 1957), now in a revised edition. Edwin Tunis, is the
author of a recent book, *Indians* (World Publishing, 1959) which
he has illustrated with more than two hundred detailed drawings.
A noteworthy author of books about individual Indian tribes
from Apaches to Seminoles, for grades four to seven, is Sonia
Bleeker. Each school library will probably need her book about
the Indian tribe whose history is connected with the school's own
region.

Those selecting material on United States history will find
names of well-known writers. On the elementary level, Alice
Dalgliesh and Alice Morse Earle both write on the colonial period,
while James Henry Daugherty's books for upper elementary and
junior high school pupils deal with pioneer days and the opening
of the West. May Yonge McNeer has several books, outstanding
among which is *California Gold Rush,* one of the Landmark
Books (Random House, 1950).

A new series of three books on American history, written by
Gerald White Johnson for his grandson, are useful for junior high
and upper elementary pupils. The first is *America Is Born; a
History for Peter* (Morrow, 1959). This is the history of America
from pre-Columbian times through the Revolution. The other two
books are *America Grows Up; a History for Peter* and *America
Moves Forward; a History for Peter,* both published by Morrow in
1960. The first of these covers the period from the Continental
Congress in 1787 to the early part of the twentieth century, and

the other from World War I to the present. These three volumes present a rare combination of sound historical scholarship and good writing for children. There are large illustrations both in black and white and in color. The books are useful for special reports on periods of American history. They would be even more helpful for study purposes if the subdivisions in their chapters were indicated by headings. The indexes are given over largely to names of people and places and have relatively few subject entries, although the latter type is important in school work.

During the Civil War Centennial, 1961-1965, a number of commemorative books are being published. One of the best accounts written for the average high school reader is Irving Werstein's *The Many Faces of the Civil War* (Messner, 1961). A definite effort is made toward an understanding of both sides, North and South. The book has maps and an index, plus a list of readings for those who wish further information on the subject.

On the high school level, there are books on American history by James Truslow Adams, Frederick Lewis Allen, Charles Austin Beard, Bruce Catton (specializing in the Civil War), Henry Steele Commager (often dealing with documentary material), William Edward Dodd, and Harold Underwood Faulkner.

Outstanding among authors of histories of other countries are Carl Lotus Becker, Lillian J. Bragdon, James Henry Breasted (a specialist in ancient history), Carleton Joseph Huntley Hayes, Anne Merriman Peck, Marjorie Courtney Quennell and Charles Henry Bourne Quennell, and Grace Sydenstricker Yaukey (under the pseudonym Cornelia Spencer).

Because school libraries always need books on costumes for history studies and other purposes, attention is called to *Costumes and Styles; 685 Examples of Historic Costumes in Color*, by Henry Harold Hansen (Dutton, 1956), covering the evolution of fashion from the days of early Egypt to 1954. The illustrations are in front in chronological arrangement with discussion in the back of the book referred to by numbers. Costume books generally are classified in 391.

Among the oldest of several outstanding series in the field of history is *Chronicles of America Series*, edited by Allen Johnson and Allan Nevins. There are fifty-six volumes, which may be purchased as a set or separately, published between 1918 and 1951 by Yale University Press. Many libraries prefer to keep this set together in 973. All of the books in this series were written by outstanding historians; they cover practically all phases of American history, and are useful on the high school level. Because the *Chronicles of America Series* contains no illustrations, another series was published to supply this lack. This is *Pageant of America; a Pictorial History of the United States,* edited by Ralph Henry Gabriel and others and published by Yale University Press between 1925 and 1929. These fifteen volumes, often classified as reference, are especially useful for the many pictures illustrating various phases of American life and times.

Landmark Books are published by Random House and are generally aimed at the junior high school level. The majority of books in this series, written by various authors who are usually eminent in their fields, are in the sphere of American history. However, there are many biographies among the Landmark Books, and others of the series are classified in the 200's, 300's, 500's, and 600's. These books are attractive and generally interesting to young readers. World Landmark Books, also published by Random House, are similar to Landmark Books, except that they deal with world-wide topics and are generally useful on the senior high school level. The books in this series are also in fields other than history.

American Heritage deserves special mention here. It is a bimonthly periodical published by the American Heritage Publishing Company, and sponsored by the American Association for State and Local History and the Society of American Historians. The articles are by authorities on popular subjects of historical interest. Each issue contains many pictures both in black and white and in color, some of which are not easily available elsewhere.

Beginning with the issue of December 1954, at which time Bruce Catton became editor, *American Heritage* has been available in book form. An annual index is ready each year in February. There has been issued one five-year combined index covering the issues from December 1954 through October 1959, and another is scheduled to appear in 1965. The publication is also indexed in *Readers' Guide to Periodical Literature*. A drawback limiting use in school libraries is the white cover of this periodical.

In addition to the magazine, the editors of *American Heritage* produce books in the field of history, published by Golden Press. Several of these have been adapted for young readers. An example is *The Golden Book of the American Revolution* (1959), adapted by Fred Cook from the *American Heritage Book of the Revolution* with narrative by Bruce Lancaster and introduction by Bruce Catton. This adaptation is for grades five to six and contains excellent colored illustrations from museums, art galleries, historical societies, and other similar sources.

The most recent venture of the editors of *American Heritage* is a series of books known as the American Heritage Junior Library, "designed to create for lively young minds a new way to experience the color and excitement, mystery and adventure, heroism and humor that make up America's past." School librarians wanting full information may address inquiries to American Heritage Junior Library, 336 West Center Street, Marion, Ohio.

o

FICTION

INTRODUCTION

In school libraries, as in others, books of fiction are usually read for pleasure and by choice of the individual reader rather than because of classroom assignment. Nevertheless, fiction is also used in school libraries in connection with the curriculum. This is especially true of historical novels, which often portray actual people of the past as well as fictitious characters and give a vivid picture of the times in which they are set. Many books of fiction by foreign authors and illustrators, or with background in foreign countries, are used to broaden knowledge of other lands and to deepen understanding of other peoples. Books about various regions of America are helpful in acquainting pupils in one part of the country with another area—North with South, East with West, city pupils with country life and vice versa. Books about racial or other groups are similarly useful.

Books of fiction with career material have long been used to interest pupils in certain careers or to acquaint them more fully with an already chosen career or one in which they are interested. A fairly recent trend in reading guidance is to consider fiction for developmental values, those factors which may help pupils in the painful process of growing up. This is rooted in the belief that books can help pupils as they read about others overcoming problems similar to their own. While this is an important consideration, it can be stressed too much in reading guidance. Selectors of books for school libraries should always bear in mind that many books of fiction are intended simply for enjoyment and deserve a place in any collection. Young readers should not only be provided with but encouraged to read fiction and should be given time to follow their own reading interests.

Books of fiction could be presented from the standpoint of their authors, and there are many noteworthy authors with whom the school librarian needs to be acquainted. He also needs to know titles that are certain to be of interest to children and young people. It seems best, however, to discuss books of fiction according to types or subjects. This is the way pupils usually approach them, and librarians must learn to do so too. Under each topic, a few outstanding authors will be mentioned and some of their titles will be cited as examples. Where all levels are concerned, books for elementary readers will be discussed before those for high schools.

ADVENTURE AND MYSTERY

A request for books of adventure and mystery may be satisfied for very young readers with almost any book containing exciting incidents. As readers mature, they desire actual mysteries, and eventually want murders with subsequent solution by detectives.

Walter Rollin Brooks injects an element of mystery into his humorous stories about talking animals in which Freddy the pig serves as the detective. *Freddy Goes to Florida* (Knopf, 1949), originally published in 1927 as *To and Again,* tells how Mr. Bean's farm animals go South for the winter. It was the first volume in this entertaining series. *Freddy, the Detective* (Knopf, 1932) is a delightful story about the animals on Mr. Bean's farm.

Pupils in grades four to six usually like the mystery stories by Helen Fuller Orton which also have some historical significance. Examples are *The Gold-Laced Coat; A Story of Old Niagara* (Lippincott, 1959), first published by Stokes in 1934, and *The Treasure in the Little Trunk* (Lippincott, 1932). A title like *Five Boys in a Cave* (Day, 1951) by Richard Church intrigues boys. They also read *The Adventures of Tom Sawyer* and other books by Mark Twain and books by Robert Louis Stevenson, notably *Treasure Island* and *Kidnapped.*

One of the few good detective stories written especially for children is *Emil and the Detectives; a Story for Children* by Erich Kästner (Doubleday, 1930), translated from the German by May Massee. The book describes the efforts of the boy Emil to apprehend a man who has robbed him, and the mystery is solved in an ingenious manner but without trickery. Another book by

Kästner portraying Emil and his colleagues as detectives is *Emil and the Three Twins* (F. Watts, 1961), translated by Cyrus Brooks.

On the junior high level, Stephen Warren Meader, whose books are largely of a regional nature or based on a historical period, has several books of adventure, *Who Rides in the Dark?* (Harcourt, 1937) being an example.

Almost any book by Howard Pease fits into the category of adventure. Two examples are *Ship Without a Crew; the Strange Adventures of Tod Moran, Third Mate of the Tramp Steamer "Araby"* (Doubleday, 1934) and *The Jinx Ship* (Doubleday, 1956), first published in 1927.

Two fairly recent mysteries recommended for the junior high school level are *Tree House Island* by Scott Corbett (Little, 1959), in which two fifteen-year-old boys uncover a forgotten crime in New England, and H. L. Lawson's *Pitch Dark and No Moon* (Crowell, 1958), about a young Coast Guardsman who risks his life to expose smugglers on the Great Lakes. *Nine Coaches Waiting* (Mill, 1959) by Mary Stewart, about a girl and her young charge in France, will appeal particularly to girls.

Standard book selection aids give few helpful suggestions for mystery and adventure stories on the high school level, though a number of books feature adventure. There is a great deal of adventure in James Arthur Kjelgaard's books, which are about animals and outdoor life. Two examples are *Swamp Cat* (Dodd, 1957) and *Stormy* (Holiday, 1959). Cecil Scott Forester has a series of sea stories which boys like about the adventures of Horatio Hornblower as, for example, *Admiral Hornblower in the West Indies* (Little, 1958); and Armstrong Sperry also writes sea stories involving adventure and sometimes a bit of mystery. Sperry prefers historical material, usually involving sea battles, privateering raids, etc. Two of his titles are *Storm Canvas* (Winston, 1944) and *Danger to Windward* (Winston, 1947). His *Call It Courage* (Macmillan, 1940) was awarded the Newbery Medal in 1941 and is read by boys of grades five to eight.

Included among mystery stories for high school are *The Moonstone* and *The Woman in White* by Wilkie Collins, a few titles by Mary Roberts Rinehart, short stories by Edgar Allan Poe, and the Sherlock Holmes mysteries by Sir Arthur Conan Doyle. Collections of detective stories, including those edited by Howard Haycraft, were discussed in the section on short stories in Chapter 8. Two fairly new writers of mystery stories for more mature readers in high school are Helen MacInnes Highet, who writes under her maiden name, Helen MacInnes, and Ralph Hammond-Innes, who uses as pseudonyms both Ralph Hammond and Hammond Innes. *Pray for a Brave Heart* by Mrs. Highet (Harcourt, 1955) involves a plot in Switzerland against several people who have escaped from behind the iron curtain. Her *North from Rome* (Harcourt, 1958) is the story of two Americans in Rome who unwillingly become involved in a spy ring. Two mysteries by Ralph Hammond-Innes are *Cruise of Danger* (Westminster Press, 1954) and *The Land God Gave to Cain; a Novel of Labrador* (Knopf, 1958).

School librarians will suggest books like *Rebecca* (Doubleday, 1938), by Daphne Du Maurier, and Rachel Lyman Field's *All This and Heaven Too* (Macmillan 1938), which girls read for the mystery element as well as for the romance.

Before adding mysteries to the school library collection, the librarian should either read them himself or trust the judgment of a reliable reader. To be avoided are those books placing undue emphasis on murder, sex, involved international intrigue, or a combination of the three. Since mystery stories are largely for recreational reading, pupils who are mystery fans probably depend on the public library for these books.

ANIMALS AND MORE ANIMALS

When young children ask for animal stories, they are interested in almost any animal. By the time they have reached junior high school, this interest has probably narrowed to books about dogs and horses.

Clarence William Anderson's books, whether fiction or non-fiction, and regardless of their level, are always about horses. Several of his books in a series featuring Billy and his pony, Blaze, are useful with small children, as, for example, *Blaze and Thunderbolt* (Macmillan, 1955). His *Lonesome Little Colt* (Macmillan,

1961) is the story of an orphaned colt who finds comfort with a mare who comes to the pasture. Anderson's books for older readers are usually about thoroughbreds with portrait-like illustrations by the author.

Anderson's books may be followed with books by Paul Brown, who also writes about horses. His *Pony Farm* (Scribner, 1948) is for grades three to four or five.

A writer of horse books for the in-between group, grades five to seven, is Glen Rounds, whose books are largely about the West. *The Blind Colt* (1960), first published in 1941, was followed by *Stolen Pony* (1948), which is also the story of a dog. *Hunted Horses* (1951) is the exciting story of wild horses and Indians. Rounds' books are published by Holiday House.

Robert Lawson uses animals as characters in many of his books. Rabbits appear in several, one of which, *Rabbit Hill* (Viking, 1944), won him the Newbery Medal in 1945. It should be noted in passing that Lawson is the only person so far to receive both the Newbery and Caldecott medals, having received the latter in 1941 for *They Were Strong and Good* (Viking, 1940), biographical sketches of his ancestors. Lawson also has written several story books based on the lives of historical characters, but in each case the story is told by an animal. The first of these was *Ben and Me; a New and Astonishing Life of Benjamin Franklin, as Written by His Good Mouse Amos; Lately Discovered, Ed. & Illus. by Robert Lawson* (Little, 1939). Amos is supposed to live in Franklin's hat.

Meindert DeJong's love of animals shines through his books, even those not classed as animal stories. Using his own Dutch background, as in *The Wheel on the School* (Harper, 1954), which was awarded the Newbery Medal in 1955, DeJong brings into his books cows, ducks, storks, rabbits. *Along Came a Dog* (Harper, 1958) is one of his recent books which have proved popular with young readers.

Mention should also be made of that inimitable story *Lassie Come-Home* by Eric Mowbray Knight (Winston, 1940) which every boy and girl, given the chance, will read. Another popular dog story is *Old Yeller* (Harper, 1956) by Frederick Benjamin Gipson. The background of this book is frontier and pioneer life in Texas.

Marguerite Henry, after trying her hand at other types of writing, seems to have found herself in writing books about horses which are appropriately illustrated by Wesley Dennis. Her books are universally popular with young readers of horse stories. Three favorite titles are *Brighty of the Grand Canyon* (Rand McNally, 1953), *Misty of Chincoteague* (Rand McNally, 1947) and its sequels, and *King of the Wind* (Rand McNally, 1948), which is based on the actual story of an ancestor of Man o' War and founder of the strain of thoroughbreds. This book received the Newbery Medal in 1949.

Walter Farley's books are all about horses, usually featuring the word stallion in each title, and are popular with both boys and girls. There are some half-dozen, the first of which is *The Black Stallion* (Random House, 1941) about one horse and his descendants. *Island Stallion* (Random House, 1948) has several sequels, one of which, *Island Stallion Races* (Random House, 1955), has an element of science fiction. *Black Stallion Mystery* (Random House, 1957), as the title implies, may serve also to satisfy demand for mysteries. Farley's latest venture is one of the Beginner Books published by Random House entitled *Little Black, a Pony* (1961).

Before his death in 1959, James Arthur Kjelgaard had written a long list of books of special interest to boys. They are filled with outdoor life, adventure, and animals, chiefly dogs that are partly wild. *Big Red* (Holiday, 1956) is the first of a series about a dog and his descendants. *Black Fawn* (Dodd, 1958) is one of two books by Kjelgaard about deer. Books by both Farley and Kjelgaard are read by elementary school children as well as those in junior high.

John Sherman O'Brien is the author of dog stories popular with both boys and girls. *Silver Chief, Dog of the North* (Winston, 1933), probably still his most popular book, begins a series of stories with a Canadian background. They involve the Royal

Canadian Mounted Police, which undoubtedly accounts for the
interest of girl readers too. Mary Alsop Sture-Vasa, writing under
the pseudonym of Mary O'Hara, is known for horse stories set in
the West. There are three in a series which senior high pupils
read and enjoy: *My Friend Flicka* (1944), *Thunderhead* (1943),
and *Green Grass of Wyoming* (1946); this series is published
by Lippincott. *"National Velvet"* by Enid Bagnold (Morrow,
1949) is the story of a girl and her horse who win the Grand
National Steeplechase. A fascinating story, especially for animal
lovers, is *The Incredible Journey* by Sheila Burnford (Little, 1961),
about a Siamese cat, an English bull terrier, and a Labrador
retriever on a journey through the Canadian wilderness.

FAMILY LIFE

Boys and girls of the early 1900's read and enjoyed books by
Louisa May Alcott, Kate Douglas Wiggin, and others who wrote
of family life and childhood experiences. Since then many others
have followed in their footsteps. Often books on family life overlap
with those on other subjects, such as school stories and historical
fiction. Their focal point, however, is the warm relationships in
the family. Books of this type appeal largely to pupils of elementary
grades with some interest continued in junior high schools.

A writer of family stories is Carol Ryrie Brink, probably best
known for *Caddie Woodlawn* (Macmillan, 1935), the story of a
girl and her brothers on a Wisconsin frontier farm at the time of
the Civil War. This was followed by *Magical Melons; More Stories
About Caddie Woodlawn* (Macmillan, 1944). Mrs. Brink is currently writing a series of books about a midwestern professor's
family, which begins with *Family Grandstand* (Viking, 1952).

One of the most widely read authors among pupils in grades
four to six is Eleanor Estes, a former children's librarian. She is
another writer on family life who apparently draws on her own
childhood experiences. A series of three books, of which *The
Moffats* (Harcourt, 1941) is the first, have long been favorites
with children. She received the Newbery Medal in 1952 for
Ginger Pye (Harcourt, 1951), which was followed by *Pinky Pye*

(Harcourt, 1958), another book about the same family. However, many school librarians feel that her most distinguished book is *The Hundred Dresses* (Harcourt, 1944), the story of a little foreign girl who suffered at school the pangs of being made to feel different.

Doris Gates, another children's librarian, has written several books on family life set in her native California. *Blue Willow* (Viking, 1940) is the heartwarming story of Janey Larkin, who migrated with her family from Texas to California, clutching a blue willow plate, the symbol of a home of their own, a dream finally realized.

Carolyn Haywood's books can be read by grades two to three and their material interests both boys and girls. There are several series of stories, the first of which begins with *"B" Is for Betsy* (Harcourt, 1939); another about a young boy, beginning with *Little Eddie* (Harcourt, 1947); and a third concerning an adopted boy nicknamed Penny, beginning with *Here's a Penny* (Harcourt, 1944).

A fairly new author, Sydney Taylor, has written several heartwarming books about Jewish family life before the First World War. *All-of-a-Kind Family* (Follett, 1951) is the story of a Jewish family with only little girls who finally get the little brother they all want. Since its publication, the author has added *More All-of-a-Kind Family* (Follett, 1954) and *All-of-a-Kind Family Uptown* (Follett, 1958).

Kathryn Worth's books are set in the South, chiefly in North Carolina, with some historical significance. *The Middle Button* (Doubleday, 1941) is the story of a little girl, the middle one in her family, who wanted to become a doctor before the medical profession was open to women. *They Loved To Laugh* (Doubleday, 1942), which is probably Miss Worth's best book, tells of a southern Quaker family during the 1830's.

Laura Ingalls Wilder did not begin writing books for children until after she was sixty years old. Before her death thirty years later, she had written eight books, all of which are double-starred in the *Children's Catalog*. The first of her books was *Little House in the Big Woods* (Harper, 1953). In this book, as in the others which follow, Mrs. Wilder uses her own experiences and those of her parents during the opening of the West in the years after the Civil War. *Little House in the Big Woods,* first published in 1932, and all her other books are now available in "newly illustrated, uniform editions" published in 1953; the illustrator is Garth Williams. Books by this author are read by pupils in junior high school as well as those in elementary grades.

While family stories are not in great demand among high school pupils, whatever need there is may be met by such books as *Mama's Bank Account* (Harcourt, 1943) by Kathryn Forbes (pseudonym of Kathryn Anderson McLean), the story of an indomitable mother which has been adapted for stage and screen by John Van Druten under the title *I Remember Mama; Papa's Wife,* by Thyra Ferré Bjorn (Rinehart, 1955), which tells of a Swedish housemaid who married her pastor and reared eight children; and *Rolling Years* (Macmillan, 1936) in which Agnes Sligh Turnbull writes a chronicle of three generations of women in a Pennsylvania Scotch family. Books of family life, as might be expected, appeal most strongly to girls.

Fun and Frolic

Humorous stories and authors who write them are so numerous that only a few will be presented as examples.

Many humorous books will be found among the picture books and easy books for grades one to three. Some of the outstanding authors and illustrators whose books can be counted on for humor are Wanda Gág, Hardie Gramatky, Theodor Seuss Geisel, Ludwig Bemelmans, and Robert McCloskey.

Heading the list of humorous books is *Winnie-the-Pooh* (Dutton, 1954) with its sequel *The House at Pooh Corner* (Dutton, 1928), by Alan Alexander Milne. Coming out first in 1926 and in 1928 respectively, these books have been reprinted many times. They are also available in one volume under the title *The World of Pooh; the Complete Winnie-the-Pooh and The House at Pooh Corner* (Dutton, 1957). Librarians should always insist on the original illustrations by Ernest H. Shepard which correlate so well with the text.

Mary Norton is a writer whose slyly humorous fantasies appeal to elementary school children. *The Borrowers* (Harcourt, 1953) is the story of very tiny people who live under a house and "borrow" their necessities from the big humans who live there. This book was followed by *The Borrowers Afield* (1955), *The Borrowers Afloat* (1959), and *The Borrowers Aloft* (1961) also published by Harcourt.

Beverly Cleary is the author of *Henry Huggins* (Morrow, 1950), the first in a series of stories about a small boy, a dog named Ribsy, their friend Beezus (for Beatrice), and her little four-year-old sister, Ramona, who get into all sorts of funny situations. Other books with these same characters, published by Morrow, are *Henry and Beezus* (1952), *Henry and Ribsy* (1954), and *Henry and the Paper Route* (1957). The illustrations of Cleary's books are by Louis Darling and help to make the characters and their situations seem altogether believable.

Mary Poppins (Harcourt, 1934) is the story of an English nurse and the remarkable happenings occurring during her stay with the Banks family. As written by Pamela L. Travers, nothing in the book seems impossible, whether it is the arrival of Mary Poppins on the east wind or her taking the children to tea with a relative who served it on the ceiling instead of the floor. The several books about Mary Poppins which have followed have been equally popular, especially with girls.

Robert McCloskey has already been mentioned as a creator of picture books whose humor appeals to young children. He is included here because of his humorous books which are popular with boys, grades five to seven. They are also useful with older boys who are retarded in reading. They are about boys and told in a simple but interesting manner. In this group are *Lentil* (Viking, 1940) and *Homer Price* (Viking, 1943) which was followed by *Centerburg Tales* (Viking, 1951), though the last does not maintain the standard of *Homer Price*.

Three additional books belong in this group, each by a different author. *Mr. Popper's Penguins* (Little, 1938) by Richard

Topper Atwater and his wife, Florence Hasseltine Carroll Atwater, with illustrations by Robert Lawson, is a very humorous book which appeals generally to children. Natalie Savage Carlson's *Alphonse, That Bearded One* (Harcourt, 1954) is "a Canadian folktale of a bear cub trained by his master to be a soldier." This is read generally by pupils in grades three to five. *Charlotte's Web* by Elwyn Brooks White (Harper, 1952) is a quiet fantasy with underlying humor about a little girl who could talk to animals, as well as about Wilbur, the pig, and his friendship with Charlotte, the spider, who could talk as well as write. In fact, the story is that of Charlotte and the words she spelled out with her web.

High school pupils who wish to read humorous material are apt to satisfy their need with nonfiction rather than fiction, with writings by Clarence Day, Ruth McKenney, Cornelia Otis Skinner, and others. However, there are compilations of humorous short stories including *Fools and Funny Fellows; More "Time to Laugh" Tales* (Knopf, 1947), *Giggle Box; Funny Stories for Boys and Girls* (Knopf, 1950), and *Fun, Fun, Fun; Stories of Mischief and Mirth, Fantasy and Farce, Whimsy and Nonsense* (F. Watts, 1953) compiled by Phyllis Reid Fenner.

History in Fiction

Books of historical fiction include those using a period of history as background or biographical novels with historical characters. Included also are stories involving frontier and pioneer life and Indians in American history. There are many writers in this field; only a few outstanding writers who have produced a number of books can be presented here.

Elizabeth Jane Coatsworth writes books of historical fiction for grades four and up. Typical of her titles are *The Golden Horseshoe* (Macmillan, 1935), a story of the colonial period of Virginia, and *Door to the North* (Winston, 1950), about fourteenth-century Vikings in America. *Peddler's Cart* (Macmillan, 1956) is set in the area of Niagara Falls in the mid-nineteenth century. While not a book of historical fiction, being based on a Japanese legend, Miss Coatsworth's *The Cat Who Went to Heaven*

(Macmillan, 1958, first published in 1930) may also be noted since it won the Newbery Medal in 1931.

Books by William Owen Steele are largely historical, dealing especially with frontier and pioneer life. They are popular with both junior high school pupils and those of the upper elementary grades. Several books include such legendary-historical characters as Daniel Boone and Davy Crockett. *The Perilous Road* (Harcourt, 1958), one of his most popular books, introduces a young boy living in the Tennessee mountains during the Civil War.

Walter Dumaux Edmonds appeals largely to boys. His books usually have New York State as their setting and often deal with Indian wars or the American Revolution. *The Matchlock Gun* (Dodd, 1941) is for grades four to six; *Two Logs Crossing; John Haskell's Story* (Dodd, 1943) is for grades five to nine; and *Wilderness Clearing* (Dodd, 1944) is for grades seven to nine. This last title and *Drums Along the Mohawk* (Little, 1951, first published in 1936) are read by senior high school pupils also.

Merritt Parmelee Allen is the author of historical novels, the scenes of several of which are set in South Carolina. He also writes of frontier and pioneer life, especially along the Oregon Trail. *Blow, Bugles, Blow* (Longmans, 1956), published after his death in 1954, is a story of the Civil War. It might be repeated that war stories, especially those about the Civil War and World War II, are popular with high school readers.

Kenneth Lewis Roberts stands high among authors of historical fiction whose works can be enjoyed by high school readers. *Northwest Passage* (Doubleday, 1937, reissued in 1959), a story of the French and Indian War, is probably one of his best known books. There is also a series of several books dealing with American history from the time of the Revolution to the War of 1812.

Some of Irving Stone's biographical novels are based on the lives of famous American women. Older girls especially enjoy his *Love Is Eternal; a Novel About Mary Todd and Abraham Lincoln* (Doubleday, 1954), and *President's Lady; a Novel About Rachel and Andrew Jackson* (Doubleday, 1951).

Though several of her earlier books dealt with experiences in teaching, Loula Grace Erdman's later books are largely about frontier and pioneer life in Texas. Probably the best known are *Edge of Time* (Dodd, 1950) and *Winds Blow Free* (Dodd, 1952), followed by *Wide Horizon; a Story of the Texas Panhandle* (Dodd, 1956), and *Good Land* (Dodd, 1959). The last three of these deal with members of the pioneer Pierce family and are popular with senior high school girls.

An older writer about frontier and pioneer life is Willa Sibert Cather, several of whose books are read by high school pupils. *My Ántonia* (Houghton, 1926), long a favorite with girls, is the story of pioneer life in Nebraska, presumably told by a New York lawyer as he recalls his boyhood days and his friendship with a Bohemian girl. Other novels by Miss Cather read by high school pupils are *Death Comes for the Archbishop* (Knopf, 1927) and *Shadows on the Rock* (Knopf, 1931). The former is the story of a French priest in New Mexico a century ago. The latter deals with life in the French colony of Quebec during the middle 1600's.

ACCENT ON PEOPLES

A writer whose name is associated with Indians is Ann Nolan Clark, already mentioned in the history section. *Little Navajo Bluebird* (Viking, 1943) is still a favorite with children. This author's most distinguished book is *Secret of the Andes* (Viking, 1952), which won the Newbery Medal in 1953. Two fairly recent books by Mrs. Clark, both published by Leibel, *Little Indian Basket Maker* (1957) and *Little Indian Pottery Maker* (1955), prove helpful in social studies for grades two and three.

Books by Arna Wendell Bontemps are about his own Negro race. *Sad-Faced Boy* (Houghton, 1937) is an excellent story of three Negro boys who leave their Alabama home to visit relatives in Harlem. *Chariot in the Sky; a Story of the Jubilee Singers* (Winston, 1951) is for junior high school age.

There are two books with Negro characters written and illustrated by Eleanor Frances Lattimore: *Junior, a Colored Boy of Charleston* (Harcourt, 1938) and *Bayou Boy* (Morrow, 1946). However, Mrs. Lattimore writes most often about China, where she lived as a child. Outstanding among books with this background are *Little Pear; the Story of a Little Chinese Boy* (Harcourt, 1931) and *Peachblossom* (Harcourt, 1943). *Little Pear and the Rabbits* (Morrow, 1956) is for slightly younger readers than her other books, grades two to four.

Various minority groups (Quakers, Mennonites, and Negroes) are depicted by Marguerite de Angeli, who writes regional books, some with historical significance, which appeal largely to girls. Some of her titles are *Bright April* (1946), *Henner's Lydia* (1936), and *Thee, Hannah!* (1940), all published by Doubleday. Attention should be called to the lovely illustrations by this author for her own books as well as those of others. Mrs. de Angeli's most distinguished book, *The Door in the Wall* (Doubleday, 1949), a story of medieval England, won the Newbery Medal in 1950.

Lois Lenski's regional stories, one for almost every part of the United States, are read by pupils in the upper elementary grades and early junior high school. Her *Strawberry Girl* (Lippincott, 1945), which won the Newbery Medal in 1946, is a story of farmers in Florida. *Judy's Journey* (Lippincott, 1947), a story of migrant workers, is probably the best of the series. *Blue Ridge Billy* (Lippincott, 1946), a story of mountain people, is one of several books in which the main character is a boy.

The books of Florence Crannell Means nearly always include characters from some minority group. Two are about Negroes: *Shuttered Windows* (Houghton, 1938) and *Great Day in the Morning* (Houghton, 1946). *Assorted Sisters* (Houghton, 1947) is about the friendship of a Mexican, a Chinese, and an American girl of high school age.

Margot Benary-Isbert is the author of several books translated from the German by Richard and Clara Winston which are suitable for, and popular with, high school readers. Two outstanding ones are *The Ark* (Harcourt, 1953) and *Rowan Farm* (Harcourt, 1954), which deal with the same characters. *The Long Way Home* (Harcourt, 1959) tells of a boy who flees from East Germany and finds a home in California.

A fairly new writer who writes about minority groups, Joseph Krumgold stands out as the first writer to have received the

Newbery Medal twice. It was first awarded to him for *And Now Miguel* (Crowell, 1953), the story of a boy's growing up in the sheep country of New Mexico. *Onion John* (Crowell, 1959), the winner of his second Newbery Medal, concerns the friendship of a twelve-year-old boy and a man who sells vegetables, does odd jobs, and scavenges in the town dump.

SCHOOL STORIES AND SPORTS

Many stories involve school experiences. For younger readers there are *Country School* (Morrow, 1955) and others by Jerrold Beim; Rebecca Caudill's *Schoolhouse in the Woods* (Winston, 1949); several of the books about Betsy by Carolyn Haywood; *Ellen Tebbits* (Morrow, 1951) and *Otis Spofford* (Morrow, 1953) by Beverly Cleary, whose books are always humorous; *Bright Island,* an interesting story about a girl in Maine by Mabel Louise Robinson (Random House, 1937); Mary Urmston's *New Boy* (Doubleday, 1950); and Catherine Woolley's series of novels of which the first is *Ginnie and Geneva* (Morrow, 1948).

On the high school level, books about school life are found among stories about teen-agers such as those by Betty Cavanna and Anne Emery for girls, and James L. Summers' books for boys. Similar stories about life at college may be found among the books for older girls by such writers as Marguerite Harmon Bro and Mary Slattery Stolz. A few individual titles are the old stand-by *Good-bye, Mr. Chips* by James Hilton (Globe Book, 1953, first published by Little in 1934); *Ride Out the Storm* (Morrow, 1951) by Margaret Elizabeth Bell; *The Luckiest Girl* (Morrow, 1958) by Beverly Cleary; and *Now That I'm Sixteen* (Crowell, 1959) by Margaret Maze Craig.

John Robert Tunis is the best-known author of sports fiction for high school readers. A former sports writer, he has a thorough understanding of athletics and can spin a yarn that interests most boys and many girls. *The Kid from Tomkinsville* (Harcourt, 1940) begins a series of several books about baseball. *Iron Duke* (Harcourt, 1938) and *Duke Decides* (Harcourt, 1939) are about Jim Wellington, who enters Harvard with a record as an excellent student and athlete in a small midwestern high school and has to learn to stand on his own. *All-American* (Harcourt, 1942) is a football story of two teams, one from a private school and one from a large public high school. The more recent books by Tunis tend to include modern social problems, such as the question of racial integration in sports.

For a slightly younger group than the readers of the Tunis books, Jackson Volney Scholz has written *Fielder from Nowhere* (Morrow, 1948), dealing with baseball, and several books about football, including *Fighting Chance* (Morrow, 1956). Senior high school pupils will also read the latter since it has to do with coaching as well as playing the game.

SCIENCE FICTION

Science fiction is not a new type of writing, as it was introduced by Jules Verne a century ago and given impetus by H. G. Wells in the 1890's. However, with the coming of the space age, there has been great demand among high school boys and some girls for books of fiction involving newer phases of science.

Although pupils in elementary grades, taking a cue from older brothers and spurred on by television programs, ask for science fiction, very little has been written for their level. *The Wonderful Flight to the Mushroom Planet* (Little, 1954) by Eleanor Cameron is the story of two boys who help restore life on a dying planet after they have worked with a neighbor to build a space ship. The story is continued in *Stowaway to the Mushroom Planet* (Little, 1956).

Several books by Ellen MacGregor, beginning with *Miss Pickerell Goes to Mars* (McGraw, 1951), are about an elderly spinster and her rather remarkable travels, including interplanetary voyages and ventures under the sea. These books contain more humor than science, but do answer the demand for science fiction by pupils in grades four to six.

Arthur Charles Clarke, himself a scientist, is the author of several books of science fiction which are avidly read by high school pupils. Two of his titles, both published in 1952, are *Islands in the Sky* (Winston) and *Sands of Mars* (Gnome Press). His *Deep Range* (Harcourt, 1957) is a book of science fiction set in the deep sea one hundred years in the future.

One of the most widely read authors of science fiction is Robert Anson Heinlein. His first book, *Rocket Ship Galileo* (Scribner, 1947), tells how a group of boys, with the help of an inventor interested in rocket airplanes, finally reach the moon. Other popular titles are *Red Planet: A Colonial Boy on Mars* (Scribner, 1949) and *Tunnel in the Sky* (Scribner, 1955). A more recent title, *Have Space Suit—Will Travel* (Scribner, 1958) has been widely read by science fiction devotees.

Alice Mary Norton, who writes many adventure stories using the pseudonym André Norton has several books of science fiction to her credit. Among these are *Star Man's Son, 2250 A.D.* (Harcourt, 1952) and *Time Traders* (World Publishing, 1958). The latter is the fantastic story of a young volunteer for "Operation Retrograde," a secret government project, who is sent back into the Bronze Age.

Other writers of science fiction are Isaac Asimov, Franklyn Mansfield Branley (who has some books in the field of science), Lester Del Rey, Alan Edward Nourse, and Donald A. Wollheim.

Groff Conklin is the editor of several collections of science fiction short stories. Experience proves that stories included in some of these collections are of uneven value. Some are by acceptable authors; others, taken from the more sensational magazines, include topics otuside the realm of science fiction and are of questionable value for high school readers.

TALES FOR TEEN-AGERS

There are many teen-age books for junior high school girls wanting love stories. They are usually about girls of their own age or a bit older, may have a school element or career interest, and always have a touch of romance.

Betty Cavanna's long list of books includes many in this category. A recent title is *Accent on April* (Morrow, 1960), the story of Cathy's fifteenth year in her Boston home with her father, a college professor who raises rare orchilds as a hobby. Miss Cavanna's *Going on Sixteen* (Westminster Press, 1946) is probably her best-known book. It has rivaled *Seventeenth Summer* by Maureen Daly (Dodd, 1942) in popularity. *Seventeenth Summer,* one of the first teen-age books to be written, is the love story of a boy of eighteen and a girl one year younger in a typical American town.

The name of Rosamond Neal DuJardin is associated with teen-age stories. *Practically Seventeen* (Lippincott, 1949) and *Class Ring* (Lippincott, 1951) are typical examples. Several of her books are about the same girl, as for example, *Wait for Marcy* (Lippincott, 1950) and *Man for Marcy* (Lippincott, 1954).

Anne Emery also writes teen-age stories for girls. *Sweet Sixteen* (Macrae Smith, 1956) is a school story in which a young girl is helped to find herself by a young teacher. *Senior Year* (1949) and its sequel, *Going Steady* (1950), both published by Westminster Press, tell the story of Sally and her friend Scotty.

Mary Slattery Stolz is another writer of teen-age romances, often based on a career or including college life. Typical titles, all published by Harper, are *To Tell Your Love* (1950); *The Organdy Cupcakes* (1951), a story of nurses in training; and *And Love Replied* (1958).

Marguerite Harmon Bro writes for older teen-agers. The story of *Sarah* (Doubleday, 1949) carries a girl intent on becoming a great pianist to young womanhood. *Stub, a College Romance* (Doubleday, 1959) tells the story of a boy's first year at college.

Margaret Elizabeth Bell has written a series of three books about Alaska which older girls enjoy. They are *Watch for a Tall White Sail; a Novel* (1948), *Totem Casts a Shadow* (1949), and *Love Is Forever* (1954), all published by Morrow.

Teen-age stories written from a boy's point of view, though not always of interest to boys alone, are created by James L. Summers. These books are designated as school stories and are published by Westminster Press. Sample titles are *Girl Trouble* (1953) and *Trouble on the Run* (1956). A more recent book with a slightly different theme bears the title *Heartbreak Hot Rod* (Doubleday, 1958). In *Gift Horse* (Westminster, 1961) Summers turns from cars to horses although still concerned with the psychology of teen-agers.

Mina Lewiton, the author of several books dealing with adolescent girls facing specific problems, such as divorced parents in *Divided Heart* (McKay, 1947) and alcoholism in the home in *Cup of Courage* (McKay, 1948), has recently written *Elizabeth and the Young Stranger* (McKay, 1961), which appeals to teen-age girls facing problems of adjustment.

School librarians may wish to read Gregor Felsen's books before purchasing because they are somewhat controversial, usually dealing with modern social problems. His most controversial book, *Two and the Town* (Scribner, 1952) relates the story of a high school boy and girl who eventually adjust to a marriage forced upon them. Other Felsen books, usually involving cars, are for teen-age boys and are very popular. Examples of these, with self-explanatory titles, are *Hot Rod* (Dutton, 1950) and *Street Rod* (Random House, 1953). *Crash Club* (Random House, 1958) is a very realistic story of automobile racing for teen-agers.

PERIODICALS

Selection of periodicals for school libraries offers some problems not encountered in the selection of books. They are subscribed for in advance, usually for the period of a year. The list of periodicals should be considered annually to take care of those that need to be dropped for any reason and to provide for others which may be added. Occasionally the policy of a magazine changes so drastically that the subscription may be dropped before it expires. When a new title is added, particularly one not well-known, the school librarian is advised to take a brief trial subscription or to buy a few issues locally in order to try out the periodical in his own library before an annual subscription is taken.

AIDS FOR SELECTION OF PERIODICALS

Among the standard selection aids, the ALA "Basic Book Collections" offer the only guides to selection of magazines, a recommended list of which appears as a section of each. For *A Basic Book Collection for Elementary Grades* and *A Basic Book Collection for Junior High Schools*, both revised in 1960, the magazines were selected and annotated by the same committee which compiled the list of books. *A Basic Book Collection for High Schools* (1957) follows an earlier plan of having the list of magazines compiled by a special subcommittee of the Magazine Evaluation Committee of the American Association of School Librarians. The next revised edition will undoubtedly follow the plan of the other two aids. It should be mentioned here that the AASL Magazine Evaluation Committee publishes reports on new magazines from time to time in *Top of the News*.

101 Magazines for Schools, Grades 1-12, a pamphlet by Ruby Ethel Cundliff, formerly of the Library Science Department of Madison College, Harrisonburg, Virginia, was issued in its third edition by the Tennessee Book Company of Nashville, Tennessee, in 1959. The very brief annotations in this rather extensive list offer only limited help in evaluation, however.

There is also *The Dobler International List of Periodicals for Boys and Girls,* published in 1960, which lists nearly 350 items; one of its four sections is devoted to periodicals for school use. This list was compiled by Lavinia Dobler, librarian of Scholastic Magazines, Inc., who has access to a very extensive collection of youth periodicals. It is a new and complete revision of a list available in mimeographed form since 1953.[1]

The October 1961 and January 1962 issues of *School Libraries* contain a bibliography entitled "Periodicals for Children and Young People." The first section of the bibliography deals with selection aids.

NEWSPAPERS

Newspapers are subscribed to by most high school libraries, although elementary school libraries seem to find little need for them. The high school library, either junior or senior, will probably need at least one local newspaper, one newspaper that gives good state coverage, and one that is adequate in national and world-wide news. Some school libraries subscribe only for the Sunday edition of a natiónal newspaper such as the New York *Times,* which is especially useful for the magazine supplement and the section devoted to book reviews.

MAGAZINES

Like books, magazines are used both for recreational reading and for reference purposes, particularly in high school libraries. Now that many high schools are dispensing with study halls and substituting either longer periods for classes or supervised study in the classrooms, pupils have less time for leisure reading in the library. On the other hand, pupils are required to work on term projects and to write term papers, both involving extensive research and more nearly approximating work on the college level. In such situations, magazines become increasingly important for reference work.

[1] Obtainable from Muriel Fuller, P.O. Box 193, Grand Central Station, New York 17.

In selecting magazines, librarians and teachers are advised to give preference to those which are indexed in either the *Readers' Guide to Periodical Literature* or the *Abridged Readers' Guide to Periodical Literature,* whichever is subscribed to by the school library. The list of magazines to be indexed in these reference tools is revised periodically by vote of the subscribers. Prior to the voting, the American Library Association Committee on Wilson Indexes makes a study of existing magazines in each subject field to be covered by the index concerned and reports its findings to the subscribers. These revisions of the coverage of the indexes help to keep them up to date in serving reference needs.

School libraries generally do not bind magazines to any extent but keep back numbers by volumes for a period of three to five years. It is conceivable that a few titles of magazines might need to be kept for more extended periods of time. A good example is the *National Geographic* in which material, even pictorial, on such subjects as ancient times never becomes outdated. After they are no longer useful for reference, magazines may be clipped for the information file before being discarded. Some school libraries follow the practice of keeping back numbers of magazines on microfilm to conserve space. However, only schools with adequate library budgets are encouraged to undertake such a project.

Magazines Suggested in "Basic Book Collections"

An overview of magazines suggested in the "Basic Book Collections" is given here to show the number suggested in various categories for each educational level. The categories also give the beginning librarian an idea of the types of magazines considered suitable for school use.

The list of magazines in *A Basic Book Collection for Elementary Grades* recommends only thirteen magazines in the following categories: Current Events; Geography and Travel; Nature, Science, and Technology; and Special Interests. There are twenty-one other suggestions for schools where additional magazines are needed. This brief list seems to emphasize the feeling of many librarians and teachers that magazines are not so essential

in the elementary school library collection as in those of junior
and senior high schools.

Most of the magazines in the above-mentioned list are actually
more suitable for junior, or even senior, high school libraries. This
selection may reflect advice in the newly adopted standards for
school libraries that the elementary school library include "some
titles in the adult field that have interest and usefulness for
children in the upper middle grades." [2] It should be noted furthermore that the reading level in *A Basic Book Collection for
Elementary Grades* extends through grade eight. Children's magazines excluded from this list because they did not meet the
standards set up for selection of books by the committee will be
discussed later.

In *A Basic Book Collection for Junior High Schools* forty-four
magazines are recommended in the following categories: General
Popular Magazines; Fashions and Homemaking; Fine Arts; Foreign
Languages; Geography and Travel; National and World Affairs;
Nature and Outdoor Life; Recreation and Sports; Science and
Technology; and Special Hobbies. Twenty-six additional magazines
are suggested for libraries that need them.

A Basic Book Collection for High Schools recommends sixty
magazines in the following categories: General; Business and Con-
sumer Research; Fashions; Fine Arts; Homemaking; Literary and
Book Reviewing; National and World Affairs; Nature and Outdoor
Life; Science; Sports and Hobbies; Technology; Travel. In several
instances, a choice is suggested between two magazines in the
same group as, for example, *Newsweek* or *Time; House and Garden*
or *House Beautiful*. This is also true in the other "Basic Book
Collections."

About half of the magazine titles recommended for junior
high schools are also on the list for senior high schools. Appearing
on lists for all three levels are *American Junior Red Cross Journal*,
which is somewhat juvenile for senior high schools; *Current
Biography*,[3] which school librarians generally think of in terms

[2] American Association of School Librarians. *Standards for School Library
Programs*. Chicago, American Library Association. 1960. p. 79.
[3] Also discussed in Chapter 4, above, "Reference Books."

of reference work rather than as a magazine for pupil use, and which is useful in any school library, especially those on the junior and senior high level; *Junior Scholastic; Life,* which many school librarians feel is too adult for use by elementary pupils; *National Geographic Magazine,* certainly a must for all school libraries; *Newsweek,* which would be useful for teachers but beyond the reading ability of most pupils below grade seven; *Popular Mechanics* and *Popular Science,* the former more suitable for use by elementary school readers; *Seventeen,* which is really on the junior high school level but could prove useful with more mature sixth grade girls; and *Sport,* which is a bit difficult for elementary school pupils but will be used by boys who stretch their reading ability to enjoy it.

Two magazines were omitted from the list in *A Basic Book Collection for Elementary Grades,* although they are included in both the other "Basic Book Collections." These are suitable for, and popular with, upper elementary as well as early junior high school pupils, but are too juvenile for most senior high school readers. They are *American Girl,* published by the Girl Scouts of the United States of America, and *Boys' Life,* published by the Boy Scouts of America, both being official publications. In addition to carrying information primarily of interest to scouts, these two magazines feature stories, some of which are written by scouts themselves, articles on many subjects, photo features, fashion and grooming hints for girls in *American Girl,* things to do or make in *Boys' Life,* puzzles, games, and special features which include a number of book reviews. Neither of these magazines, however, is indexed in either *Readers' Guide* or *Abridged Readers' Guide* and consequently their reference value is limited.

The composite list of magazines in the "Basic Book Collections" is a well-selected and fairly comprehensive basic list for schools. Selection was made by a representative group of educators and librarians from magazines proving most useful in school libraries. The annotations state the outstanding contributions of the recommended magazines and sometimes point out considerations which might limit their usefulness. The inexperienced librarian will find the "Basic Book Collections" indispensable in becoming acquainted with magazines and selecting from among them. Most school libraries will need some titles in each of the categories suggested for any particular level. The comments below, while avoiding duplication with the basic lists, attempt amplification and clarification in several areas. Addresses of publishers of magazines are given only when they are not available in the "Basic Book Collections."

Children's Magazines

Omitted from *A Basic Book Collection for Elementary Grades* are the so-called children's magazines though they are found in many collections serving children, both in public and elementary school libraries. Librarians should be acquainted with children's magazines, even though they do not meet the standards of magazines for other levels, and decide whether they should subscribe to any of them. Many librarians find them useful in elementary school library collections. They include the following: *Humpty Dumpty's Magazine,* published by Parents' Magazine; *Children's Playmate,* published by Children's Playmate Magazine, Inc. (6529 Union Avenue, Cleveland 5, Ohio); *Jack and Jill,* published by The Curtis Publishing Company; and *Highlights for Children,* published by Highlights for Children, Inc. (2300 W. Fifth Avenue, Columbus 16, Ohio), and now incorporating the former *Children's Activities.* In 1960 *Highlights for Children* was awarded the Brotherhood Certificate of Recognition by the National Council of Christians and Jews. *Wee Wisdom,* published by the Unity School of Christianity (Lee's Summit, Missouri), has understandably a strong religious slant, and belongs in church, rather than in school, libraries.

These magazines are usually published monthly except in summer, are somewhat similar in content, and are enjoyed by the younger pupils. They contain stories, sometimes excerpted from children's books; poems; puzzles of various sorts; suggested things to do, including cut-outs and coloring projects which may tempt readers to mutilate magazines; articles about well-known personages or on science and nature; and contributions by readers themselves—letters to the editors, stories, and poems.

Magazines for Classroom Use

Unless magazines designed primarily to be used in classrooms are generally subscribed to by individual pupils, they may be considered for inclusion in the school library. At any rate, school librarians, as well as teachers, should be acquainted with them.

American Education Publications publishes several magazines for classroom use. *My Weekly Reader* is published in seven editions, one for each of the six elementary grades and kindergarten. *Current Events,* the title of which is self-explanatory, and *Read Magazine,* useful for the language arts, are both suitable for grades on the upper elementary and lower junior high school levels. New in the fall of 1960 was another weekly, *Our Times,* intended for high school use. Its issues carry articles on politics, social problems, business, literature, and hobbies, including photography and hot rod cars.

Another publisher of classroom magazines is Scholastic Magazines, Inc. Its publications are usually weeklies and have a teachers' edition for each title. For the elementary grades, emphasizing social studies, language arts, and science, there are *News Explorer* for grade four and *NewsTime* for grade five. *World Week,* covering current events, is intended for use in the early grades of junior high school and could prove useful with better readers in grade six.

Senior Scholastic has long been a stand-by in high school libraries. It presents recent news, national and world affairs, forum topics for discussion, economics, science, and sports. There are also special features in line with hobbies and interests of high school pupils. Since material in *Junior Scholastic* is always similar to the contents of *Senior Scholastic,* sometimes on the same topics, high school libraries may wish to consider whether both magazines are necessary, even when both junior and senior high school pupils are served.

Other Scholastic magazines are *Science World, Edition 1,* for grades seven, eight, and nine and *Science World, Edition 2,* for grades ten, eleven, and twelve. Both magazines have similar features and departments. There are articles by and about outstanding scientists and, probably of even more interest to high school pupils, projects in science reported by teen-agers who may become the scientists of tomorrow. Departments include letters, brain teasers, science fun, and crossword puzzles, many by high school pupils.

Scholastic Magazines, Inc. also issues *Literary Cavalcade,* a monthly Scholastic magazine of contemporary literature for senior high school English classes. The December 1960 issue, as a typical example, includes the complete text of the play *Sunrise at Campobello* by Doré Schary; an article, "Christmas with Ed Sullivan"; several short stories; and five poems from the Irish by James Stephens. Neither *Literary Cavalcade* nor *Science World* is included in the "Basic Book Collections."

Homemaking Magazines

In addition to the number of magazines on homemaking recommended in the "Basic Book Collections," many school libraries include *Ladies' Home Journal,* one of the oldest of this group of magazines. Under its present editorship, *McCall's Magazine* has forged forward both in breadth and quality of coverage to rank among the best of its kind. The teacher of home economics will have to choose among these and *Good Housekeeping* (which is listed in the "Basic Book Collections"), if only one can be subscribed to. School librarians will want to know about *Forecast for Home Economists,* also published by the McCall Corporation monthly except July and August. An issue often emphasizes one phase of homemaking as, for example, "Focus on Foods." "Teacher's Notebook" is a regular feature each month.

For the junior high school age, Scholastic Magazines, Inc., publishes *Co-ed,* an attractive monthly publication covering the usual information of interest to teen-age girls. A typical issue contains such sections as Food and Festivity; Face and Figure; Friends and Family; Furnishings; Finances; Fiction and Features; Fortunes. The teacher's edition of *Co-ed* is entitled *Practical Home Economics.* However, school libraries usually do not include professional magazines and those strictly for the faculty in their regular budgets.

Glamour, "the 'how-to' fashion magazine for young women," which has taken over Street and Smith Publications' *Charm,* is published by Condé Nast Publications, Inc. In addition to material on fashions, this magazine covers other phases of homemaking. There is usually an article on how an actual young couple lives in an interesting place such as "Space-Age Boom-Town" (Huntsville, Alabama) and a travel article. Letters and other special features are also a part of each issue. Suitable for junior high school use, *Glamour* also appeals to senior high school pupils.

Magazines of Science and Technology

There is a great demand at the present time for magazines of science and technology. School librarians continually receive queries as to why certain magazines are not included and requests for subscriptions to additional titles. There is a wide variety of magazines in this category by a varied group of publishers. Two companies, each of which publishes several of these, are Fawcett Publications and Ziff-Davis Publishing Company. The "Basic Book Collections" offer a very good selection of magazines in this field.

These magazines are somewhat similar in content. They cover recent news of inventions and discoveries, scientific developments, and progress in communication and transportation, especially space travel. There are many illustrations, usually charts and drawings or photographs, and the pages devoted to advertising bulge with things any boy would like to have. (Coupons to order articles advertised should probably be stamped with the school library stamp to prevent mutilation.) Titles selected at random demonstrate varied material offered through interesting articles: "Brain Surgery by Ultrasonics" "Lightning, Nature's Mysterious Display of Pyrotechnics"; and "What Is Your Car's Traffic Ability?" The bulk of their contents, while probably outside the ken of the average female school librarian, is readily intelligible to the average high school boy. Elementary pupils get a great deal from the pictures and retarded readers are often interested in these magazines, even though they cannot read their own textbooks.

Fawcett Publications, Inc., publishes *Electronics Illustrated* and *Mechanix Illustrated*. The latter uses as a subtitle "the how-to-do-it magazine." The two are almost identical in format, feature brief articles, and include a great many illustrations. *Mechanix Illustrated* is more nearly confined to the world of electronics. The latter is not included in any of the "Basic Book Collections."

In this subject area, *Popular Electronics*, published by Ziff-Davis Publishing Company, is recommended and *Electronics World* suggested if others of this type are needed. *Electronics World*, also published by Ziff-Davis, was formerly *Radio and TV News* and is recommended under that title in *A Basic Book Collection for High Schools* (1957). Contents cover new developments in radio, television, high fidelity, and similar topics. Some attention is given to the amateur in communications. A number of departments appeal to high school readers. There are numerous diagrams to be pored over and the advertisements are striking. It is for senior high school pupils and the more advanced ones in junior high schools.

Whether *Hot Rod* is classified as sports or technology and whether the school librarian likes it or not, a copy will probably be included in most high school library collections. The issues are filled with articles on car racing and ways and means to equip cars for this sport. This magazine is published by Petersen Publishing Company. A similar magazine, although it gives more attention to regular cars than to racing, is *Motor Trends*, also published by Petersen. This would interest the more mature high school readers, although it is not suggested by the "Basic Book Collections."

Two other magazines in this general grouping are mentioned for emphasis because they are more generally useful than their titles indicate. *American Modeler*, a Street and Smith publication, has had two previous titles, *Air Trails Pictorial* and *Young Men*. The present title appeals to junior high school pupils and this is probably the first magazine of this type from which elementary pupils could profit. *Today's Health*, a magazine of the American

Medical Association, contains a wealth of material, not all of it strictly of a medical nature, which is useful for reference purposes in both junior and senior high schools.

Digest Magazines

There are two schools of thought about so-called digest magazines in school libraries. One holds that pupils should read the original articles, many of which are condensed from magazines in the school library. The other maintains that it is better for pupils to get the gist of many articles than to read only a few in full. Besides, the condensed article might lead a pupil to pursue the original in an available magazine.

The argument probably started over the *Reader's Digest*, which is now included in most high schools. However, it is no longer wholly a digest because many of its articles are written directly for publication in its pages. Since selections from the *Reader's Digest* are now published in several foreign languages, these versions are proving useful in foreign language classes, in addition to magazines from foreign countries, some of which are suggested in "Basic Book Collections."

The *Science Digest*, published by Science Digest, Inc., serves to introduce readers to the more serious type of science writing and to awaken their interest in the subject. The articles are brief and interesting, and many are written by outstanding science writers.

The *Children's Digest*, published monthly except June and August by Parents' Magazine, is hardly a digest. Although it has a few stories taken from well-known books or collections of stories and an occasional article by a well-known writer, most of its contents are of the things-to-do variety with an element of the comic book characteristic of several magazines published by Parents' Magazine. For this reason, subscription to *Children's Digest* by the individual child seems best. Some librarians, however, regard it as useful in the elementary school library.

The convenient size of digest magazines may tempt some pupils to appropriate them for use outside the school library without benefit of charging. To prevent loss of magazines, school libraries usually require that pupils sign at the circulation desk for any titles that seem prone to disappear, even when only being used in the library.

Professional Magazines

As a general rule, the budget for materials in the school library is not sufficiently generous to provide magazines of a professional nature. If they are to be purchased for use in the school library, additional funds should be made available for them. In some schools, teachers contribute to a fund to cover the cost of subscriptions to magazines for faculty use and a committee decides which should be included. It is possible to ask teachers also to contribute to the library their own professional magazines, once they have read them, to be shared by others in the school.

School librarians should become acquainted with professional magazines, in both the educational and library fields. Some are received as a part of membership in professional organizations. Others must be secured through regular trade channels by subscription. Some professional magazines are very general in nature; others confine themselves to one subject area, such as English, mathematics, social studies. All help the reader keep abreast of educational trends and offer practical help for teachers and librarians.

Periodicals useful in current book selection are a necessary part of any school library collection. Most of these are discussed in Chapter 2, "Book Selection Aids"; others are in an additional list in the Appendix. While kept in the library, these should be readily available to teachers, who should be encouraged to use them. Subscriptions to those magazines are usually included in the school library budget.

MAGAZINES AS GIFTS

Nearly all school libraries receive a few magazines for which they do not pay. Such magazines fall into these categories: those sent free by the publisher, sometimes without solicitation; subscriptions paid for by organizations or individuals; and back numbers of magazines. The first group usually consists of promotional magazines from business firms, chambers of commerce, highway departments, etc. These may be of reference value because of their local interest. A few publications of this type are available only through subscriptions. When an individual or an organization offers to pay for a subscription for the library, the librarian should suggest a title which the library actually needs, or, better still, request that money be donated to the library so that the subscription can be ordered through the usual channels. Back numbers of magazines donated to the library may provide materials for filling gaps in back files maintained by the library or for building up files of magazines not taken by subscription. They may also provide material to be clipped for the information file.

Generally speaking, the school library should accept as gifts only magazines which the school library actually needs. This rules out the possibility of getting into the collection magazines that are unsuitable for school library use. It also saves time in looking over or processing such material. Some libraries stamp "Gift" on any material not obtained by purchase.

NUMBER OF MAGAZINES

The number of magazines needed in any school library will depend on the use of library materials. This, in turn, will depend on the amount of time which pupils spend in the library for leisure reading and research, teachers' use of current magazines in connection with classwork, and pupils' use of back numbers for research and term papers.

When standards for school libraries were first set up in the 1920's, a stated sum ($75 in the case of the Southern Association of Colleges and Secondary Schools) was suggested for magazines. Later it came to be generally accepted that 10 to 15 per cent of the library budget should be devoted to magazine subscriptions. Still more recently a number of state standards, which in practice appear to be replacing regional standards, have suggested that so much money per pupil should be allotted for magazines.

In the summary of quantitative standards in the newly adopted standards for school libraries prepared by the American Association of School Librarians, suggestions are made for the actual number of magazines as follows: Schools having grades from kindergarten through grade six, at least 25 magazines; kindergarten through grade eight, 50 magazines; junior high schools, 70 magazines; and senior high schools, 120 magazines.[4] Elsewhere the standards suggest that "Schools having a special program in technical, vocational or other areas need larger periodical collections so that magazines in the special fields are included."[5] In addition it is suggested that each school have at least five titles of magazines in the areas of librarianship and instructional materials.

School librarians are advised to subscribe to magazines according to the needs of the individual schools, which vary widely, rather than to attain a minimum number set by any standards. Generally speaking, few elementary school libraries will need 25 magazines. Not many junior high schools could afford or make wise use of 70 magazines. Only the largest senior high school libraries would need 120 magazines even if that many suitable ones were actually available. Selection of magazines should be done realistically. There seems no real point in having more magazines in the school library than are actually needed.

The Stern Family Fund Magazine Project

In the fall of 1958 and again in 1959, the American Association of School Librarians administered a grant of $5,000 from the Edgar B. Stern Family Fund, a nonprofit educational and charitable foundation of New Orleans. This grant provided that some selected periodicals be placed in high schools in order that their impact on an educational program might be studied.

The participating schools were selected by a committee established for this project by the American Association of School Librarians. In 1958-1959, 54 schools participated; in 1959-1960, there were 57 schools, 46 participating for the second year. These

[4] American Association of School Librarians, *op. cit.*, p. 24-5.
[5] *Ibid.*, p. 79.

schools differed greatly in enrollment and in library budgets, both general budget and amount designated especially for magazines. While some schools of grades one to twelve were included, the majority of participating schools were grades seven to twelve or nine to twelve. The number of magazines regularly subscribed to before the experiment ranged from 6 to 80, 36 schools subscribing to 35 magazines or fewer and 14 schools to from 40 to 60 magazines. Participating schools were asked to fill out a questionnaire at the end of each school year of the project, results of which were summarized in a meaningful annual report.

Attention of school librarians is called to this project for two reasons. The annotated list of periodicals from which titles were selected by participating schools was "carefully chosen by the Magazine Evaluation Committee of the Young Adults Services Division of the American Library Association." [6] This list will prove helpful in acquainting high school librarians with magazines not listed in "Basic Book Collections." Some magazines on this list are from other countries; many are not found in the average school library collection. The mimeographed reports, more particularly that of 1959-1960, should prove helpful in analyzing the use of magazines in any school library and suggesting additional uses. Evaluation of the project for 1958-1959 was made by Mary Louise Mann in "Widening Horizons Through Periodicals." [7]

According to these reports, the project was deemed of value to the school curriculum, the teaching staff, and the pupils. School librarians reported a wide variety of methods used to stimulate use of these additional magazines by both teachers and pupils, in classes and as individuals. Teachers found a vast array of stimulating methods to assure use of the magazines generally and in connection with various subject divisions of the curriculum. Though the project was chiefly concerned with magazines in high school libraries, use made by elementary pupils who had access to the magazines was also reported. The consensus was that the magazines were used most extensively by gifted or above average pupils, especially those preparing for college work.

[6] *Top of the News.* p. 15. December 1958.
[7] *School Libraries.* 9:12-14. January 1960.

PART III

PROBLEMS IN SELECTION

CHAPTER 12

o

THE CLASSICS—YESTERDAY AND TODAY

PROBLEM OF THE CLASSICS

"A classic is normally a work of literature written in the past, the qualities of which are notable enough to have kept it alive in the memory of later generations or centuries as an example of excellence," wrote Robert Emmons Rogers.[1] To Rogers we are also indebted for the following excellent advice: "A catholic and eclectic knowledge of the best-loved literature of the past is the safest assurance that you will know how to discriminate in the present. Your horizon will be infinitely wider and your compass will point true North." You can learn "how weary, flat, stale, and unprofitable is most of the mass production writing of our age, the hundreds of machine stories undistinguishable in the memory from one another." [2] The trouble is that such advice, admirable as it is, today falls on deaf ears. With a few exceptions, both as to books and readers, children and young people no longer read the classics unless they are forced to do so by classroom assignments.

An analysis of this situation may prove helpful. Before 1900, very few books had been written exclusively for young readers. Most of the books on school library shelves today bear dates since the turn of the century. A great many of them have been written since 1940. Before books designed specially for them became a part of their heritage, children and young people of necessity chose books which they could read and enjoy from those written on the adult level. In the childhood of many parents, teachers, and school librarians, any list of books to be read on the high school level would have comprised works by Jane Austen, the Brontë sisters, Cooper, Dickens, Dumas, George Eliot, Hawthorne, Victor Hugo, Howard Pyle, Sir Walter Scott, General Lew Wallace, and others.

[1] *The Fine Art of Reading.* Boston, Stratford Company, 1929. p. 118.
[2] *Ibid.,* p. 133-4.

For younger readers there were books by Alcott, Lewis Carroll, Mrs. Ewing, Washington Irving, Kipling, Stevenson, Mark Twain, and so on.

There would have been such single titles as *Hans Brinker; or, The Silver Skates,*[3] by Mary Mapes Dodge; *Robinson Crusoe,* by Daniel Defoe; *Swiss Family Robinson,* by Johann David Wyss; *Lorna Doone,* by Richard Doddridge Blackmore; *Don Quixote de la Mancha,* by Miguel de Cervantes; and *Last Days of Pompeii,* by Edward Bulwer-Lytton. The list would doubtless have included *Black Beauty,* by Anna Sewell, which was written as propaganda for the prevention of cruelty to animals, drips with sentimentality, and by all standards should never have become a classic in the first place. Surprisingly, this book is still read by youngsters today, despite the automobile age and despite the fact that many better horse stories are now available. It is also among the classics most frequently adapted. The point is again made, however, that, when so few books for children and young people existed, they read those which were available.

Most of the above books and authors are included today in the *Children's Catalog* and the *Standard Catalog for High School Libraries,* as well as in other standard lists. They are usually found in school library collections. Parents, teachers, and librarians, remembering how their own childhood was enriched by these classics, want their children to read them too. This refers chiefly to older adults, because many of the younger parents, teachers, and librarians are themselves not familiar with the classics. The simple fact is that modern-day children and young people do not of their own volition read the classics in great numbers unless adults who work with them in reading guidance see that they read them.

School librarians and teachers will find helpful the revised edition of *Children's Classics* (Horn Book, 1960) which contains Alice M. Jordan's essay on the qualities which enable certain books to attain the status of classics. The list of recommended editions has been brought up to date by Helen Adams Masten.

---

[3] The publisher and date of books written before 1900 are not included because these books are available in various editions.

WHY CLASSICS ARE NOT READ

One reason classics are not read has already been suggested: modern children and young people may choose from so many good books—books written recently, designed for them, and about things in which they are interested. Many of such books are themselves on the way to becoming classics of the future. Any experienced school librarian could compile a list of them, and a creditable one.

Many of the classics, especially those written before 1900, seem old-fashioned to modern young readers and deal with a way of life which no longer has meaning for them. The vocabulary used is often unfamiliar and sometimes the words are archaic, even obsolete. The sentences are long and involved. Older books are filled with long descriptive passages, beautiful to those interested in poetical words or literary style. The modern reader, however, accustomed to learning things quickly, wants to get on with the story, to find out what happens next. Unless urged, he gives up on the first thirty to forty pages of John Buchan's *Prester John* (Houghton, 1928, first published in 1910), an exciting story after one gets into it.

Some teachers unfortunately have driven young readers from the classics by constantly including them on required lists and forcing pupils to read certain titles without choice. If teachers had to revert to childhood and follow their own assignments, it might change their views.

School librarians must bear their part of the blame also. So many copies of classics in school library collections are old, worn, and unattractive, with fine print and yellowed pages. Just because the library has a copy of the title, it is often not deemed necessary to replace it with a new, more attractive edition. Hence young readers come to regard the classics as books to be avoided.

It must also be remembered that modern youngsters see versions of the classics, however distorted and watered down, in comic form, in abridgments and adaptations, and as programs on television—all of which may take the edge off reading them.

ADAPTATION OF THE CLASSICS

As a solution to the problem of what to do about the classics, several publishers have undertaken the publication of adapted classics. Two companies which are in this field are Globe Book Company, with from fifty to sixty titles in a series known as Adapted Classics, of which 100,000 copies a year are reported to be sold; and Laidlaw Brothers, who offer thirteen titles in their simplified Classics for Enjoyment Series. Webster Publishing Company has five titles for the third grade level in the Junior Everyreader Series and eleven titles in the Everyreader Series on the fourth grade level. These stories are retold by William Kottmeyer, Assistant Superintendent of Instruction in the St. Louis Public Schools, and others. Mr. Kottmeyer is outstanding for his work in the field of remedial reading and these books are advertised as "interesting material adapted for high-interest, low-difficulty for retarded readers" through high school. Other series of adapted classics are Famous Story Series, adapted and retold by Frank Lee Beals, who also is the author of simple books for older readers, and published by Benjamin H. Sanborn; and Simplified Classics published by Scott, Foresman.

The process of adapting a classic includes some or all of the following changes. The book contains fewer pages because long descriptive passages, considered nonessential, have been removed. The vocabulary has been adjusted to the reading level of the age for which the adapted story is intended, often in conformity with some well-known word list or formula for readability. Long, involved complex sentences have been simplified. According to one publisher's catalog, "unnecessary and unknown historical references and allusions have been removed." Ease of reading is further enhanced by use of large type, uncrowded pages, and illustrations, although they are not always appropriate, often being from the movie version of the story. The adapted classics are advertised as being "high in interest value, simple in readability." Accompanying each book are usually questions and other materials to aid teachers in making maximum use of these adaptations.

Typical of classics which have been adapted are *Lorna Doone,* by Richard Doddridge Blackmore, for grades five to six; *Count of Monte Cristo,* by Alexandre Dumas, for grades seven to eight; and *Moby Dick,* by Herman Melville, for grades nine to ten. Other titles, chosen at random, are Charles Dickens' *David Copperfield, Oliver Twist,* and *A Tale of Two Cities; Silas Marner,* by George Eliot; and Jules Verne's *From the Earth to the Moon, and a Trip Around It,* listed as being in especially simplified vocabulary. It is somewhat surprising to find in adapted form books by Louisa May Alcott, Mark Twain, and other writers, since they are simple enough to be read in the originals and are interesting to modern children who still read some of them.

There are widely divergent opinions about the present trend of abridging and adapting the classics. Many parents, teachers, and librarians, especially librarians, agree with the opinion expressed by J. C. Furnas in a recent *Saturday Evening Post* article. His belief, as summarized by the magazine, is that "misguided editors, who water down the classics to make them 'easier' for young readers are doing irreparable harm to the literary appetites of our future adults." [4]

Those who oppose adaptation of the classics claim that only the plot of the story is retained—bare bones without meat in the retelling. This would necessarily follow when a book is cut from 100,000 to 8,000 words. Consequently, readers miss the author's creative writing and literary style. With all unusual and difficult words removed, children have nothing left with which to exercise their minds. Everyone who works with children and books knows that young readers love the sound of words, even when they do not understand their meaning. Camomile tea administered by Peter Rabbit's mother is much nicer than ordinary tea and the white palfrey on which Prince Charming rides by in fairy tales is far superior in the young reader's mind to a mere horse.

On the other hand, there are many teachers and some school librarians who believe that adapted classics are useful in in-

[4] "Must They Spoil Children's Books?" *Saturday Evening Post.* 232:20. December 12, 1959. Two other interesting articles on this subject are "Old Favorites and the New Look," by Richard T. Hurley in *Senior Scholastic.* 71:11T. November 1, 1957; and "Pre-Chewed Classics," *Time.* 72:55. July 7, 1958.

troducing children to the classics at an earlier age than they could read them in the original form. Presumably they will read the complete version later; if not, they have the gist of the story. They find abridgments useful in teaching literature classes in that pupils become acquainted with a larger number of classics in less time. Yet the strongest justification for adaptations of the classics is that they can be read by retarded readers who will probably never be able to read the originals which can still be read and enjoyed by the normal, certainly the better, readers.

Looking at the problem from the practical side, readers do not *always* distinguish between the originals and the abridged editions. Sometimes there is nothing on the title-page of the book itself to differentiate between them. High school pupils often use the simplified version to prepare a book report instead of reading the full text. (This can also be done with the comic version of the classic in question.) Better readers also sometimes prefer the adapted classic to the original book pleading lack of time—and no doubt because of a touch of indolence.

TIME-HONORED ADAPTATIONS

Students of literature for children and young people should be aware that retelling the classics is not altogether a modern trend. *Tales from Shakespeare,* by Charles and Mary Lamb, has become a classic itself. The same thing is true of *A Wonder Book* and *Tanglewood Tales,* retellings of Greek myths by Nathaniel Hawthorne, and *The Aeneid for Boys and Girls; Told from Virgil in Simple Language* (Macmillan, 1908), *The Iliad of Homer* (Macmillan, 1951, first published in 1907), and *The Odyssey of Homer* (Macmillan, 1951, first published in 1906) by Alfred John Church. But for the retelling of folk tales in the latter part of the nineteenth century by such writers as Andrew Lang, James Baldwin, and Howard Pyle, the King Arthur stories, the adventures of Robin Hood, and fairy tales from many countries would not have been available to many later generations of young readers.

Retelling of folk literature still goes on. *Tales from Grimm,* freely translated and illustrated by Wanda Gág (Coward-McCann,

1936) is one of the best renditions of the German household tales collected by the Grimm brothers and written down in the early part of the nineteenth century. Even the Grimms retold these tales, after their first rendition proved so scholarly that few could read and enjoy them, in the simple words of the storytellers from whom they had collected them.

One of the best modern adaptations of a classic is that of John Bunyan's *Pilgrim's Progress*, first published in 1678, which only the most optimistic would expect modern-day young people to read, as it recounts the story of Christian's struggle toward the celestial city. Robert Lawson did a set of illustrations for this book which was combined with a version of *Pilgrim's Progress* that in 1884 had been "retold and shortened for modern readers" by the daughter of an English vicar under the pseudonym of Mary Godolphin. Although the essence of the story was retained, much moralizing was omitted and the book was cut to one fifth of its original length. Robert Lawson's illustrations are like music to the words of a song. This adaptation, published by Lippincott in 1939, can be and is read by children today.

To one brought up on the Uncle Remus tales, it seems a sacrilege to change even a single word. Yet, when it is realized that few children and not many teachers can read the difficult dialect, one must face the fact that the beloved tales are on their way out. *The Uncle Remus Book*, retold by Miriam Blanton Huber, an authority on reading, with the original illustrations by A. B. Frost, was published by Appleton-Century in 1935. This small book contains the best-known stories from Uncle Remus retold in simple language which retains the spirit of the original dialect without its extreme difficulty. These are two good examples of adapted classics which might well be on school library shelves. It is unfortunate that *The Uncle Remus Book* has been allowed to go out of print.

Generally speaking, however, simplified classics are better suited to classroom use and the school library should have the original versions of these books. Before choosing adaptations of the classics, the book selector should consider what title has been adapted, by whom the adaptation was made, the age level for which it is intended, and the purpose for which it is being added to the collection. There is no particular value attached to the adapted classic *per se*. There are some acceptable adaptations of the classics. Others are only one step above the comic version of the book which no school library should include in its collection. If possible, the adapted form of any classic should be examined and compared with the original before being purchased. Both teachers and librarians should make every effort to encourage pupils to read classics in their original form.

SUGGESTIONS FOR SOLUTION

There are some things which can be done to accomplish this end. An attractive, readable copy of each desired title goes a long way toward making readers examine classics in the library and check them out for reading. Introduction to the classics, often accomplished by reading a section or telling a story from each book, interests young people in reading these books for themselves. An annual PTA program might be used to interest parents in purchasing unabridged classics, rather than comics or fiction series, for their children. At school, sharing experiences with books among pupils is better than formal book reports and broadens acquaintance with the classics.

Reading should not, however, be confined to the classics. Pupils need access also to more recent books, some of which are as good as the classics by any standard. *Publishers' Weekly* conducted a survey of librarians, reviewers, and booksellers to determine which of the children's books published between 1930 and 1960 qualify as modern classics. In the results, published November 14, 1960, E. B. White's *Charlotte's Web* (Harper, 1952) was the overwhelming favorite, mentioned twice as often as the second two favorites, *Mary Poppins* by Pamela L. Travers (Harcourt, 1934) and Laura Ingalls Wilder's *Little House in the Big Woods* (Harper, 1953). Others were *Homer Price* (Viking, 1943) and *Make Way for Ducklings* (1941) by Robert McCloskey, *Mr. Popper's Penguins* by Richard and Florence Atwater (Little, 1938), *Stuart Little,* also by E. B. White (Harper, 1945), Eleanor Estes'

The Moffats (Harcourt, 1941), and *The Little Prince* (Harcourt, 1943) by Antoine de Saint-Exupéry.

A well-rounded collection in the school library and time for pupils to browse and read under guidance will go far toward solving many reading problems, including that of what to do about the classics.

o

SERIES IN FICTION AND NONFICTION

FICTION SERIES

Books in many and varied fiction series are not actually a problem in book selection for school libraries, except as they are related to reading guidance. Most school librarians, certainly those who rely mainly on standard book selection aids, simply do not include such series, though pupils request them and often ask why they are not available.

It should be stated at the beginning that this section of the chapter deals principally with fiction series written to order by publishers' writers, usually under a "house" name, that is, a name thought up by the publisher for the supposed author of the series. The writing is done by a prescribed formula in which there is little or no room for anything original or creative, either in plot or literary style.

Series books are read largely at home (sometimes in school libraries under guise of other reading) and passed around from one pupil to another. Children often receive series books as gifts from adult relatives who either recall such books from having read them in their own childhood or are urged to purchase them by some bookseller on the plea that children "just eat them up." As indeed they do! Once in a while a teacher encourages pupils to bring their favorite books to school for exchange reading, a practice which invariably widens contacts with series books. School librarians should know about fiction series if they are to help teachers, pupils, and their parents aim at more solid reading.

Older Series

Fiction books in series have for a long time been a part of the publishing business. The type of series varies with the times. One series dies out only to be replaced with another. Fiction series flourished in the latter half of the last century, though most of these are no longer read by young readers. Jacob Abbott wrote the Rollo books for boys and their counterpart, the Lucy books, for girls, as well as the Franconia Series. There were also the books by William Taylor Adams (under the name Oliver Optic); the Little Prudy books and the Dotty Dimple series by Sophie May, whose real name was Rebecca Sophia Clarke; the Elsie Dinsmore books by Martha Finley (who used the pseudonym Martha Farquharson); and many more series.

Gilbert Patten, who also wrote under the name of Burt L. Standish, "was probably the first to exploit self-perpetuating series for boys, about boys." [1] His best known series was initiated with *Frank Merriwell, or First Days at Fardale* (Street and Smith, 1896). In 1941, *Mr. Frank Merriwell* was published by Alliance Books. It had taken forty-five years for the boy hero to reach manhood and assume the role of citizenship. Patten has been credited with having written "775 more Merriwell books that had an average weekly sale of 125,000 copies." [2] The *United States Catalog of Books in Print January 1, 1928* (Wilson, 1928) listed the Frank Merriwell series as containing 98 volumes.

In addition to the Frank Merriwell books, Patten wrote another series, the chief character of which was Dick Merriwell, and the Big League Series about a baseball pitcher, Lefty Locke. Howard Garis has probably run Patten a close second, having "written 400 juveniles, including the famous Uncle Wiggily books." [3] No count was available of titles credited to Laura Lee Hope, author of the Bobbsey Twins, Blythe Girls, Bunny Brown stories, Outdoor Girls, Six Little Bunkers, and perhaps other series.

Another example of a perpetuating series is furnished by Victor Appleton's Tom Swift books, which have supplied reading matter for several generations of boys, and some girls. Thirty titles of the Tom Swift books were listed in the *United States Catalog of Books in Print January 1, 1928*, after which for a number of years they continued to be published. Then the series

[1] "For It Was Indeed He," *Fortune.* 9:233. April 1934.
[2] *Ibid.*
[3] *Ibid.*

was apparently dormant for a while. At least, no titles were listed in the *Cumulative Book Index* for the years 1943 to 1956. However, beginning with *Tom Swift on the Phantom Satellite* (Grosset, 1957) the New Tom Swift, Jr., Adventures was launched with Victor Appleton II listed as author.

Present-day Series

There are many fiction series being written, published, sold, and read today. A fairly recent check shows the following series, all issued by Grosset, each comprising twenty or more titles: The Bobbsey Twins series by Laura Lee Hope; the Hardy Boys series by Franklin W. Dixon; the Honey Bunch series by Helen Louise Thorndyke, who also writes the Norman books; Nancy Drew mystery stories by Carolyn Keene, also author of the Dana Girls series. And this list does not include the Judy Bolton books by Margaret Sutton; the Lone Ranger series by Fran Striker; and the Tarzan books by Edgar Rice Burroughs. These all have more than ten titles each and are issued by the same publisher as the group mentioned above.

As indicated previously, several authors are credited with more than one series. Thornton W. Burgess, whose books, also published by Grosset, have an element of nature, has written series known as Green Forest, Green Meadow, Mother West Wind, and Smiling Pool series, all for children ages four to eight. On the other hand, a series may be written by more than one author. The Pollyanna books have been written not only by the original author, Eleanor Hodgman Porter, but also by Elizabeth Borton, Margaret Rebecca Piper Chalmers, Virginia May Moffitt, and Harriet Lummis Smith in a series known as the Pollyanna Series. One of the more recent titles, which appeals to teen-age girls, is *Pollyanna and the Secret Mission* (Grosset, 1954) by Elizabeth Borton. When Frances Boyd Calhoun, author of *Miss Minerva and William Green Hill* (Reilly & Lee, 1916), died, the series was continued by Emma Speed Sampson, who has also used the pseudonym Nell Speed. Despite the fact that Miss Minerva was pictured in the original book as Billy's spinster aunt, readers have since followed her through a marriage to the Major and at least one offspring. *Miss Minerva Broadcasts Billy* (Reilly & Lee, 1925) is one of the subsequent titles by Mrs. Sampson.

One author, either real or supposed, may write under more than one name, as suggested earlier. In fact, it is difficult to know when an author's name is real or when it is only assumed. Victor Appleton, always listed as a pseudonym, is, according to an article in *Fortune*[4] which school librarians would do well to read, a collective pseudonym used by Edward Stratemeyer, his family, and others to write the Tom Swift books and other series. They also used the names Ralph Bonehill, Roy Rockwood, and Arthur M. Winfield. The feminine names of Laura Lee Hope, Mary Hillis Burton, and perhaps others were also used by the writing syndicate headed by Edward Stratemeyer. A great deal of ghostwriting goes on in connection with fiction series. One person provides the plots while others develop them into whatever pattern is set for the series.

Appeal of Series

Most children at some time in their growing up come into contact with series books. The age of ten to twelve is the time when they usually meet series books and read them voraciously. However, quite a few series are slanted at teen-age pupils. And this does not take into account the love stories which adolescent girls explore, or the western stories which appeal to boys—series books on the adult level. Most pupils, however, with the years, outgrow the series books if other reading matter is available. The great pity is that valuable time has been spent in reading the mediocre which might have been spent on some of the fine books chosen from standard lists and actually present on school library shelves.

Fiction series have certain features which appeal to young readers. The books are about children their own age and are generally filled with adventure. That the boys and girls are given impossible roles and accomplish things far beyond their abilities

[4] *Ibid.,* p. 86-9+.

does not deter the young series devotees. The presence of the same characters in book after book after book gives readers a feeling of security as they identify themselves with these characters, but, since the characters never change, there are no examples of normal character development. Series books are usually easy to read, requiring a minimum of mental effort and less time than books which stretch young people's reading capacity. Series books are ordinarily cheaper than the average book for young readers, a fact which appeals to the pocketbooks of both children and adults who buy books for them. To buy several books, even two, for the price of one has definite appeal.

Objections to Series

Nevertheless, series books are cheap in things other than price. They are usually printed on a poor quality of paper with few, if any, illustrations and those of a cheap nature, often from the movie versions. In reading series books solely, or even largely, children miss the fine qualities of good bookmaking which encourage them to acquire and care for books of their own.

There is a great sameness in the stories in series books. One book may have the seashore for background; another covers a trip to the mountains. In one book the children visit the country; the next may take them to the city. Regardless of the number of titles in or the period of time covered by the series, the characters remain essentially the same. There is, as suggested above, little or no character development, so important for young readers, themselves in the process of growing up. Because series books offer easy reading, growth in vocabulary building or in language development is limited. Probably the most important objection is still that time spent in reading series books is lost for the many good books which the child might read. That children like series books is beside the point. They also prefer candy to spinach but no one advocates a diet of pure sweets as being well-rounded or suitable for children.

On the whole, and this is important to school librarians, series books of fiction are written hastily and published for mass sales rather than because they exemplify fine creative writing and contain lasting values for young readers. As an example of hasty writing, at least five Don Sturdy books by Victor Appleton were published in the same year. That more than one person writes books in the same series, that the author's name is not always that of a real person, that a name serves as a collective pseudonym for a group of writers—these are all part of the confused picture of fiction series publishing.

Suggestions for Series Readers

There are many books listed in standard book selection aids which offer some of the same features that children like in series books. Usually they have the same characters in several books. When an author writes three books in a series, school librarians should become watchful lest he also run into the snares common in series writing.

There are many recommended authors of books in series of two, three, or even four. A number of these were mentioned in Chapter 10. A few of the outstanding characters in good series books for young readers are Jo of *Little Women* and other books by Louisa May Alcott; Madeline in picture books by Ludwig Bemelmans; Henry Huggins in books by Beverly Cleary; Betsy, Eddie, and Penny in three series by Carolyn Haywood; Dr. Dolittle, created by Hugh Lofting; Mary Poppins, the English nurse, in books by Pamela Travers. Sometimes the main character is an animal, such as Freddy, the pig who is a detective in books by Walter Rollin Brooks; Angus, the lovable Scottie dog in Marjorie Flack's picture books; Curious George, the monkey created in words and pictures by Hans Augusto Rey; and Big Red, a dog in several books by James Arthur Kjelgaard. A few other writers of appealing books in series for the elementary grades are Elizabeth Enright, Eleanor Estes, Maud Hart Lovelace, Arthur Ransome, Noel Streatfeild (who uses "shoes" in titles involving careers, e.g., *Circus Shoes,* published by Random House in 1939), and Laura Ingalls Wilder, whose *Little House in the Big Woods* (Harper, 1953) and other books are a continuing delight.

In addition to the above, some of which are read also on the junior high school level, there are authors of several series of books for the senior high school level, some of which were mentioned in Chapter 10. Roy Chapman Andrews' books like *Quest of the Snow Leopard* (Viking, 1955), Edward Ellsberg's stories of diving and salvaging treasure in the sea, and the books about Horatio Hornblower by Cecil Scott Forester all emphasize adventure. In historical fiction, there are writers of series such as Elswyth Thane Ricker Beebe, using the pseudonym Elswyth Thane, whose books describe life in Williamsburg, Virginia, in Revolutionary times and in the period of the Civil War; Conrad Richter, who writes largely of pioneer life; Kenneth Lewis Roberts, the author of two books on the War of 1812 and three dealing with the American Revolution; and Paul Lewis Anderson, author of several books in the Roman Life and Times Series first published by Appleton and reissued in 1957 by Biblo & Tannen. Several writers of regional books in brief series are Margaret Elizabeth Bell with books about Alaska; Loula Grace Erdman, who writes about Texas; Martha Rebecca Harper, whose *Bittersweet* (Longmans, 1948) and *Winter Wedding* (Longmans, 1950) portray the same girl, first in Pennsylvania and later in Iowa; and Hubert Skidmore's two books about West Virginia which also have career interest. John Roberts Tunis and, more recently, Scott Young have written several series about sports which boys and some girls enjoy. Animal books in series include not only books by James Arthur Kjelgaard, mentioned earlier, but also Walter Farley's Black Stallion books, John Sherman O'Brien's series of dog books which begins with *Silver Chief, Dog of the North* (Winston, 1933), and the several horse books by Mary Alsop Sture-Vasa (using the pseudonym Mary O'Hara) of which *My Friend Flicka* (Lippincott, 1941) is the first and probably still the most popular. Many other examples could also be cited.

School librarians should list titles by outstanding authors, as they are added to the collection, which will appeal to pupils addicted to the series, and, where possible, guide them to reading better books with the same interests. Otherwise, the students will reach adulthood knowing only Tom Swift and Nancy Drew and thus be easy prey for cheap mysteries, light love stories, and roaring westerns.

SERIES IN NONFICTION

Current Problem

One of the current problems in selecting books for children and young people is the unusually large number of series in non-fiction. When not actually designated as belonging to a series, books published with similar titles are often considered by a book selector as a series. And such a maze of series exists! Most of these series have been initiated since 1940. The 1961 fall children's book number of *Publishers' Weekly,* as an addition to its regular "Forecasts" section, listed by publishers the new titles in juvenile series.[5] Although not a complete list, it included 99 nonfiction series by leading publishers, 13 marked with an asterisk to indicate that they were new that season.

Nonfiction series, both publisher and subject series, have always existed but until recently have presented no particular problem in selection. There were not too many of them and each series was usually self-explanatory. By way of example, Famous Biographies for Young People, a series of collective biographies originated by A. S. Barnes and later taken over by Dodd, is sufficiently described by its title. Landmark Books by Random House, largely in the field of history, present no special problems. The Children's Illustrated Classics series, which includes some non-fiction, comprises books that are similar in format.

The present trend in series, however, presents problems not only because of the vast number of series being published but also because of great similarity among series. This trend is not confined to any one publisher nor does the publisher necessarily issue only one series. Indeed it seems to the book selector who makes any effort to sort out series that each publisher has said: "So-and-So is making a killing"—or whatever publishers say when they grudgingly admire the success of a competitor—"with Such-and-Such series. Why don't we start one along the same lines?" Thus,

---

[5] "Juvenile Forecast—Series." *Publishers' Weekly.* 180:189-95. July 3, 1961.

apparently, a new series is started, often duplicating, certainly approximating, an already existing series.

A good example of two very similar series is presented by Initial Biographies published by Scribner and Signature Books, a product of Grosset and Dunlap. The former is a series of individual biographies by Genevieve Stump Foster, on the covers of which appear the initials of the biographees. The latter is also a series of individual biographies, edited by Enid LaMonte Meadowcroft, with individual volumes by different authors. The cover of each volume is decorated with a facsimile of the signature of the person about whom the book is written.

Books are sometimes published with similar titles with no apparent indication of a series. An example is found in books with titles beginning "All About," published by Random House. Although the earlier books were not designated as a series, current titles do bear a series note, Allabout Books, the spelling of which is in itself confusing. To further complicate the situation, other publishers have several books with titles beginning "All About." Since a book's title is not covered by copyright, any author or publisher is at liberty to use "All About" in a title.

One group of books published by Franklin Watts is now actually called the Terrific Triple Title Series, after being so nicknamed by librarians. The name derives from the use of a word three times in the titles of collections of fairy tales and short stories compiled largely by Phyllis Reid Fenner. Recently a number of books of nonfiction have been published in this series, for example *Science, Science, Science,* edited by Russel Hamilton (1960).

In addition to those designated as series, other groups of books have titles so similar that in the minds of book selectors they constitute a series. Some of these groups are "Fun with" published by both Lippincott and Random House, "Here Is" published by Scribner, "Made in" published by Knopf, "What's Inside" published by Morrow, "You and" published by Childrens Press. Books whose titles begin with "Let's" are too numerous to list. They begin variously—for example, "Let's Go," "Let's Look," "Let's Make." Books published by Fideler whose titles began "Let's

Read About" now constitute the Life in Other Lands series and each title has been shortened to include only the name of the country each tells about.

Confusion in Similarity

One further, and perhaps the best, example of confusion in series titles is presented. Holiday publishes a Lands and Peoples Series, the titles of which are names of individual countries, as, for example, *Turkey* (1945) by Vernon Ives. Macmillan also has a Lands and Peoples series. Some titles of this series consist only of the name of the country, as, for example, *Norway* (1957) by John Dent, while others have titles similar to *Land and People of Denmark* (1958) by Reginald Spink. However, a group of books published by Lippincott, the titles of which begin "The Land and People of," as, for example, *The Land and People of Australia* (1959) by Godfrey Blunden, belongs to the Portraits of the Nations Series. Titles in this series at one time began with "The Land of," as, for example, *The Land of the Polish People* (1952) by Eric Philbrook Kelly, now in a revised edition but first published in 1943. None of these series is related to a seven-volume set published in 1961 by the Grolier Society under the title *Lands and Peoples: The World in Color* (1929-1960). It should be noted that McGraw has a series of books in the field of travel called The World-in-Color Series.

First Books—Longest List

One of the largest current series is the the First Books series published by Franklin Watts. The fall catalog for 1961 listed nearly 150 titles available, and others continue to be added. The First Books group presents a problem for the selector not only in the large number of titles published but also in grade level. A few are for very young readers, as the series title suggests, and most are for the elementary grades. However, some books in this series are for readers as advanced as ninth grade and on subjects as difficult as archaeology or the United States Congress. *The First Book of Baseball* by Benjamin Brewster, pseudonym of Mary

Elting, the second revised edition of which is dated 1958, is for grades one to four. Yet *The First Book of Basketball* by Don Schiffer (1959), which one would normally expect to be of similar grade level, is for grades five to eight. Librarians and teachers will find some help in the matter of grade level of the First Books series on a chart, available from the publishers, "suggesting the elementary school grade levels at which First Books may be used in attaining socially desirable curriculum goals developed through appropriate classroom units or projects." This chart was prepared by Harold G. Shane, Professor of Elementary Education at Northwestern University.

Problem for Young Readers

The major problem, however, in any long list of titles all beginning alike, is presented for the young readers themselves. Elementary pupils, and even some in high school, invariably remember and call for books by titles. In consulting the card catalog, which pupils are taught to use from the third grade up, they are confronted by card after card after card with titles beginning, "All about," "The First Book of," "What's Inside of," or whatever. It is difficult to teach young pupils to look for the first word of the title which is different. To thumb through similar cards even when one understands the process proves a tiresome exercise.

Confusion in Multiplicity

This is not to intimate that nonfiction series in themselves are objectionable. But their multiplicity is confusing and librarians find it difficult to become acquainted with all of them. Through experience school librarians learn to know which series are more and which are less helpful for particular pupils. They learn, for example, that books in the Childhood of Famous Americans series published by Bobbs are helpful in introducing pupils to biography in grades four to six, even though pupils continue to read them after they are in more advanced grades; that the Landmark Books and the companion series, World Landmark Books, written by authors outstanding in the field of history and published by Random House, are likely to be consistently good; that books published by Fideler are copiously illustrated with good photographs; that the "Made in" books published by Knopf are useful in several fields of study which include the cultural side of countries and their people. They will learn also that some series with many similarities on many varied topics at different grade levels are not so easily evaluated. This knowledge, however, comes only from experience and at present there is little help for the librarian in reading about series.

What school librarians deplore whenever they meet to discuss books and exchange experiences in using books with boys and girls is the apparent current trend to publish everything in some series. The net result must of necessity be similarity rather than individuality. When a new book is announced, the tendency is to say, "Another series book," rather than to welcome a fresh title which pupils can remember and find when they want it.

Advice to the Selector

In actual practice, the librarian is advised to judge every book on its own merits. The same criteria should be used in evaluating any book, whether in a series or not. It must be considered in relation to the school's needs and evaluated in comparison with other books covering the same subject matter and at the same reading level. Librarians are cautioned against ordering all books in a series, or even adding the latest title merely because the first books in the series are outstanding. Later titles may prove inferior, as often happens with a successful author's books. In a series, a great many authors are represented. It cannot be emphasized too strongly that each book must be considered individually, even though its title is similar to many others.

o

THE COMICS

Like fiction series, comic books are a problem in reading guidance rather than in book selection so far as the school librarian's work is concerned. School libraries do not include comics in their magazine collections, and generally pupils are not allowed to bring comics to the school library to read. It should be made clear in the beginning that this chapter does not consider the comic strips which many pupils follow in newspapers. Facts about comic books, however, should be available to librarians and teachers who want to encourage pupils to read more worth-while material. School librarians seem to be agreed that comics are not the problem at present that they were some years ago. This may be an indication that interest in them is on the wane; on the other hand, it may be due to the extensive comic element in many programs on television and in movie cartoons.

DEVELOPMENT OF THE COMICS

Comic books seem to have been initiated in 1922 by M. C. Gaines, a former principal of schools, at that time on the staff of Eastern Color Printing Company. Mr. Gaines later devoted his entire time to comic books for use in schools, preparing such material as *Picture Stories from American History* with an accompanying manual for teachers. The four-color comics, usually about one character, came out in 1929 and were published by Dell Publishing Company, still one of the largest publishers of comic books. These were called funnies and were at first distributed by various firms as a medium of advertisement. By 1936, the comic magazine had become sixty-four pages long; since then it has remained generally uniform in length.

Comics probably came to full flower in 1938 with "Superman," created by two young Cleveland men, Jerry Siegel and Joe Shuster, who began working together about 1929, one as a writer and the other as an illustrator of cartoons. In one year the circulation of "Superman" exceeded a million—a remarkable feat considering the hard road traveled by juvenile magazines. "Superman" began to be published as a comic strip feature in newspapers in 1939, was heard as a radio program the following year, and for some years was a television program. "Superman" has been the subject of animated cartoons in movies; has had all sorts of merchandise named for it; has been used to advertise many articles, including books; and furnished part of the name for Superman-Detective Comics, one of the largest publishers, and the largest seller, of comics.

Comics grew in a few years to be big business. *Publishers' Weekly* quoted Ronald Mead, a research consultant, as having estimated that 45 million comics were produced monthly in 1946. [1] This adds up to 540 million for the year, a number larger than the highest estimate for the total book production in the United States to that date. Peak figures for different comics published finally reached a total of more than 400 titles. In 1957 alone $9 million was spent for comic books. According to a survey made some years ago by the National Market Research Company of America, comic books were at one time read regularly by 95 per cent of the boys and 91 per cent of the girls between the ages of six and eleven; and by 87 per cent of the boys and 81 per cent of the girls between twelve and seventeen. When it is reckoned that, to be a regular reader of the comics, boys and girls had to read an average of twelve to thirteen comics a month, some idea of the tremendous extent of comic reading becomes apparent.[2]

COMICS AN EDUCATIONAL ISSUE

The comics and their use by and with young readers eventually became a major educational issue. A few outstanding educators not only advocated the comics but served on advisory boards of publishers of comics, writing book reviews and making word studies for comics. These educators generally took the view that reading

[1] "540 Million Comics Published in 1946." *Publishers' Weekly.* 152:1030. September 6, 1947.

[2] Harvey Zorbaugh, "The Comics—There They Stand." *Journal of Educational Sociology.* 18:196-203. December 1944.

the comics marks a normal stage in development which children will safely pass or outgrow. Some of them maintained that such reading has positive value, both educational and emotional. Others in the educational world felt that children are going to read the comics anyway and that the sensible thing was to take steps to improve the quality of comics generally.

Opponents of the comics were more numerous. This group was composed of parents, teachers, librarians, social and religious workers, and others. Between 1941 and 1944 alone, more than one hundred articles criticizing the comics appeared in educational and nonprofessional periodicals. Most of these dealt with the sociology of the comics or were concerned with possible effects on emotional or moral behavior or with problems of taste and ethics.

One of the first to speak out against the comics was Sterling North, book reviewer and author of several books for children, in an editorial, "National Disgrace and a Challenge to Parents," in the Chicago Daily News of May 18, 1940. This has been quoted so often as to have become a classic. North, elaborating on the editorial in National Parent-Teacher, March 1941, commented that it had been republished in forty newspapers and magazines and that requests for reprints averaged one thousand daily.[3]

Almost immediately following North's editorial, the Congress of Parents and Teachers launched an attack on comics. The chairman of reading and library service of this organization enlisted parents and teachers in a crusade against the comics which became nation-wide. Parents barred comics from the homes or limited purchase to a few approved titles. In many schools, pupils were forbidden to bring comics to classrooms and teachers were instructed to confiscate comics found in desks and lockers. Librarians made every effort to use, as a substitute for comics, books with similar appeal. As one writer put it, "Critics of the comic books, however, found that their thunder was without much notice by the public and especially without any notice by the children whose millions of noses remained buried in the books as before."[4]

[3] Sterling North, "Antidote for Comics." National Parent-Teacher. 35:16-17. March 1941.

[4] Coulton Waugh, The Comics. New York, Macmillan, 1947. p. 344-5.

THE COMICS

235

In 1941, Parents Institute, publishers of *Parents' Magazine*, began the publication of *True Comics* as a substitute for the less desirable comics. The experiment was evidently considered successful by the publishers of *True Comics*, who later expanded to the publication of eight magazines for children and young people, either partly or entirely in comic form. Many people saw in the substitute comics a solution to the problem; others, with Stanley J. Kunitz, at that time editor of the *Wilson Library Bulletin*, deplored the necessity of fighting comics with comics as he predicted that *True Comics* would seem to young readers the "pale imitation of 'the real thing.' "[5] It has been the experience of those working with children and young people that the comics published by the Parents Institute were accepted and read like any other comics, as evidenced by the fact that early in 1944 paid circulation was reported to be 1.75 million.

Sources of Materials for Comics

Publishers of comics have invaded many sources for material. At various times they have used folklore, biography, and history. There is a comic magazine which portrays the lives and works of great scientists. *Picture Stories from the Bible* has been issued in comic form and is reported to be used by some churches.

Probably the publication most deplored by school librarians was *Classic Comics*, whose publishers began with the intention of issuing over three hundred of the world's greatest books in comic form. In three and one half years, *Classic Comics* had sold in all about 100 million copies of its twenty-eight titles based on famous novels and tales for young people.[6] With the issue of March 1947, the title *Classic Comics* was changed to *Illustrated Classics*, a name already associated with well-illustrated books. The first issue under the new title was a comic book version of *The Last Days of Pompeii* by Bulwer-Lytton that gave a rather sketchy idea of the book itself.

[5] Stanley J. Kunitz, "Libraries to Arms! the So-Called Comic Magazines." *Wilson Library Bulletin.* 15:670. April 1941.
[6] "Classic Comics Sell a Hundred Million." *Publishers' Weekly.* 149:1736. March 23, 1946.

At present, *Classics Illustrated* is being published by Gilberton Company, Inc.,[7] which also publishes *Classics Illustrated Junior* for ages nine to eleven. The latter series seems to feature folk tales and has grown rapidly for the issue of February 1960, *The Salt Mountain,* was numbered 564. The May 1960 issue of *Classics Illustrated* was a comic book version of *The Conquest of Mexico* by Bernal Diaz del Castillo, number 156 in the series.

COMICS IN CHILDREN'S READING

The appeal of comics to children is almost universal. They are also read by many adolescents and some adults. They require no mental effort, hence any child can read them, if such an exercise can be called reading. Comics contain a large amount of drama; they are colorful, filled with adventure and romance. They often appear in series having the same characters in various situations which children like. All the reading matter is in the form of conversation, though the pictures themselves usually tell the story. The pictures, in spite of the fact that they seem harsh and garish to adults, appeal to children, especially when humorous. Humor is stressed, justice triumphs over wrong, and the story always ends right. Comics also provide much entertainment for a small amount of money, ten to fifteen cents being the usual price and only a nickel for a used copy.

The objections to the comics are many. The physical format is very inferior. The paper is pulpy and of poor quality and the art work is crude with too bright colors. The print is generally so bad that eyestrain may result. The grammar is repeatedly faulty, the spelling is often incorrect, and the language sometimes objectionable. The stories are fantastic and unreal, encourage undue daydreaming or wishful thinking, and are generally bad for maladjusted children. Frederic Wertham in his *Seduction of the Innocent* (Rinehart, 1954) maintained that there is a definite relation between juvenile delinquency in the United States and comic books. In many comics, crime is considered to hold too prominent a place and, while justice finally triumphs over wrong,

[7] 101 Fifth Avenue, New York 11.

methods used to obtain good results are sometimes open to question. To put the problem of subject matter even more strongly, the stories in some of the comics featuring horror or romance are unbelievably depraved.

Parents and teachers agree that constant reading of comics prevents a variety of interests for the children and leads to neglect of school work. Some teachers hold that the balloon type of reading in the comics deters pupils from learning to read normally across the page. Another problem is that older pupils fool themselves that they have read a book (reduced to comic form) and unfortunately are able to fool an unwary teacher by handing in a book report on it. Librarians rather consistently fear that the too easy reading of comic books will leave no time and destroy incentive for reading the worth-while books which are a part of childhood's rich heritage.

EVALUATION OF COMIC BOOKS

Attention should be called to the work of the Committee on Evaluation of Comic Books.[8] Organized in 1948 in response to a request from the National Council of Churches that something be done to improve comic books, a permanent executive committee, composed of nine persons representing community service institutions and professions, directs the work assisted by a hundred additional citizens who review and evaluate all comic books on the market. This committee has published "Criteria for Evaluating Comic Books," revised June 1961. The criteria are applied in three general areas: cultural, moral, and emotional, with special concern for morbid emotionality. As a result, comics are grouped by title under each area as producing "no objection" or "some objection" or being "objectionable." A leaflet, "An Evaluation of Comic Books," published March 1956, listed a total of 268 titles in the various areas and categories. Since then the committee's service has been rendered largely through spot checks of comic books and reports to the public press which are made annually in mimeographed form.

[8] 6302 Kincaid Road, Cincinnati 13, Ohio.

The report for the fall of 1961 is entitled "How Good Are the Comic Books?" To answer this question, the committee reviewed 191 comic books published in May 1961. "The check revealed that the comic books are getting better with 78 per cent falling in the 'no objection' category"; according to the report, this is the best record since the committee began reviewing in 1949 and in direct contrast to the year 1953 when 72 per cent of 418 comic books were rated objectionable. Gratification was also expressed over the apparent continued improvement in comic books which in 1961 were on the following subjects: adventure, 6 per cent; children's and teen-age cartoon comics, 40 per cent; crime, 2 per cent; mystery and space, 19 per cent; romance, 12 per cent; war, 5 per cent; and western, 16 per cent.

READINGS

Only book references on the subject of comics are listed here. There are hundreds of periodical references easily found through indexes.

Frank, Josette. *What Books for Children? Guideposts for Parents.* Rev. ed. New York, Doubleday, 1946. Chap. 7, "The Comics."

Martin, Laura Katharine. *Magazines for School Libraries.* Rev. ed. New York, Wilson, 1950. p. 28-33, "The Comic: Its Place in Current Children's Literature."

Waugh, Coulton. *The Comics.* New York, Macmillan, 1947. Chap. 20, "Comic Books."

Wertham, Frederic. *Seduction of the Innocent.* New York, Rinehart, 1954.

BOOKS FOR BEGINNING READERS

The Problem

Another type of material which may prove a problem for those selecting books for elementary school libraries is books for beginning readers. For many years there were very few books, exclusive of primers and readers designed to teach children to read, which pupils in grades one and two could actually read for themselves. Consequently, the publishing of books for beginning readers is long overdue and the idea has been welcomed by both teachers and librarians. The potential problem lies in the fact that so many publishers are now publishing so many books of this type that it is difficult to evaluate them. Some books for beginning readers are very good, some very poor; others are in the in-between category of the mediocre.

Beginner Books from Random House

The trend toward books for beginning readers was initiated in 1957 by several publishers almost simultaneously. Among the first was Beginner Books, Inc., whose books were distributed by Random House, which subsequently became the owner of the Beginner Books imprint. The trademark of this series is the picture of a child seated behind an open book on the cover of which is printed "For Beginning Readers." Outside a circle around the figure is the caption "I Can Read It All by Myself." The first title in this series was *The Cat in the Hat* (1957) by Theodor Seuss Geisel, who writes under the pseudonym Dr. Seuss and is an all-time favorite of most small children. It is the story of a fabulous cat in a tall hat who visits Sally and her little brother and does wonderful stunts while they are at home alone. This was followed by *The Cat in the Hat Comes Back* (1958) which continues the story with other adventures of the cat. Both books are written in the familiar verse of Dr. Seuss, a device which is emulated in several other books of the series, and illustrated with the author's characteristic humor. Other titles among the first published include *Sam and the Firefly* (1958) written and illustrated by Philip D. Eastman. This is the story of Sam, the owl, and Gus, the firefly who writes words in the sky with his light, thus confusing drivers in traffic. Finally Gus stops a train just in time to avoid a serious accident. Another is *A Fly Went By* (1958), of which Marshall McClintock is author, with pictures by Fritz Siebel. This tells the story of a fly, followed by a frog, a cat, a dog, a cow with her "little cow," a fox, and a man, each of whom in turn thinks the other is after him until the boy solves the puzzle. There are now quite a number of books in this series, each employing about two hundred words, on a wide variety of subjects. *You Will Go to the Moon* (1959), which describes a trip to the moon, is by Mae Blacker Freeman and Ira Maximilian Freeman, outstanding writers in the field of science.

Some of the more recent books in this series, all published in 1960 and advertised as being for "beginning beginners," use a more limited number of words. Some examples are *Green Eggs and Ham* by Theodor Seuss Geisel using fifty words, the smallest number encountered so far in any one book; *Put Me in the Zoo* by Robert Lopshire; and *Are You My Mother?* by Philip D. Eastman, author and illustrator of the above-mentioned *Sam and the Firefly*. These last two books include one hundred words each.

HARPER BOOKS FOR BEGINNERS

About the same time as Random House, Harper began a series entitled the I Can Read Books, advertised as being appropriate for four-year-olds who will, of course, not yet have entered school. Several of these are by Sydney Hoff, including *Danny and the Dinosaur* (1958). This is the story of a modern boy who meets a dinosaur on the street and goes for a ride on his back, or, more correctly, on his neck, and gets into modern traffic problems. Probably the best of this series is *Little Bear* (1957), followed by *Father Bear Comes Home* (1959) and *Little Bear's*

Friend (1960). These are written by Else Holmelund Minarik, author of several other I Can Read Books with appropriately delightful pictures by Maurice Sendak. Another recent title is *Harry and the Lady Next Door* by Gene Zion (1960), the story of a dog's efforts to drown out a lady's singing. This, however, does not measure up to the author's earlier books about Harry.

Within this series are the Science I Can Read Books for pupils in kindergarten through grade three. Two of the titles are *Seeds and More Seeds* (1959) and *Plenty of Fish* (1960), both by Millicent Ellis Selsam, an outstanding writer in the field of science. Each book uses about two hundred words.

Recently Harper has added the Early I Can Read Books to the series, these being designed for still younger readers. An example is *Who Will Be My Friends?* by Sydney Hoff (1960) which contains only sixty words. On the whole, the books for beginning readers published by Harper and Random House are superior to many of the others.

Books from Benefic Press

In 1958 a series called Easy To Read Books was initiated by Benefic Press, the publishing division of the Beckley-Cardy Company. These books are written by Sarah Derman with pictures by Jack Boyd or Dave Gillis. Representative is *Poker Dog* (1958), a group of stories involving a dog named Poker and his many adventures before he finally finds a home. In writing this book, the author used 147 words, exclusive of proper names, of which only 30 are of first grade level or above, the others being below first grade level. These books have the appearance of readers both in content and format though the texts do have some continuity similar to that of story books.

Another series by Benefic Press which bids fair to become more useful in school libraries is the What Is It series. There are now a number of these, some of which are for beginning readers, each about an animal, plant, or other topic in science. Typical is *What Is a Fish?* (1958) by Gene Darby, an elementary teacher in Redding, California, with pictures by Lucy and John Hawkinson.

In simple language, the author explains what fish are, how they swim, and how they reproduce. At the end the reader learns how a fish is a helper. Scientific names of fish used are included at the back of the book. There is a vocabulary of 235 words, 39 of which are on the second grade level, 21 above, and the remaining ones below.

FOLLETT BEGINNING-TO-READ BOOKS

A Beginning-To-Read Book series is published by Follett. A seal on the books' covers pictures two children seated with books, around which is the inscription "The Follett Beginning-To-Read Series." Below each seal are one, two, or three dots indicating the level of readability. Level one is for pupils in the latter half of the first grade. *Mabel the Whale* (1958), written by Patricia King and illustrated by Katherine Evans, is an example on the second grade level and is advertised as having been tested in grade two where it was read with ease. It has a vocabulary of 161 words. The story is based on a true incident in which a whale was transported from the ocean to a tank at Marineland. Mabel, the whale, after necessary adjustments, is happy when children come to visit her. One of the better titles in this series is *Nobody Listens to Andrew* (1957), by Elizabeth Guilfoile, on the first grade level. Andrew can get no one to listen to him until he finally blurts out that a bear is in his bed.

There are now some twenty Follett Beginning-To-Read Books. Many are publicized as having been written by elementary teachers. Manuscripts are constantly sought and there is an annual Follett Beginning-To-Read award of $2,000 for the manuscript considered best. At least one is a reference book, *Follett Beginning-To-Read Picture Dictionary* (1959) by Alta M. McIntire, a consultant in primary education. This contains a list of words with colored pictures to illustrate each object. At the end is a group of sentences with the words used in the dictionary printed in blue, other words in black. Four books in this series, including *Nobody Listens to Andrew,* have been published in French and Spanish and two in German. These are available on records so that pupils may hear the correct pronunciation in studying the language.

DOLCH FIRST READING BOOKS

Another series initiated in 1958 is the Dolch First Reading Books published by the Garrard Press. These books are written by Edward William Dolch, formerly of the University of Illinois and an authority in the field of reading, assisted by his wife, Marguerite Pierce Dolch. They are "written especially for the first reader to encourage independent reading on the beginner level" and are recommended by the publisher for "supplemental class-room reading and for recreational reading in the library." They contain the easier half of the Dolch 220 Basic Sight Words and the 95 commonest nouns, a total of 205 words. On a reading level of first grade, the interest level is described as being up to grade four. Five books were published in 1958, including *On the Farm* and *Zoo Is Home*. They resemble readers rather than trade books both in content and format. More recently the Dolch team has written several First Reading Books of the folklore type, an example of which is *Once There Was an Elephant* (1961). The Dolch books would probably be most useful with retarded readers.

BOOKS BY THE CHILDRENS PRESS

The Childrens Press publishes a series of books "designed to encourage independent reading on the beginner level." There are some thirty books written by Carla Greene with Dr. Paul Witty of the Psycho-Educational Clinic of Northwestern University as consultant. Called the I Want To Be books, they are on subjects ranging from airplane hostesses to zoo keepers. One of the more recent titles is *I Want To Be a Librarian* (1960). They are recommended by the publisher for first independent reading in grades one to two and the vocabulary used is said to be chosen from the "first 1000 words for children's reading." It is open to question, however, how many children in the first and second grades would be vitally interested in any given career other than that of policeman, fireman, or some other community helper. The Carla Greene books are useful in social studies when directed by the teacher. These books also would seem useful for older readers who read poorly but need career interest.

HOLT'S A BOOK TO BEGIN ON SERIES

Holt has also recently started a series of beginner books, A Book To Begin On series. Of the first books of this series, two were written by Eunice Holsaert, *Outer Space* (1959) and *Dinosaurs* (1960). Many others have been written by Leslie Waller, including *Weather* (1959) and *Numbers* (1960). These were announced as being suitable for ages six to eight, except the one on numbers, which is placed at ages six to ten.

SEE AND READ BOOKS FROM PUTNAM

The most recent series noted for beginning readers, See and Read Books, is really two-fold with story books based on a first grade vocabulary and biographies based on a second grade vocabulary. These books were published by Putnam, all with the 1960 imprint. Of the story books announced, *How Many Bears?* is by Laura Zirbes, whose name is well known in educational circles. Four of the biographies are by Gertrude Norman. May C. Ihnken calls *A Man Named Lincoln* and *A Man Named Washington* "informative, enjoyable stories that will be welcomed in all libraries for primary school children." [1]

Still other series may be used with beginning readers. Also there are books for beginning readers that belong to no series. A good example is John Ciardi's *I Met a Man* (Houghton, 1961) which the poet and editor wrote for his own child to read but which readers of every age will enjoy.

BOOK CLUB FOR BEGINNING READERS

Indicative of increased interest in material for beginning readers is the Book Club for Beginning Readers established by Parents' Magazine. Club members receive one book each month at a discount of 50 per cent of the list price.

EVALUATION OF MATERIAL FOR BEGINNERS

So far school librarians have had little guidance or direction in selecting books for beginning readers. Very few of the titles have yet been included in standard book selection aids, and so far

[1] *Junior Libraries.* 6:60. April 1960.

there has been no real evaluation of the many series. The 1960 edition of *A Bibliography of Books for Children,*[2] compiled and published under the auspices of the Association for Childhood Education International, includes for the first time a brief list of books for beginning readers, covering both factual material and stories.

CHOOSING MATERIAL CAREFULLY

Elementary teachers and school librarians alike agree that material which young children can read for themselves is badly needed. Yet much of that which is at present being published is fairly similar to primers and readers which school librarians have consistently regarded as classroom rather than library material. School librarians will want to consider carefully how much of the material for beginning readers is actually material to be purchased with library funds and how much is supplementary reading material for the classroom, which is usually purchased with other school funds. Chapter 5, "For the Very Young," should also be of help in selecting beginning books.

Books for beginning readers, regardless of publisher or name of series, show marked similarity. They have been written with a closely controlled vocabulary which has been checked against some well-known list of words, formula for readability, or both. In the back of the book there is usually a list of words used.

High interest level is stressed in books for beginning readers. The many uses suggested for them include enrichment of the basic reading program and use in individualized reading programs as well as for leisure-time reading, thus improving independent reading. These books should also prove useful for beginning retarded readers. Pupils in second and third grades who have not yet learned to read can read these simple books. However, teachers and librarians are discovering that the grade level set by the publishers of books for beginning readers is apt to be misleading.

[2] Discussed with other book selection aids in Chapter 2.

CHAPTER 16

o

BOOKS FOR RETARDED READERS

Statement of the Problem

One of the most persistently troublesome problems which face the school librarian, particularly the inexperienced school librarian, is that of selecting books for the reader who has not learned to read as he should. The problem is more acute now than formerly because retarded readers are enrolled in all schools, and in increasingly large numbers.

Much printer's ink has been used in discussion of the reading situation, particularly as to causes of the present problem of retardation. Among the causes suggested are absence from school during the early school years, crowded conditions in classrooms, the vast number of emergency teachers in the present shortage of fully qualified teachers, and especially the methods of so-called progressive education which fail to stress phonics and other phases of the process held to be essential in learning to read. Studies made of a wide sampling of cases of severely retarded readers seem to indicate conclusively that emotional problems, present in home or school conditions or perhaps in both, often contribute to the pupil's inability to learn to read. Some educators hold that a few children simply fail to read under ordinary conditions and with presently known methods of teaching reading.

Whatever the causes, there are numbers of retarded readers in modern schools where compulsory attendance laws hold them, often without any specific help toward solving their problems. A child who fails to learn to read at the proper time, normally in his first year of school, becomes increasingly handicapped because of educational requirements that all pupils make wide use of library materials. The pupil who is retarded in reading reads slowly, often haltingly, sometimes without comprehending what he has read. He develops little or no ability for attacking a new or difficult word, either to pronounce it or determine its meaning.

The printed page eventually becomes an enigma for him and he is likely to develop a complex about making the effort to decipher it. He probably has never read a book in its entirety and has small desire to do so. He develops other methods of learning where he can, and invents cover-up devices in cases where he cannot. Yet assignments demand that he, along with others of his class who enjoy the reading process, must read. Besides, there are many things about which the retarded reader would like to read if books were only available in sufficiently simple language for him. The school librarian hopes to help him select books to read on his own, just as in the case of other pupils, and, with the teacher, must work to find what the individual child can and will read. The whole problem is an involved one and often seems insoluble because each retarded reader needs individual help and attention, for which the teacher or librarian never has sufficient time.

QUALITIES OF BOOKS FOR RETARDED READERS

While it is true that any book which a child can read and enjoy will improve his reading and furnish the satisfaction which comes from the reading process, there are certain qualities that make a book peculiarly suitable for the retarded reader.

In the first place, while the interest level must be sufficiently high for the pupil's age and grade level, the vocabulary level must be sufficiently low so that his reading ability can reach it. This simply means that material written in third grade vocabulary must interest a sixth grade boy who can read nothing more difficult. A book that meets both requirements is characterized by "high interest-low vocabulary," or some similar term.

Since the printed page is a deterrent to the retarded reader, efforts must be made to make it less forbidding. The reader who complains of "too much reading on the page," as does the average retarded reader, states his problem as simply as he knows how. The school librarian looks for books that have not too many pages, with large print and generous leading between the lines, and the pages interspersed with illustrations and broken with conversation, usually in short lines.

Despite this concern with simple vocabulary and other devices for obtaining reading simplicity, the book needs that certain something which kindles enough enthusiasm to hold the reader's attention and insure perseverance even when the going is tough. In the final analysis, interest is the strongest determining factor in getting any pupil to read. There are not too many books for retarded readers which have this last quality but, when the school librarian finds a choice item, he adds it to his list of books certain to be successful and continues to search for others.

SELECTION OF MATERIALS FOR RETARDED READERS

In selecting materials for retarded readers, the situation of the school librarian is further complicated by the fact that so little help is available. Books included in standard book selection aids are chosen for the readers who read normally on their grade level, as they should be. It is seldom noted that a book would prove suitable for a retarded reader—or for an advanced reader, so far as that goes. There are some lists of books suggested especially for retarded readers and several of those are included in the appendix. *Gateways to Readable Books: An Annotated Graded List of Books for Adolescents Who Find Reading Difficult,* by Ruth Strang and others, now in its third edition (Wilson, 1958), is, as its title shows, useful only on the high school level. The February 1961 issue of *Elementary English* has an excellent list for younger retarded readers. Often the books suggested in such lists, including those published in library periodicals, are not very helpful selections. As one school librarian puts it, "When I pick up a list of books for retarded readers and find books by Alcott and Mark Twain included, I know I cannot trust it." To repeat, any book which the retarded reader can and will read is helpful. The trouble is that he often cannot or will not read most of the books which school librarians know and suggest. Furthermore, reading guidance with retarded readers is such an individual matter that a book which helps with one reader will not with the next one whose case seems similar.

While it is neither possible nor practical to submit here a list of books for retarded readers, some suggestions of types of books with representative titles may prove helpful.

Lower Level Books

The most obvious material for use with retarded readers is books intended for reading in grades below the one in which the reader is enrolled: third grade material for the retarded sixth grader, sixth grade material for the ninth grader, and junior high school material for the retarded senior high school reader. There is an advantage when working with retarded readers in having a school library collection serving all pupils, first through twelfth grades. Such use of material also presents an argument against labeling either books themselves, or the shelves on which they stand, as being definitely for one grade. In book selection for a collection serving only one level (elementary, junior high, or senior high school), as is the situation in most schools, the librarian should see that books on given subjects are included on various reading levels to take care of variations in reading ability, advanced as well as retarded.

For example, among biographies it is possible to find a book about an outstanding person on various levels of reading difficulty. There are three biographies of George Washington, each using his name as title. The one by the d'Aulaires (Doubleday, 1936) is for normal readers in grades three to five; the Initial Biography by Genevieve Stump Foster (Scribner, 1949) for grades four to six; and Clara Ingram Judson's *George Washington, Leader of the People* (Wilcox and Follett, 1951) for grades five to eight. On the subject of stars, for another example, *Find the Constellations* (Houghton, 1954) by Hans Augusto Rey can be read by good fourth graders, yet because of the material included and the illustrations, especially the "sky views" showing constellations in the sky throughout the year, the book will appeal to pupils as advanced as eighth or ninth grade.

Titles in Childhood of Famous Americans, a series of biographies published by Bobbs-Merrill for grades four to six, are good to use with older retarded readers as high as junior high school.

The Landmark Books published by Random House, mostly in the fields of biography and history and intended for junior high school readers, are valuable in getting retarded readers in high school interested in reading. These latter books are usually by distinguished writers and, while simply written, provide interesting reading as well as valuable information.

School librarians also search among books for beginning readers, discussed in the previous chapter, for titles that might also appeal to older, retarded readers.

Picture Books

Books with numerous pictures are useful in supplying information without taxing unduly the reading ability of the retarded reader. Such picture books must be on subjects interesting and challenging to older readers who often read several grades below where they should read. Illustrated books on subjects that appeal to readers somewhat older than those for whom they were intended are the Hardie Gramatky books about mechanical objects with human characteristics in amusing situations, published by Putnam; horse stories with pictures for very young children by C. W. Anderson, Paul Brown, and Wesley Dennis; Hans Augusto Rey's books about the engaging monkey introduced in *Curious George* (Houghton, 1941); and Virginia Lee Burton's *Katy and the Big Snow* (Houghton, 1943) and other books which have to do with mechanical objects, change of seasons, and similar subjects. Margaret Wise Brown has several picture books, especially *Wheel on the Chimney* (Lippincott, 1954), that appeal to older boys and girls. Books by the Beims (Jerrold and Lorraine), intended for pupils in grades one to three, are usually about modern social problems and are suitable for older readers. Their *Two Is a Team* (Harcourt, 1945) is the story of a Negro boy and a white boy who find that they get along better by working together. *The Biggest Bear* by Lynd Ward (Houghton, 1952) will be enjoyed by readers as high as sixth grade, though it was written for kindergarten through third grade.

For retarded readers in the upper elementary grades, biographies by the d'Aulaires sometimes prove useful, though readers may not choose them because they seem like picture books. Similar books for older readers by Daugherty, with many large colored illustrations, likewise are a possibility for retarded readers in junior high school. On the senior high school level, one looks for pictorial material in the field of science for boys, who compose about three fourths of the retarded readers. A good example is *Exploring the Weather* by Roy A. Gallant (Garden City Books, 1947) which has many large colored illustrations and charts.

Books Written Especially for Slow Readers

Some books have been prepared especially for slow readers. At least two such were prepared by Helen Heffernan, a school supervisor in California, in collaboration with others, and published by Harr Wagner in San Francisco. The first half of each book is an exciting and interesting story; the latter half is factual material, connected to the story and intended to be useful for geography, history, or science. An example is *Desert Treasure* (1939), a mystery story for which the Mohave Desert furnishes the setting, with subsequent chapters on desert people, plants, and animals.

Scott publishes an easy reading series of books for slow readers. One of the most popular is *Boxcar Children* (1950, first published in 1942) by Gertrude Chandler Warner, about a family of orphans who, until they discover the identity of their grandfather, improvise a home for themselves in a railroad boxcar. Using only six hundred words to write the book, the author managed to invent a fairly interesting story which children enjoy reading. There is now a brief series of books about the same children, including *Surprise Island* (1949), *The Yellow House Mystery* (1956), and *Mystery Ranch* (1959).

Wheeler for a number of years published the American Adventure Series of which the reading expert, Emmett A. Betts, is editor. These books are intended for about fifth grade level but are on subjects which interest older readers. Frank Lee Beals, who has also adapted a number of classics for Sanborn, is one of the authors of this series. Some of Beals' titles are *Davy Crockett* (1941), *Kit Carson* (1941), *Buffalo Bill* (1943), *Chief Black Hawk*

(1943), and *Rush for Gold* (1946). One book in this series, *Cowboys and Cattle Trails* (1948), was written by Doris Shannon Garst and her husband, Warren Garst. Several of Mrs. Garst's books, which are included in standard book selection aids, interest slow readers. Another writer, Anita Melva Anderson, has written *Wild Bill Hickok* (1947), *Squanto and the Pilgrims* (1949), and *Fur Trappers of the Old West* (1946). The progression of the reading level in the Wheeler series is shown on a list. Now that Wheeler has been acquired by Row, the American Adventure Series is handled by the latter.

Row also publishes a series of biographies in pamphlet form, thirty-six pages each, in groups of six, ranging in subject matter from "Explorers and Early Settlers" to "Heroes of Modern Times." The editor of this Real People Series is Frances Cavanah, who has also written several of the individual biographies. Quite a few outstanding authors have contributed to this series. In addition to other illustrations, each pamphlet has at least one map and a picture calendar of events in the life of the biographee and his times.

Adapted Classics

If ever there is justification for adapting classics and for adding them to school library collections, it would be the fact that there are readers who cannot read classics in the original. What to do about the good readers who prefer the simplified classics poses a problem, as discussed in Chapter 12, "Classics—Yesterday and Today."

A number of publishers have already published classics with a simplified vocabulary. The trend will no doubt continue, may even be expanded if demand justifies it. Classics are adapted by the following publishers: Heath, Globe Book, Laidlaw, Row, Sanborn, Scott, and Webster.

School librarians needing this type of material might like to secure from each publisher a complete list of titles available, with the grade level for which each is intended, and order a few titles with which to experiment. The school librarian should use his judgment in selecting titles, choosing those whose originals would interest modern-day pupils.

As an example, one of the most useful of the adapted classics is the 1938 Scott adaptation of Richard Blackmore's *Lorna Doone* made by Rachel Jordan and others. It is read by girls, both normal readers in grades four and five and older girls who are retarded in reading. Despite its title, boys will also read this version of *Lorna Doone* especially when they see the picture on the front and realize it is a book about outlaws.

Books with Large Print

Large print on the page makes material more easily readable and at the same time assures that the page will not offer too much text. Both of these attributes appeal to the poor reader, and the school librarian will help locate books with large print. *Books for Tired Eyes; a List of Books in Large Print,* compiled by Charlotte Matson and Lela Larson, is out of print after its fourth edition (A.L.A., 1951) but still useful in schools which have a copy. Selected for readers with poor eyesight, the titles may also be useful with retarded readers. Selections in the section "Juvenile Books" prove helpful in identifying books with large print for young readers and a few titles listed in the section for adults are simple enough to be read by retarded readers of high school age.

A number of books for elementary readers are published in fairly large print. Some of these are books by Ernest Ralph Norling and his wife, Josephine Stearns Norling, with such titles as *Pogo's Fishing Trip; a Story of Salmon* (Holt, 1942) and *Pogo's Truck Ride; a Story of Motor Freight* (Holt, 1954), the latter by Mrs. Norling alone and both for grades two to four; George Frederick Mason's books about animals, such as *Animal Clothing* (Morrow, 1955) and *Animal Tools* (Morrow, 1951), both for grades five to eight; and Naomi Buchheimer's books—for example, *Let's Go to a School* (Putnam, 1957) for grades two to three or four. Some of the science books by Herbert Spencer Zim, whose books are generally popular with children, are in large print. A good example is *Owls* (Morrow, 1950), for grades two to four, which also has many large illustrations in black and white by James Gordon

Irving, some of which are around the page, others interspersed among the printed material. Several of the Zim books, including *What's Inside of Me?* (Morrow, 1952), were published in two sizes of type. One page is simply written and is printed in large type for a child to read himself; the next is in smaller type and with greater detail on the subject for an adult to read to the child. School librarians who hoped to use these books for two levels of reading ability in the same grade found instead that they tended to prove frustrating to both groups. This experiment in printing has not been continued, so apparently did not prove successful.

Benefic Press, the publishing division of Beckley-Cardy Company, has published some books in large print which, although they are not included in standard book selection aids, may prove useful in getting boys in upper elementary grades to read. A rather long series, by Edna Walker Chandler, begins with *Cowboy Sam* (1951); a recent title is *Cowboy Sam and Big Bill* (1960). As the titles indicate, these books are about western ranch life and, though the reading level is aimed at grades two and three, the subject matter, plus the illustrations of teen-age boys in blue jeans, appeals to pupils in grades five and six. A more recent series by William J. Hurley, a reading specialist in the Chicago Public Schools, begins with *Dan Frontier,* which was published in 1959, also by the Benefic Press. On the same reading level as *Cowboy Sam,* these books are based on pioneer life with pictures of woodsmen in buckskin and they appeal to older pupils, especially boys.

Thin Books

The request for a thin book consistently evokes a smile from the school librarian who usually recognizes its source as a reader who is either lazy or has postponed an assignment until almost too late. The same plea from a retarded reader should be given more consideration because a thin book is about all he is capable of reading. In the *Wilson Library Bulletin* for October 1960 (35:151-3), Mrs. Eloise B. Oakes, Librarian, Lyndenville Central School System, New York, suggests a list under the title "Slim, Trim *and* Terrific" to "provide reading of high quality with strong appeal for young people," yet with format that would make the books appear thin. Since selection was not made with retarded readers in mind, not all of the titles suggested would prove suitable for those in high school but a quick survey shows that many would. What school librarian has not used, and with good results, the exciting *Adrift on an Ice-Pan* (Houghton, 1909) by Sir Wilfred Thomason Grenfell, Mary Raymond Shipman Andrews' *The Perfect Tribute* (Scribner, 1956, first published in 1906), or *Good-bye, Mr. Chips* (Little, 1934) by James Hilton? A retarded reader does not ask for the latest best seller nor scorn a book off the press more than ten years; he asks only for something he can read and enjoy. However, there are some recent books in this category which also interest slow readers. *Hold Back the Night* by Pat Harry Hart Frank (Lippincott, 1952), a book of fiction dealing with the Korean War, interests boys in high school. Ben Hecht's *Miracle in the Rain* (Knopf, 1943) appeals to slow readers among the girls. It is a love story with a bit of religious mysticism which seems to fascinate them through the book's fifty-one pages. On the other hand, three recent books on Mrs. Oakes' list would probably not be popular with slow readers: *Gift from the Sea* by Anne Morrow Lindbergh (Pantheon Books, 1955), because of its philosophy; Doré Schary's *Sunrise at Campobello* (Random, 1958), since it is in dramatic form; and *The Old Man and the Sea* (Scribner, 1952) by Ernest Hemingway, which contains symbolism; these factors tend to make reading difficult.

Simply Written Books

There are many books so simply written, and also so interesting, that even slow readers on the reading level for which the books were intended are able to read and enjoy them. The school librarian works consistently to identify such books in the library collection and to add others. While one does not want to overwork one author as an example, it is true that many books on science by Herbert Spencer Zim could meet these requirements. Having taught science in elementary schools, Zim writes simply and clearly so that his books are not too difficult for retarded readers. Other good examples are the books by William

Maxwell Reed, *The Earth for Sam* and *The Stars for Sam*, as well as *The Sea for Sam* by Reed and William Swancourt Bronson. These have long been popular with boys, grades six to nine. All three are in attractive revised editions (Harcourt, 1960) edited by Paul F. Brandwein.

Another of this type is *Volcanoes, New and Old* (Day, 1946) by Satis Narrona Barton Coleman. The author usually writes in the field of music but has succeeded in writing effectively on a far different subject. Written for grades seven to nine, the book is simple enough for slow readers of that group, yet is also useful for slow readers in high school because of its interesting material.

Books of Special Appeal to Retarded Readers

There are a few books that somehow have a special appeal for readers who find the reading process difficult. It is not easy to tell what constitutes the appeal of such books nor to predict one that will appeal. Only in working with retarded readers can the school librarian ascertain the criteria—often by the method of trial and error. *Homer Price* by Robert McCloskey (Viking, 1943) is probably the outstanding example. Simple enough to be read by a good fourth grade reader, the story will interest pupils as high as grade seven. The book has humor and abiding interest, so that a slow reader virtually "sweats out" his reading of it. A similar book for somewhat older readers, grades five to eight, is *Henry Reed, Inc.* by Keith Robertson (Viking, 1958). This relates the story of a boy who spends the summer with an aunt and uncle in New Jersey and meets an enterprising neighbor girl; it is read with enjoyment by both sexes. The pictures by Robert McCloskey help to make the happenings seem quite true to life. Beverly Cleary's books are generally useful with retarded readers in grades five and six.

Any school librarian with experience in helping retarded readers find books they can read could add many additional examples. The beginning librarian will find the search for others interesting and rewarding as he meets the enthusiasm of a retarded reader returning a book which at long last he has been able to read for himself and asking for another just like it.

o

CENSORSHIP AND THE SCHOOL LIBRARY

INTRODUCTION

In the early days of school library development, the problem of censorship did not figure prominently. Books for children and young people were then somewhat limited in number. They were not written on almost every topic found among adult books, including those in the controversial realm. Books from the adult field which found their way onto school library shelves were most often selected from the classics and were thus highly acceptable. School library collections were indeed rather specialized and, with their perennially limited budgets, only the most essential books could be purchased. Thus there was some tendency on the part of school librarians to feel that censorship was hardly their concern.

The past decade has changed the above factors. Each succeeding year a great outpouring of books for children and young people issues from presses. New publishers specializing in books for young readers have sprung up. These books are for all levels and on almost every conceivable subject. Even the elementary grades demand material on a wide variety of topics. Young people have easy access to adult books in public libraries, and high school libraries find it necessary to purchase a selected number of adult books for advanced pupils. No longer can the school librarian afford, like the ostrich, to bury his head in the sand and comfort himself with the belief that his library is not concerned with the problem of censorship.

EVIDENCES OF THE PROBLEM

Anyone who has read newspapers and magazines in the past ten years or so must realize that the problem of censorship looms large in importance for all librarians. A survey of library and educational periodicals proves how often schools and their libraries are involved in censorship cases, because whatever concerns one involves the other. A brief bibliography follows this discussion; other articles may be located through periodical indexes. In the present climate of general criticism of modern schools, their programs and their products, books both for use in classrooms and for school libraries have been attacked.

No school librarian has forgotten the prolonged attack on the series of textbooks by Harold Rugg of Columbia University used in junior high schools, nor the less successful attempt to remove as a textbook on the senior high school level *American Government* by Frank Abbott Magruder, a standard in its field, revised after the author's death by William A. McClenaghan (Allyn, 1957), and still in many school libraries.

Attacks on materials used in schools have occurred in areas as widely separated as California and New Jersey or Texas and Massachusetts. They have occurred in individual school systems and on a state-wide basis. Attacks have been made on an individual book, often because of a single, brief statement; in other instances, all the books of a given author are brought under attack.

Any school librarian could contribute one instance from his own experience in which objection has been raised to a book on his library shelves. Such objection most often stems from a parent or other person in the community, though objection may occasionally be voiced by administrators or teachers. Isolated objections can usually be resolved. It is when pressure is brought to bear either by an individual or an organized group and wide publicity is given that real trouble arises and serious damage may result.

In some states state-wide legislation has been proposed in order to control what types of library books may, or may not, be circulated. Demands have been made that books of certain authors be removed from library shelves. In some cases, books have been removed, even though temporarily, because of pressure. In extreme cases, library materials have been destroyed.

It is most deplorable when an attempted purge is directed against certain authors whose books are in school libraries. No author's books are all of equal value. Besides, it is the book, not the author, that is on the school library shelf. To remove, for instance, Dorothy Canfield Fisher's standard books of fiction because of some objection to *A Fair World for All; the Meaning of the Declaration of Human Rights* (McGraw, 1952) does not make sense. To take off the shelves Howard Fast's *Goethals and the Panama Canal* (Messner, 1942) which, in addition to being a good biography, has an excellent description of the operation of canal locks, just because of disapproval of another book by the same author seems equally unreasonable. Yet the attitudes of book banners often are unreasonable.

AREAS OF CENSORSHIP IN SCHOOL LIBRARIES

To deal in specifics and focus the problem of censorship as it affects the school library, the areas in which objection to books usually arises are (1) the various "isms" as found in theories and practices of government, particularly any statements held to be un-American or insufficiently pro-American (a common practice is to label communistic any material contrary to the beliefs of those bringing pressure); (2) books designed to promote sex education; (3) books in the field of art which display the human figure in the nude; (4) books that appear to indicate conflict between scientific findings and religion, especially as regards the evolution of man; and (5) books of a literary nature, usually on the adult level, which present "seamy" phases of life, especially those that deal specifically and at length with sex, or contain certain words considered taboo in our society.

The most recent area in which censorship has intruded is that of race relations, especially in states resisting the school integration imposed by the Supreme Court's 1954 desegregation decision. Furor has been raised over such innocuous books as *The Swimming Hole* (Morrow, 1951) by Jerrold Beim, in which a Negro boy goes swimming with white boys, and Garth Williams' picture book, *Rabbits' Wedding* (Harper, 1958), because one of the rabbits happens to be white and the other black. In one state the legislature passed a resolution requesting that the state Library Board "remove from circulation such books as are antagonistic and inimical to the traditions and customs" of the state.

THE SCHOOL LIBRARIAN AND CENSORSHIP

The school librarian, who, in the final analysis, regardless of who takes part in selection, is responsible for what goes on the library shelves, finds that he is on the horns of a dilemma. His stand on censorship must lie sensibly between that of the person who feels that the reading of children must be strictly supervised to exclude anything against which there might be objection and that of the one who holds that children should be allowed to read anything they wish, or that may fall into their hands. A few representatives of both extremes can be found among school librarians.

The school librarian, along with parents and teachers, recognizes that children of school age are immature and that guidance in what they read is just as necessary and as important as guidance in what they eat, what they wear, and what they do. He knows that children arrive at maturity of judgment largely by making decisions that are based on mounting experiences. Thus, in learning to evaluate information for themselves, children need to read from many different sources with a variety of viewpoints. The school librarian believes that the printed page does play a large part in what people believe and that it develops creative thinking perhaps to a greater degree than does any other medium of communication. At the same time, young, immature readers must have guidance in deciding what is good and what is bad and how much of what they read should be taken at face value. Otherwise, they will be buffeted about by every whim of opinion expressed in black and white.

Furthermore, arrival at maturity is not altogether a matter of any certain age or grade nor is it consummated with the event of going to college. Any school librarian realizes that subjects from which pupils in grade and high school may have been shielded are taught on the college level. Some books deemed not suitable by teachers and librarians on the high school level are required reading on the college level. The elementary school is preparatory to high school as high school is to college. Where better than in the school library will pupils receive preparation for adult reading?

Problem Outside the School Library

Yet it is not usually the readers themselves who present a problem for the school librarian and the school library collection. Young readers tend to take what they read in their stride and seem not to be influenced by things which adults hesitate to present to them. This is more true in the modern world where children are conditioned to practically everything that conditions the adult world. They see the same television programs and many of the same movies as their parents. They have a great deal of information on most current subjects.

An example is offered by the expurgated edition of *The Big Sky* (Houghton, 1950) prepared for high school use by the author, Alfred Bertram Guthrie, Jr. A high school librarian, whose collection already contained a copy of the regular edition, added a copy of the high school edition. Pupils interested in the title or the author read whichever edition was on the shelves. No rush for the unexpurgated copy was apparent. Whenever the expurgated copy was requested, it was probably because it was shorter, not because of the nature of the omissions. The foregoing leads to the comment that librarians themselves shift their ideas of what is suitable for school library collections. Has anyone forgotten that *Gone with the Wind* (Macmillan, 1936) by Margaret Mitchell, at first deemed unsuitable for high school use, was later considered almost required reading for any study of the Civil War?

It is rather the adults in the community, the politician who sets himself up as censor, the fanatic on religious dogmas, the organized group, often with outside funds, who keep any book selector, especially the school librarian, on his guard. It is therefore important to know the general tone of the community in which the school is situated, and to make selection for the group which will be using the library collection. There are, for instance, elementary school libraries in which a copy of Marie Hall Ets' *The Story of a Baby* (Viking, 1939) with its accurate scientific information, direct presentation, and realistic illustrations could circulate. There are others in which the librarian would do well to shelve this book with others to be used with children by their teachers. There may be other libraries which would not purchase a copy. School librarians generally believe that pupils need to get both sides of a controversial topic. Yet not many would actually place on high school library shelves a book which openly and unequivocally advocated the Communist way of life. Nor does this mean to imply that school librarians should not be free in selection. In practice, they must understand that consideration should be given also to selection for what purpose, in what school library, and in what community.

Suggestions for Solving the Problem

The uninitiated at this point will be asking: What, then, is the solution? While no one has a magic formula, a few suggestions may be offered:

1. Learn, by reading and discussing with other librarians, what persons or organizations are active in censoring school and library collections, the methods which have been used and how other librarians have met similar situations. The school librarian can never be too sure that "it can't happen here" and must be prepared for such an eventuality.

2. Belong to educational and library organizations, local, state, and national, which give support to the fight for intellectual freedom in schools and libraries. Become familiar with the policy statement of the National Education Association's National Commission To Defend Democracy Through Education. This statement is available under the title "The Public School and the American Heritage," and has been endorsed by other organizations, including the American Library Association, which also has its Library Bill of Rights. At its council meeting in July 1955, the American Library Association also endorsed the School Library Bill of Rights, prepared by the American Association of School Librarians. This document is quoted in full at the end of this discussion and should be in every school library.

The March 1962 issue of the *Wilson Library Bulletin* (36: 500+) carried in full a statement entitled "How Libraries and Schools Can Resist Censorship," adopted by the American Library

Association Council at the Association's midwinter meeting in Chicago "as a guide to librarians and others threatened by the current wave of censorship activity." The statement has been "approved in principle by the executive board of the American Association of School Librarians."

3. In the light of the above documents, and with the cooperation of teachers and administrators and advice from school library supervisors of the local system and of the state, prepare a statement of policy regarding book selection for the school library. The Board of Directors of the American Association of School Librarians at the 1961 midwinter conference of the American Library Association approved a statement entitled "Policies and Procedures for Selection of School Library Materials," later endorsed by the ALA Council at their meeting in Cleveland. Copies of this statement together with several examples of policy statements made by groups of school librarians and administrators are available from the AASL office in Chicago.[1] This statement could be adapted to the needs of a particular school, or the system of which the school is a part. Such a statement would serve as a basis for defending the principles adopted and assure that the administration knows and approves them and will support the librarian if there is any criticism.

4. Rely on standard book selection aids, which represent the seasoned judgment of many people, for most of the materials for the school library. Other materials should be known by either the librarian or teacher who recommends them. If possible, examine publications in controversial areas before ordering them.

5. Become familiar with material as soon as it arrives in the school library. Ask teachers and administrators to look over any books about which there might be some doubt. It helps in discussing materials with parents to be able to point out that certain materials were chosen by teachers for use with their classes. An example in point is a brief paragraph in a book on prehistoric man which some teachers feel is presented too abruptly and too briefly for the concepts of fourth grade children who will be reading it. If the decision should be, as is most likely, that the remainder of

[1] 50 East Huron Street, Chicago 11.

the book outweighs this small portion in importance, the book will be added to the collection. Then both librarian and teachers will have a basis for defending the choice if any question should arise.

6. Make sure that prejudices and enthusiasms of individuals —librarians or teachers—do not play too large a part in selection of school library materials. The collection, as has been emphasized before, is for all levels of reading ability and maturity, and for all interests represented in the school. It should contain materials for all classes, on a wide variety of subjects, expressing various viewpoints. Selection is both wide and deep; it must also be fair and unbiased.

7. On controversial subjects, make every effort in selection to present both sides of the issue, choosing materials which will help pupils arrive at their own opinions and formulate principles for propaganda analysis. To quote from "The Public School and the American Heritage":

> Teachers and administrators must encourage young people to locate, use and evaluate materials of instruction as they identify and analyze significant contemporary problems and form judgments about them. However, they must not direct or compel any particular judgments.[2]

8. Try to bring about an understanding among all concerned that different books serve different purposes in the school library, that they are intended for different uses. Books dealing with sex education, for example, are best used by the adult, parent or teacher, with the child. Works of art are intended for art classes where an understanding teacher guides pupils toward maturity of judgment in distinguishing between art and pornography. The adult novels by modern writers are for the senior class whose teacher is introducing pupils to the best in modern literature. The purpose behind selection is important, determines major use in any school library, and may be the deciding factor as to where material is housed.

9. Be prepared to defend selection policies and the selections made in light of the policies. While the librarian makes every effort to understand the motives behind censorship, he does not need to condone motives or the resulting action. He must not be

---

[2] *National Education Association Journal.* 40:557. November 1951.

swayed by every objection which reaches the library. Otherwise the task of removing books and replacing them after the storm has passed would be added to the school librarian's already full load.

10. Enlist the unqualified support of administrators in facing the possibility of censorship and reach agreement with them on action to be taken if books in the library are criticized. In the final analysis, it will undoubtedly be the administrator, not the librarian, who must deal with the problem. In most systems, each book order is checked by the school principal, the school library supervisor, or both. This practice offers an opportunity to discuss books which might prove targets for censors.

The problem of censorship pressure does not arise in every school library. Many schools have existed for years without even one instance of criticism against the library collections. There are at present seemingly less frequent attacks than there were in the 1950's. All librarians have added support on the national level for withstanding pressures. Yet, as long as the possibility of attack remains, school librarians, like others, must be prepared to meet it.

School Library Bill of Rights

A School Library Bill of Rights was presented to the ALA Council on July 8, 1955, by the American Association of School Librarians and was endorsed by the Council. The text of the bill is as follows:

School libraries are concerned with generating understanding of American freedoms and with the preservation of these freedoms through the development of informed and responsible citizens. To this end the American Association of School Librarians endorses the Library Bill of Rights of the American Library Association and asserts that the responsibility of the school library is:

To provide materials that will enrich and support the curriculum, taking into consideration the varied interests, abilities, and maturity levels of the pupils served.

To provide materials that will stimulate growth in factual knowledge, literary appreciation, aesthetic values, and ethical standards.

To provide a background of information which will enable pupils to make intelligent judgments in their daily life.

To provide materials on opposing sides of controversial issues so that young citizens may develop under guidance the practice of critical reading and thinking.

To provide materials representative of the many religious, ethnic, and cultural groups and their contributions to our American heritage.

To place principle above personal opinion and reason above prejudice in the selection of materials of the highest quality in order to assure a comprehensive collection appropriate for the users of the library.

BRIEF BIBLIOGRAPHY ON CENSORSHIP AND THE SCHOOL LIBRARY

Asheim, Lester E. "Not Censorship but Selection." *Wilson Library Bulletin*. 28:63-7. September 1953.

Brown, Mrs. Clifford. "Censorship in School Libraries: A Statement of Belief." *Michigan Librarian*. 21:30-4. October 1955.

Dunkley, Grace S. "Selection Policies Defined to Allay Fears of Censors." *Junior Libraries*. 2:3-5. December 15, 1955.

Fiske, Marjorie. *Book Selection and Censorship; a Study of School and Public Libraries in California*. Berkeley, University of California Press, 1959. Chapter 6, "Paradox in School Librarianship."

Gannon, Richard D. "Censorship and High School Libraries." *Wilson Library Bulletin*. 35:46-7. September 1960.

Lees, Gladys L. "Censorship As It Affects the School Library." In Harold Lancour, ed. *The School Library Supervisor; a Report of an Institute on School Library Supervision Held at the University of Illinois Library School*. Chicago, American Library Association, 1956. p. 39-51.

Oman, William. "Book Banning: Theory and Practice." *University; a Princeton Magazine*. p. 25-7. Fall 1960.

Rogers, Virgil M. "Don't Let Censors Take You Unaware." *Junior Libraries*. 2:1-3. December 15, 1955.

Rogers, Virgil M. "Toward Intellectual Freedom." *ALA Bulletin*. 51:243-7. April 1957.

Schmitt, Gladys L. "Censorship and the Immature." *Library Journal*. 75:652-5. April 15, 1950.

Srygley, Sara K. "Schools Under Fire." *Library Journal*. 76:2049-50. December 15, 1951.

PART IV

FACTORS RELATED TO SELECTION

BOOK WEEK AND NATIONAL LIBRARY WEEK

BOOK WEEK

Development and Significance

The idea of an annual Book Week originated with the late Franklin K. Mathiews, Chief Librarian for the Boy Scouts of America. Interested in making books and reading a meaningful part of the Boy Scout program, Mr. Mathiews traveled widely during 1915 to ascertain by survey what Boy Scouts were reading and from what sources their reading material was being obtained. None too well pleased with his findings, he compiled and had printed a list of books suitable for boys and encouraged book stores to set aside one week prior to the Christmas holiday season to promote reading for them. This marked the beginning of interest in Book Week, now an important annual event in the world of books and reading. At first known as Boys' Book Week, it was later renamed Children's Book Week. Today it is called Book Week to include all interested in books and reading.

Little was done to promote the idea of Book Week further during the First World War. In 1918, however, Mr. Mathiews discussed plans with Frederic G. Melcher, at that time co-editor of *Publishers' Weekly* and secretary of the American Booksellers Association. (Mr. Melcher is now chairman of the board of the R. R. Bowker Company, publishers of *Publishers' Weekly* and the *Library Journal.*) Interested in books and reading for all children, Mr. Melcher suggested that girls also be included in plans for Book Week. With help from Clara Whitehill Hunt, then children's librarian of the Brooklyn, New York, Public Library and herself an author of children's books, Mr. Mathiews and Mr. Melcher prepared a booklist entitled *The Bookshelf for Boys and Girls,* which for a number of years proved to be a valuable tool, especially for bookstores.

In 1919 Mr. Mathiews addressed a meeting of the American Booksellers Association at Boston and, as a result, the group adopted a resolution hoping to arouse interest in more and better reading materials for children. Later, at the first meeting of the Children's Librarians Section of the American Library Association at its conference in Asbury Park, New Jersey, the first Book Week Committee was appointed to publicize Book Week and to supply some material for its observance in libraries.

During the American Library Association meeting at Swampscott, Massachusetts, in 1921, with Frederic G. Melcher as speaker, the Children's Librarians Section discussed the topic "Children's Book Week—a National Movement." It was at this meeting that Mr. Melcher, in an effort to encourage higher quality in books for children, offered to award annually a medal for the most distinguished book for children published during the preceding year. The Newbery Medal, as it was called, has been awarded annually since 1922 to many notable authors, and in 1938 Mr. Melcher added the Caldecott Medal for the most distinguished picture book. (These awards are discussed in Chapter 19.)

Each year a slogan is chosen to characterize Book Week. This slogan is made the subject of a poster which is always designed by an outstanding artist. The first theme chosen, "More Books in the Home," with a poster by Jessie Wilcox Smith, was used for the years 1919 to 1923 and again for the years 1929 and 1930, when the original poster was also used. Other Book Week themes have been "Reading for Fun" (1935) and "Reading Is Fun" (1952 and 1953); "Books to Grow on—The Modern World for Young Readers" (1936); "Reading—The Magic Highway to Adventure" (1937); "Forward with Books" (1941 and 1942); "United Through Books" (1944 and 1945); "Explore with Books" (1957 and 1958). "Hurray for Books!" was the slogan in 1960 and again in 1961.

Book Week was sponsored by the National Association of Book Publishers during the period 1920-1934. In 1934 the Association ceased to exist, and for the next ten years, the R. R. Bowker Company assumed office responsibilities for Book Week with a committee of children's book editors to carry on the program and with the financial backing of publishers. In 1945 the Children's Book Council was organized on a nonprofit basis to serve as national headquarters for Book Week.

For the celebration of Book Week each year, material, including a Book Week manual, a poster and streamers carrying out the theme of Book Week, and bookmarks listing winners of the Newbery and Caldecott medals, is furnished at a nominal price by the Children's Book Council.[1]

During the year, the Council serves as an information center for the promotion of books and reading. It publishes quarterly and distributes free on request a Council Calendar of events throughout the year to be tied in with special library displays, which indicates sources from which material may be obtained.

From a small beginning in 1919, Book Week has spread from coast to coast in the United States and is observed by all types of libraries, especially school libraries and the children's departments of public libraries. Book Week is also observed in a number of foreign countries.

It would be difficult to overestimate the influence of Book Week in concentrating attention on books and reading. Its celebration is participated in by schools, libraries of all kinds, many national organizations, bookstores, and book dealers. Book publishers and their editors vie with each other in producing fresh, attractive books for display during Book Week and for subsequent sales. Most newspapers and many magazines carry articles about Book Week and feature book reviews for the occasion. Book Week offers an opportunity for book reviewing periodicals to present a special Book Week issue. The *Wilson Library Bulletin* and other library periodicals feature pictures of displays from many libraries and offer suggestions for the observance of Book Week. Programs are presented in schools and libraries, over radio and television— all promoting books and reading.

Readings

Beust, Nora E. "Books Around the World." *School Life.* 25:40-1. November 1939.

[1] Order from the Council, 175 Fifth Avenue, New York 10.

Bush, Mildred. "Book Week Comes of Age." *Illinois Libraries.* 21:29-32. December 1939.

Children's Book Council. *World of Children's Books.* New York, The Council, 1952. "History of Book Week and the Children's Book Council," p. 108-13.

Heaps, Willard A. "On the Joys of Owning Books and Their Companionship." New York *Times Book Review.* p. 3. November 10, 1940.

Melcher, Frederic G. "Working Together: Publisher, Bookseller, and Librarian." In Frances L. Spain, ed. *Reading without Boundaries.* New York, New York Public Library, 1956. p. 85-7. Also in New York Public Library *Bulletin.* 60:619-21. 1956.

NATONAL LIBRARY WEEK [2]

The first National Library Week was celebrated March 16-22, 1958. This was in line with a resolution submitted to the United States Senate on August 22, 1957, by Senator Lister Hill of Alabama, on behalf of himself and seventeen other senators, urging the President to designate these dates as National Library Week. The first observance enlisted the support of five thousand communities in a variety of activities which, according to the official report, "awakened a sense of personal need as well as responsibility for the status of reading in the community." Activities on the national level included: 22 magazine articles reaching 68 million people; 11,607 major newspaper stories in a three-week period; 14 radio and television shows going into 170 million homes; and more than $800,000 worth of spot time donated by broadcasters. Perhaps never before in the history of America had such a concerted effort, using various media of communication, been made to emphasize the importance in modern civilization of books and reading—and the book trade and library service which bring books to the public.

The story behind National Library Week is an interesting one. For several years prior to 1954, the American Library Association and the American Book Publishers Council had worked

[2] This section was prepared largely from material furnished by the National Book Committee, Inc., 24 West 40th Street, New York 18.

together for such needs as "improved copyright protection for American writers; the extension of public library facilities to unserved rural areas; and the encouragement of needed research studies in the field of book distribution and use." As a result of these combined efforts, there was organized in 1954 the National Book Committee which, in cooperation with the American Library Association, sponsors National Library Week.

This committee has eighteen cooperating organizations including the National Congress of Parents and Teachers, the National Council of Teachers of English, and the National Education Association. There are also nine industry groups which cooperate, including, besides the American Book Publishers Council, such organizations as the American Booksellers Association, the Children's Book Council, and the Religious Publishers Group. The president and the president-elect of the American Book Publishers Council regularly serve on the National Book Committee, which is limited to 150 members and embraces men and women from many professional and business groups.

During the years 1954 to 1958, before the first National Library Week was observed, activities of the National Book Committee included: (1) preparing a parents' handbook on children's reading;[3] (2) developing and promoting the Reading Aloud Bookshelf idea;[4] (3) conducting conferences of educators to discuss the development of lifetime reading habits; (4) organizing conferences on American Books Abroad; (5) sponsoring a special inquiry into the theory of censorship and the freedom to read; (6) organizing and promoting National Library Week.

Important as are all these undertakings, it was National Library Week which received nation-wide publicity and fired the imagination of all those interested in books and reading.

April 12-18 was designated as National Library Week for 1959. As in the first observance, the slogan used was "Wake Up and Read" with an official poster featuring the theme "For a

[3] Nancy Larrick, A Parent's Guide to Children's Reading. New York, Doubleday, 1958. See entry in bibliography in the Appendix for further information on this book.
[4] Gilbert W. Chapman, "An Experiment in Reading." Harper's Magazine. 213: 73-5. December 1956.

Better-Read, Better-Informed America." The program for 1959 was greatly expanded with cooperation from "national civic, cultural, and fraternal organizations, business groups and labor unions." A statement of the aim of National Library Week issued by the Steering Committee said that "it is devoted to the importance of libraries of all kinds—public, school and university libraries, and the libraries maintained by individuals in their own homes." National Library Week was observed for the third year April 3-9, 1960, with the motto "Open Wonderful New Worlds ... Wake Up and Read."

The fourth National Library Week was set for April 16-22, 1961, stressing the theme "For a Richer, Fuller Life—Read!" and its observance was reported to be extremely effective. Over 5,000 communities in 50 states participated with more than 50 national organizations taking part. It was notable for coverage in various media. A long-playing record featuring National Library Week messages from nine celebrities sold over 700 copies intended for placement with local radio stations. A film spot on reading and libraries, available for television and motion picture theaters, was widely used. More than 50 magazines, including some of the nation's best known periodicals, scheduled National Library Week features which reached 109 million people and other National Library Week messages reached millions of newspaper readers through articles contributed by noted authors.

John S. Robling, director of National Library Week since its beginning, resigned during 1961 and was succeeded by Beryl L. Reubens, former director of public affairs for Brandeis University.

While National Library Week has so far had only a slight impact on the work of school libraries, as compared to that on the work of public libraries, many school libraries do observe it. A full-page article, "National Library Week: A Backward Glance Suggests Future Activities," in *School Libraries* for October 1959, recounts various types of activity engaged in by school libraries and school librarians as reported through thirty state representatives for National Library Week of the American Association of School Librarians. The 1961 National Library Week "focused on the special emphasis being given this year to both the development of school libraries and continued accent on young adult reading."

An editorial in *ALA Bulletin* for January 1961 discusses the committee, with Margaret Monroe of the Rutgers University Graduate School of Library Service as chairman, appointed by the American Library Association to make an evaluation of National Library Week. The ALA Committee on Evaluation of National Library Week presented its report to the ALA Council at the June 1961 meeting and the report was adopted by the Council. Copies have been distributed to state directors and coordinators of National Library Week. The February 1962 issue of the *ALA Bulletin* includes the gist of the report with some account of how ALA has worked to implement the recommendations.

MEDALS AND AWARDS

THE NEWBERY AND CALDECOTT MEDALS

The complete story of the Newbery and Caldecott medals, both for outstanding books for children and young people, is unfolded in *A History of the Newbery and Caldecott Medals* by Irene Smith (Viking, 1957). The following brief sketch is intended merely to acquaint readers with the medals and their place in book selection.

Both medals, presented annually, were established and endowed by Frederic G. Melcher, for many years an ardent promoter of better books for young readers. The Newbery Medal has been offered since 1922 for a book "original in conception, fine in workmanship and artistically true," published in the United States during the previous year. It was named in honor of John Newbery, an English bookseller and printer who in 1744 with *A Little Pretty Pocket Book* began publishing a series of small books for children. The Caldecott Medal has been offered since 1938 for the "most distinguished American picture book for children" published during the preceding year. This medal honors Randolph Caldecott, an English artist (1846-1886), one of a small number including Walter Crane and Kate Greenaway who set high standards in picture books for children. *Randolph Caldecott's Collection of Pictures and Songs* (2 volumes) and *Caldecott Picture Books* (4 volumes), both published by Frederick Warne, are still found in many school library collections.

Books to receive the two medals each year are chosen by the American Library Association's Newbery-Caldecott Committee, sometimes referred to as the Awards Committee, though all librarians who are members of the ALA Children's Services Division have the privilege of voting in an advisory capacity. The committee is composed of officers of the Children's Services Division, chairmen of several designated committees, three members-at-large elected annually, and five members from the American Association of School Librarians. The chairman is always the chairman-elect of the Children's Services Division.

Announcement of the winners of these medals is made about the middle of March each year and the awards are presented at an award dinner held each year during the summer meeting of the American Library Association. Acceptance speeches made at this dinner and biographical sketches of the winners are published annually in the *Horn Book Magazine* and are also made available in volumes known as the Horn Book Papers,[1] edited by Bertha Mahony Miller and Elinor Whitney Field.

A complete list of medal winners is carried in each edition of the *Children's Catalog* and kept up to date by the supplements. Books that have won the medals through 1956, together with the runners-up for each year, form the appendix of the above-mentioned book by Irene Smith. The 1960 edition of *Bibliography of Books for Children,* published annually by the Association for Childhood Education International, carries a list of Newbery and Caldecott awards. Bookmarks listing the medal winners are also available from the Children's Book Council, whose work is discussed in Chapter 18. Since lists of medal winners are easy to locate and many of the winners are mentioned in Part II, the titles of these medal books are not included here.

Perhaps no single undertaking has done more than the establishment of Newbery and Caldecott medals to stimulate the production of good books for boys and girls. Children's editors, writers, librarians, and teachers all take great interest in the awards. The books chosen over the years constitute a distinguished group. Most of them are for elementary children, though a few are on the high school level. In fact, the appeal—or lack of appeal—of some selections remains a favorite subject whenever librarians meet. In all such discussion, it should be remembered that the awards have never been made on the basis of popularity with children. They are made rather for distinction. It would be impossible to select from a given year's output any one book which would agree

---

[1] *Newbery Medal Books: 1922-1955; Caldecott Medal Books: 1938-1957.* Boston, The Horn Book, Inc., 1955, 1957.

with everybody's idea of a winner. On the other hand, many of the Newbery and Caldecott medal winners—perhaps the majority of them—have proved popular with the readers for whom they were intended and continue to be read and enjoyed by succeeding generations.

The school library does not necessarily need to have a complete set of the Newbery and Caldecott medal winners, or to choose a book because it received an award. These books should be selected, as are other books, because of their potential contributions to the school in which the library is located. Some correlate nicely with subjects studied in school, some supplement materials in more factual books, while others provide just pure fun, nonsense, or solid enjoyment—all of which are factors in the well-balanced school library collection.

OTHER AWARDS FOR CHILDREN'S BOOKS

In addition to the Newbery and Caldecott medals, there are a number of other awards for children's books given by various donors under a variety of regulations. Salient facts about these awards are summarized here because librarians working with children and young people should know about them and keep up with the books and the authors receiving awards. With the exception of one international award, those included are American awards. Some are donated by individuals, others are under the auspices of organizations—educational, library, religious, and welfare. Several are state-wide in scope, some are regional, but the majority are offered on a national basis. Most winners are selected by organized committees; in a few instances, the choice is based on votes by the young readers themselves. A few which seem purely local in interest have not been included.

The Children's Spring Book Festival Awards

The Children's Spring Book Festival Awards are combined with a seasonal celebration, somewhat comparable to the two special weeks discussed in Chapter 18.

Since its beginning in 1937, the Children's Spring Book Festival has been sponsored annually by the New York *Herald Tribune*. Its purpose is "to give children's book activity a push in the spring." Prior to its establishment, the prevailing tendency had been to publish children's books largely at Christmas and about the time of Book Week in the fall.

Each year during the third week in May cash prizes of $200 are awarded to each of the three children's books judged best of those published between the first of the year and the last of May. These books are in the following groups: (1) picture books for ages 4 to 8; (2) books for middle-age children, 8 to 12; (3) books for older boys and girls.

In addition to the three prize-winning books, four honor books in each group are chosen. These and other leading books for children are featured in a special Children's Spring Book Festival issue of the New York *Herald Tribune Books,* presenting the best of children's books for the first five months of the year.

For the festival, two prominent persons in the field of children's literature who know both children and books serve as judges for each of the three groups of books. An outstanding artist is selected to design an appropriate poster for the festival. There are also bookmarks and various types of display materials.[2] Libraries, schools, and book stores cooperate by centering attention on children's books during the festival.

In 1937, the first year of the Children's Spring Book Festival, only 50 books were entered for the awards. The list of books competing in 1956 numbered more than 300 and about the same number were reported as having been entered in the 1960 contest. In 1956 a complete list of the award-winning books of the first twenty years was displayed on a chart. A rather remarkable record was established by the fact that all but six of these books were at that time still in print.

The Jane Addams Children's Book Award

The Jane Addams Children's Book Award Committee was first appointed in 1953 by the United States Section of the

[2] Available from the New York *Herald Tribune,* 230 West 41st Street, New York 36.

Woman's International League for Peace and Freedom, and has remained as one of the organization's standing committees.

The purpose of the Jane Addams Children's Book Award is to encourage the publication of books for children which have both literary merit and constructive themes, including solving problems calmly, breaking down suspicion and fear, overcoming prejudices, understanding destructive impulses, and approaching life constructively through sympathy and understanding.

The committee members read and evaluate books submitted by various publishers on the basis of established criteria. Their judgments are then pooled for a combined list of the top ten books from which the final award is made. A list arranged by grades and entitled *Books for Youth Which Build for Peace* is published annually and the winning book is featured in this list.

The author of the chosen book is presented with a hand-illuminated annual award certificate and the publisher is supplied with award seals for use on the book jackets. Time and place of presentation of the award vary with circumstances. A permanent exhibit of books that are winners and the runners-up has been established at the International Friendship Center.[3]

The first award was presented to Eva Knox Evans for her *People Are Important* (Capitol Publishing, 1951). *Champions of Peace* (Little, 1959) by Edith Patterson Meyer received the 1960 award and in 1961 it went to Shirley L. Arora for *What Then, Raman* (Follett, 1960).

Hans Christian Andersen Award

Every two years the International Board on Books for Young People presents the International Hans Christian Andersen Youth Book Award "to a living author who merits an award for his efforts in the promotion of good children's and youth literature by means of an outstanding work." For this award, fiction, especially from the preceding two years, is considered.

The Hans Christian Andersen Medal was first presented to Eleanor Farjeon for *The Little Bookroom* (Oxford, 1956). In 1960

[3] 306 North Aurora Street, Ithaca, New York.

it was presented to Erich Kästner, a German writer, for all his works, especially *When I Was a Little Boy* (Clarke, Irwin, 1959). The award was made during the Congress of the International Board on Books for Young People in Luxembourg, September 26-29, 1960.

Annual Children's Book Award

Since 1943, the Child Study Association of America,[4] an organization devoted to parent education, has presented the Annual Children's Book Award for "a book for children which reflects realistically the world in which they are growing up and some of the vital problems they encounter there."

The award book is selected annually by the Children's Book Committee, who also evaluate new children's books and prepare a booklist, *Books of the Year for Children,* published by the Association to help parents guide their children's reading. A scroll of award is presented to the winning author at the annual conference of the Association. *Keystone Kids* by John R. Tunis (Harcourt, 1943) won the first award in 1944. In 1951, awards went to two authors, Eleanor Roosevelt and Helen Ferris, for their joint production, *Partners; the United Nations and Youth* (Doubleday, 1950), and in several years two awards have been presented to authors of different books.

In 1960, Zoa Sherburne's *Jennifer* (Morrow, 1959) was selected for the award. A citation was also given to the book *Mary Jane* by Dorothy Sterling (Doubleday, 1959). The 1961 award went to *Janine* by Robin McKown (Messner, 1960).

Aurianne Award

The Aurianne Award was donated by Miss Augustine Aurianne, a New Orleans school librarian who died in 1947, in honor of her father and sister. This award was conferred for the first time in 1958 on John and Jean George for their *Dipper of Copper Creek* (Dutton, 1956).

[4] 9 East 89th Street, New York 28.

The Aurianne Award is an annual prize of $200 which goes to the author of an animal book, either fiction or nonfiction, that develops humane attitudes in children eight to fourteen. A committee to serve a three-year term is appointed by the president of the Children's Services Division of the American Library Association to select the book to receive this award. This committee works on a calendar year basis and the new chairman is announced each year at the midwinter meeting of the American Library Association. The committee found no book which it considered worthy of the award in 1959, but in 1960 the award was made to Meindert DeJong for *Along Came a Dog* (Harper, 1958). The 1961 award was made to Agnes Smith for *An Edge of the Forest* (Viking, 1959).

Lewis Carroll Shelf Award

The University of Wisconsin School of Education, cooperating with state organizations, has initiated the Lewis Carroll Shelf Award, to be given annually.

Publishers were invited in 1958 to select one book from their lists "worthy to sit on the shelf with *Alice in Wonderland*." From a total of forty-five books submitted, a committee of six librarians, teachers, parents, and writers chose sixteen titles as the first award books. A vote of five was necessary to qualify any book for an award.

The February 1959 *Horn Book Magazine* features a list of these winners, containing many old favorites and a few surprises. A composite list of award winners for 1958, 1959, and 1960 is available from the University of Wisconsin School of Education. The collection of winning books is available for exhibiting from the Wisconsin Free Library Commission.[5] The awards for 1960 include *Johnny Crow's Garden* by L. Leslie Brooke (Warne, 1903), and the more recent Newbery Medal winner *Onion John* by Joseph Krumgold (Crowell, 1959).

[5] 706 Williamson Street, Madison, Wisconsin.

Thomas Alva Edison Foundation Awards

The Edison Foundation [6] with the cooperation of sixty-two national organizations has established the National Mass Media Awards "to encourage improved quality in the mass media especially for juvenile audiences." Among these the following awards are offered in the field of books for young readers: (1) the best children's science book; (2) the best science book for youth; (3) a book of special excellence in portraying America's past; and (4) a book of special excellence in contributing to the character development of children. The award consists of a scroll plus $250 for the author and a scroll for the publisher.

In 1960, the awards were presented for: (1) *Experiments in Sky Watching* by Franklyn Mansfield Branley (Crowell, 1959); (2) *IGY: Year of Discovery; the Story of the International Geophysical Year* by Sidney Chapman (University of Michigan Press, 1959); (3) *The Great Dissenters: Guardians of Their Country's Laws and Liberty* by Fred Reinfeld (Crowell, 1959); and (4) *Willie Joe and His Small Change,* by Marguerite Vance (Dutton, 1959).

Award books for 1961 were *Animal Clocks and Compasses* by Margaret O. Hyde (McGraw, 1960); *Saturday Science,* edited by Andrew Bluemle (Dutton, 1960); *Peter Treegate's War* by Leonard Wibberley (Farrar, Straus, 1960); and *Touched with Fire; Alaska's George William Steller* by Margaret Elizabeth Bell (Morrow, 1960).

Dorothy Canfield Fisher Children's Book Award

The Dorothy Canfield Fisher Children's Book Award is sponsored by the Vermont Congress of Parents and Teachers and the Vermont Free Public Library Commission and administered by a committee of five. The award consists of an illuminated scroll and is presented to the author of the winning book at the annual convention of the Vermont Congress of Parents and Teachers, Vermont Library Association, Vermont Education Association, or

[6] Suite 806-7, 8 West 40th Street, New York 18.

another professional organization in the field of children's reading or library service. Its purpose is to encourage Vermont school children to read more and better books, as well as to honor one of Vermont's most distinguished authors, some of whose books are for children.

A master list of books, with ages for which they are intended, is compiled by a committee representing both school and library organizations, plus several members at large interested in children's reading and library service. Pupils of Vermont schools, grades four through eight, are encouraged to read books from the master list and before May 1 to cast a ballot for the book each likes best.

The Dorothy Canfield Fisher Children's Book Award was first given in 1957 to Mildred Mastin Pace's *Old Bones, the Wonder Horse* (McGraw, 1955). The winner in 1960 was *Double or Nothing,* by Phoebe Erickson (Harper, 1958), and in 1961 was *Captain Ghost* by Thelma Harrington Bell (Viking, 1959).

Jewish Book Council of America Award

The Jewish Book Council of America has since 1952 made several annual awards, including a juvenile award, under various names, to authors of books that are of particular interest to Jewish readers. The Book Council is sponsored by the National Jewish Welfare Board, which also sponsors Jewish Book Month. The Jewish book award consists of a citation and $250. The first book to receive this award was *All-of-a-Kind Family* by Sydney Taylor (Follett, 1951), which begins a series of books about a Jewish family. For 1960 this award was presented to *Keys to a Magic Door* by Sylvia Rothchild, a biography of Isaac Loeb Peretz (Farrar, Straus, 1959).

Junior Book Awards

In 1945, the Boys' Clubs of America established Junior Book Awards as part of a national reading program. These bronze medals are awarded annually for five or more books published during the preceding year receiving the highest recommendations from club members in the United States. Winners are announced dur-

ing National Boys' Club Week in April. Selection of winners is
made by an Awards Committee from books accorded the best
reviews by members of Boys' Clubs all over America. Awards went
to six books in 1948, ten in 1950, nine in 1951, and twelve in
1952, and again to six in 1960. Because of the number of awards
in a given year, no authors and titles of winners have been
included here.

To cite an example of how books are chosen for awards, in
1957 over four thousand boys reported on nearly five hundred
current books. Of the total list, sixteen of the most highly recommended books were considered by the adult committee for the
final selection of five winners.

Regina Medal

On March 30, 1959, the Regina Medal was awarded for the
first time by the Catholic Library Association at its annual meeting
in Chicago. This award is given annually "to single out for
recognition and emulation those writers, editors, and illustrators
who have given unstintedly of their creative genius to children's
literature, finding in that field a challenge worthy of their talents
and demanding always their best." It is not limited as to country
of birth or creed and is to be awarded for the lifetime work, rather
than a single work, of the recipient.

The first Regina Medal went, appropriately, to Eleanor Farjeon
whose lilting poems and fanciful stories have for many years
delighted children and adults who work with them, both in her
native England and in America, which she also claims through
her mother, daughter of the American actor Joseph Jefferson. In
Miss Farjeon's absence, the award was accepted by Edward
Ardizzone, who has illustrated Miss Farjeon's books.

In this connection it may be interesting to note that *The
Little Bookroom* (Oxford, 1956) in the year of its publication
received the Carnegie Medal, the English counterpart of the
Newbery Medal, and, as has already been mentioned, the International Hans Christian Andersen Medal.

Anne Carroll Moore was chosen to receive the second Regina
Medal "for her pioneer work for children in public libraries, her

influence upon children's literature through the quality of her literary criticism, and her recognition and encouragement of many promising young writers and artists." [7] Miss Moore was appointed in 1906 as supervisor of work with children in the New York Public Library, the first such position in the United States. Her books about books for children have influenced the entire field of book selection for young readers, in school as well as public libraries.

The 1961 award was made to Padraic Colum, the Irish author who has done so much to preserve legends for young readers.

Sequoyah Children's Book Award

The Sequoyah book award is part of "a reading program to encourage Oklahoma school children from grades four through nine to read more and better books." It is sponsored by the Oklahoma Library Association, the Oklahoma Education Association, the Oklahoma Congress of Parents and Teachers, the State Department of Public Instruction, the Oklahoma Council of Teachers of English, the Oklahoma State Library, and the University of Oklahoma Library School. The Children's Book Award Committee is composed of one representative from each of the sponsoring organizations.

A master list of books is compiled by this committee and school children may read all or any books from this list before casting a vote for the best book. Only books by American authors are included on the list, and neither picture books nor textbooks are considered. First presented in 1959, the award went to *Old Yeller* by Fred Gipson (Harper, 1956). The 1960 winner was *Black Gold* (Rand McNally, 1957) by Marguerite Henry. In 1961 the award went to Robert Heinlein's *Have Space Suit— Will Travel* (Scribner, 1958).

The medal accompanying the award was designed by Dick Palmer of the University of Oklahoma, where the annual award is made.

[7] *Library Journal.* 85:128. March 15, 1960.

The William Allen White Children's Book Award

This award is an example of a state-wide undertaking that since its establishment has been emulated by other states. Its purpose is two-fold: (1) to encourage Kansas school children to read, and (2) to honor the memory of William Allen White (1868-1944), the famous editor of the Emporia *Gazette*. His editorial, " Mary White," a tribute to his sixteen-year-old daughter after her untimely death, is often included in anthologies for high school pupils. The William Allen White Children's Book Award was the first to be based on the choice of children themselves.

The book selection committee compiles a master list of books which the children in grades four through nine read and from which they select the book to receive the award by voting for the book they like best. Committee members are either specialists in children's literature or representatives of various state-wide organizations interested in books and reading for children.

This award, consisting of a medal and at least $250, was announced in April 1952 at the dedication ceremonies of the new William Allen White Library of the Kansas State Teachers College in Emporia. It was first given to *Amos Fortune: Free Man* by Elizabeth Yates (Dutton, 1950). The 1958 award was presented to Elliott Arnold for his *White Falcon* (Knopf, 1955) in a special ceremony at Kansas State Teachers College in Emporia on October 16, 1958, when the Children's Library Division of the William Allen White Library was named the Mary White Room.

Over 54,000 Kansas school children from grades four to nine named *Old Yeller,* by Fred Gipson (Harper, 1956) the 1959 winner of the William Allen White Children's Book Award. The 1960 award winner was William O. Steele's *Flaming Arrows* (Harcourt, 1957). In 1961 this award went to *Henry Reed, Inc.* by Keith Robertson (Viking, 1958).

Laura Ingalls Wilder Award

The Children's Services Division of the American Library Association offers a bronze medal designed by artist Garth Williams as the Laura Ingalls Wilder Award. This medal is presented every five years to an author who has contributed substantially to children's literature and whose works have been published in the United States. The work of an author or illustrator receiving the award may be in one field or several, fiction or nonfiction. The medal is given for a person's total contribution, though there is no restriction as to the number of years he must have worked.

The first award was made in 1954 to Laura Ingalls Wilder. At the ALA conference in Montreal in June 1960 the second award was given posthumously to Clara Ingram Judson, author of many excellent biographies. Mrs. Judson had died on May 24 at the age of 81.

Young Readers' Choice Award

Another award based on the reading of children is the Young Readers' Choice Award sponsored by the Division of Work with Children and Young People of the Pacific Northwest Library Association, which embraces the states of Washington, Oregon, Montana, Idaho, and Utah, and the province of British Columbia in Canada. This award is a hand-painted parchment scroll. To insure recency, selection is limited to books published during the previous two or three years. The books must be of universal appeal, liked by both girls and boys, and read by children grades four to eight.

The committee consists of the chairman and the vice-chairman of the Division of Work with Children and Young People and of the School Librarians Section of the Pacific Northwest Library Association. Both large and small libraries are represented and the final choice is made on the basis of votes by librarians and teachers who express the opinions of children with whom they work as to the popularity of the books read.

The first award went in 1940 to Dell J. McCormick for *Paul Bunyan Swings His Axe* (Caxton Printers, 1936). In 1960 the award went to *Henry and the Paper Route* by Beverly Cleary (Morrow, 1957). *Danny Dunn and the Homework Machine* by Jay Williams and Raymond Abrashkin (McGraw, 1958) won the 1961 award.

Awards for Children's Books Offered by Publishers

In addition to the numerous awards donated by individuals or organizations, there are several awards made by publishers to encourage writing for children and young people. These will not be discussed in full, however, because the awards are commercial in nature and not too closely related to book selection for school libraries. There is usually involved a sum of money tied up with rights of publishing and/or the royalty to the author. School librarians interested may write to each publisher for details of these awards.

Some awards by publishers for books for young readers are as follows:

Since 1954, Dodd, Mead has offered the Librarian Prize Competition Award to the best book, fiction or nonfiction, for an American boy or girl, age nine to sixteen. The winning book must be written by an American librarian who is working, or has worked, with children and young people. Since 1950 Dodd, Mead and *Boy's Life* magazine have offered an award for a "story or biography of distinctive literary merit for boys from twelve to sixteen." For several years starting in 1954 Dodd, Mead and *Compact, the Young People's Digest* have offered annually a Seventeenth Summer Literary Competition award for novels for young people on contemporary life.

Follett, formerly Wilcox and Follett, presents the Charles W. Follett Award to stimulate more interest in children's literature among good authors. The award is given annually to the author of a book, either fiction or nonfiction, for children ages eight to sixteen. There is also a Follett Beginning-to-Read Award given to the author of a book for children in grades one to three.

Franklin Watts has since 1958 offered annually the Franklin Watts Juvenile Fiction Award for a "noteworthy work of fiction suitable for children to read themselves," with age limits approximately eight through twelve, or grades three, four, and five.

Sources of Information About Awards

Information about awards and their winners is found currently in various educational and library periodicals. Each year the annual *Literary Market Place* (Bowker) in a section entitled "Literary Prizes and Awards" lists children's book awards, among others, with the following information: name of award, its nature, date of presentation, by whom and under what conditions the award is made. Useful for the names of winners as well as for general information about awards is *Literary and Library Prizes* (Bowker, 1959).

A comprehensive study, *Awards in the Field of Children's Books,* was undertaken under the auspices of the Department of Library Science, Kent (Ohio) State University. Edited by E. M. Portteus, it was issued as a pamphlet in the fall of 1959. In addition to other information, a chronological list of authors and titles of books which have won each award is included.

In 1961 the Children's Book Council published a list of almost fifty children's book awards, compiled by the Westchester Library System, Mount Vernon, New York, under the title *Children's Books: Awards and Prizes, 1960-1961.*[8] The pamphlet includes a statement of the history and purpose of each award, as well as a list of winners. The list is to be kept up to date by annual supplements. School librarians interested in awards not discussed in this chapter may find a copy useful.

BOOK AWARDS IN SELECTION

Book awards are one of many factors in the complicated business of book selection. Those which go to children's books and their authors indicate what adults consider worthy of note and what interests young readers themselves. In checking award winners, the school librarian widens his knowledge of authors and their books. Sometimes through awards he is introduced to unknown authors and to titles of which he is not aware. Once in a while he adds an award-winning book to the collection because readers have heard about it and ask for it. However, like any other book, an award winner should be selected for the school library collection only if it seems likely to make a real contribution to it.

[8] Order from the Council, 175 Fifth Avenue, New York 10.

o

BOOK CLUBS

Book clubs represent an effort to increase the number of readers and to multiply book sales. They were begun on the adult level, but there are now many for children and young people. The first of these to attain success was Junior Literary Guild which began in 1929 and is still probably the best known and most popular. It is rather difficult to compile a complete list of such clubs. The April 15, 1955, issue of *Junior Libraries,* now *School Library Journal,* carried an evaluation, now somewhat out of date, entitled "Children's Book Clubs," by Rhoda Kruse, assistant librarian of Girls High School, Brooklyn, New York. At one time each monthly issue of *Junior Libraries* listed the current selections of a number of book clubs for younger readers but this service was discontinued May 15, 1959.

The following are some of the principal book clubs for children and young people which are currently in operation: Arrow Book Club, Campus Book Club, Catholic Children's Book Club, the Junior Heritage Club, Junior Literary Guild, Parents' Magazine's Book Club for Beginning Readers, Parents' Magazine's Book Club for Children, Science World Book Club, Teen Age Book Club, the Weekly Reader Children's Book Club, Young Folks Book Club, Young Adults' Division of the Literary Guild, and Young Readers of America, a branch of the Book-of-the-Month Club.

Four of the above-mentioned clubs are divisions of clubs for adult readers. It is obvious which club sponsors the Junior Literary Guild, the Junior Heritage Club, and the Young Adults' Division of the Literary Guild. As stated above, Young Readers of America is a branch of the Book-of-the-Month Club. Young Readers of America confines its selections to books of two series published by Random House, Landmark Books and Allabout Books, largely in the fields of history and science respectively.

Seven clubs are sponsored by periodicals, as follows: Parents' Magazine's Book Club for Children and Parents' Magazine's Book Club for Beginning Readers; the Arrow Book Club, Campus Book Club, Science World Book Club, and Teen Age Book Club sponsored by Scholastic Magazines; and the Weekly Reader Children's Book Club by *My Weekly Reader,* a classroom newspaper with Charles E. Merrill Books (publisher) as co-sponsor. All four clubs sponsored by Scholastic Magazines limit their selections to paperback books, a large percentage of which are published by Scholastic Magazines and are not available through regular trade channels. The Arrow Book Club appeals to pupils of the fourth, fifth, and sixth grades, the Teen Age Book Club and the Science World Book Club to junior and senior high school pupils, and the Campus Book Club to high school pupils interested in more adult reading. The Weekly Reader Children's Book Club serves two age groups, five to eight and eight to twelve.

Selections for the Catholic Children's Book Club are made from books approved for young Catholic readers in any of five groups as follows: Picture Book, Intermediate (nine to eleven), Older Boys (twelve to sixteen), Older Girls (twelve to sixteen), and Knowledge Builders, this last consisting of nonfiction books appealing to various ages.

Young Folks Book Club, a division of Seasonal Promotions, Inc., offers selections for children from kindergarten through the sixth grade in two groups: kindergarten to third grade, and fourth to sixth grade.

School librarians interested in book clubs for children and young people may secure information from the clubs themselves. A great deal of similarity appears in the operation of all book clubs. A certain number of books are offered for consideration and usually a stated number must be purchased within a given period of time. A bonus or dividend book is often given to new members and occasionally to those who are already members. The school library may be given a free book for some specified number of books bought by pupils. A printed sheet describing the books is available for librarians and teachers, and in some clubs for pupils also. There is usually a discount on the price of books to club members, either individually or collectively through the classroom group or the library. Among other inducements, free book plates, often designed by outstanding artists, are given to encourage the building of individual libraries. A few clubs offer a special gift, such as a small bookrack, a "school size" microscope with manual of instructions, or a weather thermometer and barometer.

School librarians differ in their attitude toward book clubs. Some favor membership to insure the regular arrival of a few new books during the school year. Others do not approve of membership in any book club on the theory that many of the books selected are not suitable for school library needs. It is certainly true that any school library can secure good discounts on all books ordered from regular book dealers.

Books selected for the school library from whatever source should be, in the opinion of teachers and librarian, the very best available to meet the needs of the school. The most satisfactory book selection results from the use of standard book selection aids and other reliable sources and subsequent orders submitted to regular book dealers.

APPENDIX

o

BOOKS AND READING FOR CHILDREN AND YOUNG PEOPLE: A BIBLIOGRAPHY

Adams, Bess Porter. *About Books and Children; Historical Survey of Children's Literature.* New York, Holt, Rinehart & Winston, 1953. 573p. $7.50.

> Notwithstanding the subtitle, more than half of this book deals with modern books for modern-day readers. The appendix contains extensive lists of books for parents and teachers and for children and young adolescents. Index.

Arbuthnot, May Hill. *Children and Books.* Rev. ed. Chicago, Scott, Foresman & Company, 1957. 684p. $6.50.

> Prepared as a textbook for children's literature courses, this book contains a wealth of material for students, teachers, and librarians. A bibliography of books mentioned in each chapter is included. Index.
> The same publishers have issued a supplementary bibliography, *Keeping Up with Children and Books,* by Margaret Clark, which lists books published in 1957-59. 25c.

Becker, May Lamberton. *First Adventures in Reading; Introducing Children to Books.* New rev. ed. Philadelphia, J. B. Lippincott Company, 1947. 286p. o.p.

> The various chapters are on types of books, ranging from "Singing to the Baby" to "The Mystery Story." A brief list of books is found at the end of each chapter. Especially helpful for information about older books.

Burton, Dwight L. *Literature Study in the High Schools.* New York, Holt, Rinehart & Winston, 1959. 291p. $4.25.

> The author, in charge of English education at Florida State University, Tallahassee, and formerly a teacher of high school English, offers excellent help in teaching literature to high school pupils. The first part of the book is devoted to a discussion of books and their values for young readers. The author knows high school literature, and school librarians will be glad to find him in agreement with many of their opinions.

Duff, Annis. *"Bequest of Wings"; a Family's Pleasures with Books.* New York, The Viking Press, 1944. 204p. $3.

A former children's librarian tells of her experience in sharing books with her own small son and daughter. Appendix lists by chapters the books and other materials mentioned in the book.

Duff, Annis. *"Longer Flight"; a Family Grows Up with Books.* New York, The Viking Press, 1955. 269p. $3.

This book continues the account of the experiences of the author in guiding the reading of her son and daughter through adolescence. Books mentioned are listed in the appendix.

Eaton, Anne Thaxter. *Reading with Children.* New York, The Viking Press, 1940. 354p. $4.

The former librarian of Lincoln School, Teachers College, Columbia University, discusses books on various subjects in chapters with such titles as "Through Magic Doorways" and "Round-about the Earth." Books mentioned are listed at the end of each chapter and there is an index.

Fenner, Phyllis Reid. *The Proof of the Pudding: What Children Read.* New York, John Day Company, 1957. 246p. $4.50.

A chatty sort of book about a great many books and their appeal to young readers under catchy chapter headings such as "The Foolisher the Better" (funny stories) and " 'I Get Enough Reading in School' " (books for nonreaders). There is an index of authors and titles.

Frank, Josette. *Your Child's Reading Today.* Rev. ed. Garden City, N.Y., Doubleday & Company, 1960. 391p. $3.95.

Basing her study on her work as children's book consultant for the Child Study Association of America, the author writes for parents concerned with providing good reading experiences for their children. She discusses reading problems and ways to deal with them, as well as books for children of various ages. There is an index of authors and titles.

Hanna, Geneva Regula and McAllister, Mariana Kennedy. *Books, Young People, and Reading Guidance.* New York, Harper & Brothers, 1960. 219p. $3.50.

Designed for use by all concerned with books and reading for pupils of junior and senior high school age. Covers reading interests of young people, growth and characteristics of adolescents, and book selection for young people as well as methods of reading guidance. A list, "Recommended Books Referred to in the Text," appears at the end.

Huck, Charlotte S. and Young, Doris A. *Children's Literature in the Elementary School.* New York, Holt, Rinehart & Winston, 1961. 522p. $6.75.

A textbook by professors of education for a course in children's literature, this book promises to be helpful to school librarians. In addition to the usual material on types of books, there are sections on book selection aids, criteria for selection, and children's interests. Three chapters deal with using literature with children, and there are lists of helpful books.

Larrick, Nancy. *A Parent's Guide to Children's Reading.* Garden City, N.Y., Doubleday & Company, 1958. 283p. $2.95. (Pocket Books, 35c)

This book was sponsored by the National Book Committee "in consultation with advisers from eighteen national organizations—educational, civic, youth, and business." Discusses what parents can do to help reading progress and suggests books for various levels. Index.

Larrick, Nancy. *A Teacher's Guide to Children's Books.* Columbus, Ohio, Charles E. Merrill Books, 1960. 316p. $4.95.

Based on the author's experience as a teacher, lecturer, and editor, this book is filled with practical suggestions for using books with elementary school children. Addressed to the teacher, this guide will also benefit the school librarian. A very full index and a list of children's favorite books are included.

Moore, Anne Carroll. *My Roads to Childhood; Views and Reviews of Children's Books.* Boston, The Horn Book, 1961. 399p. $3.50.

Reprint of a book which was out of print for ten years. Comments on children's books by the first superintendent of Children's Work, New York Public Library. Most useful for selection of older books.

Munson, Amelia H. *An Ample Field; Books and Young People.* Chicago, American Library Association, 1950. 122p. $3.

Addressed primarily to young people's librarians in public libraries, the book contains help for school librarians as well. The three parts are Challenge, Resources, Techniques. Index.

Smith, Lillian Helena. *The Unreluctant Years; a Critical Approach to Children's Literature.* Chicago, American Library Association, 1953. 193p. $4.50.

The author, supervisor of children's work in the public library of Toronto, Canada, deals interestingly with book selection for children, her primary purpose being to examine the qualities which make children's books good literature. There is an index but no lists of books.

Spain, Frances Lander, ed. *The Contents of the Basket, and Other Papers on Children's Books and Reading.* New York, New York Public Library, 1960. 83p. $1.50.

> "A series of nine lectures given between 1954 and 1960 by well-known people in the children's book field."

Spain, Frances Lander, ed. *Reading Without Boundaries.* New York, New York Public Library, 1956. 104p. $1.

> "Essays presented to Anne Carroll Moore on the occasion of the 50th anniversary of the inauguration of library service to children at the New York Public Library."

Tooze, Ruth. *Your Children Want To Read; a Guide for Teachers and Parents.* Englewood Cliffs, N.J., Prentice-Hall, Inc., 1957. 222p. $5.25.

> The author is concerned mostly with modern-day reading problems and the use of books to meet children's needs and interests as they adjust to the physical and social worlds and meet emotional, esthetic, and spiritual needs. Lists of books discussed are found throughout the book.

Walsh, Frances, ed. *That Eager Zest; First Discoveries in the Magic World of Books.* Philadelphia, J. B. Lippincott Company, 1961. 252p. $3.95.

> An anthology, containing both prose and poetry, of "autobiographical reminiscences of childhood reading experiences" by nearly fifty outstanding writers, many of whose books are for children and young people. Inspirational for librarians, teachers, and more discerning pupils. No index.

White, Dorothy Neal. *Books Before Five.* New York, H. Z. Walck, Inc., 1954. 196p. $3.75.

> An account in diary form, covering a period of two years, based on a mother's notes on her daughter's early contacts with books. A list of books mentioned in each chapter appears at the end. Many of the books referred to by Mrs. White are British and so are not well known in this country.

ADDITIONAL LIST OF BOOK SELECTION AIDS FOR SCHOOL LIBRARIES

Chapter 2, "Aids for Selection," lists and discusses at some length a number of the more important book selection aids useful in school libraries. This bibliography contains additional book lists which the school librarian will find helpful. Many of these are mentioned throughout the text but are listed here for convenience in ordering.

In addition, the school librarian will probably wish to order a copy of *Aids in Choosing Books for Young Children,* compiled by Alice Dalgliesh and Annis Duff for the Children's Book Council, 175 Fifth Avenue, New York 10 (5c).

GENERAL BOOK SELECTION AIDS

Best Books for Children. New York, R. R. Bowker Company. Issued annually. $3.

> Lists and annotates books on all levels, preschool through high school, including adult books of interest to young people, arranged by grades and by subject.

Books for the Teen Age. New York, New York Public Library. Revised annually. 50c.

Books To Build On. Elvajean Hall and others. 2d ed. New York, R. R. Bowker Company, 1957. 79p. $2.

> "First books to buy for school libraries: elementary, junior high, high school."

Children's Books Too Good To Miss. May Hill Arbuthnot and others, comps. 2d rev. ed. Cleveland, Ohio, Press of Western Reserve University, 1959. 64p. $1.25.

Growing Up with Books. New York, R. R. Bowker Company. Revised annually. 10c.

LJ Recommended Children's Books of ——. New York, R. R. Bowker Company. Issued annually. $3.

> *Library Journal* reviews of recommended children's books published from May to May. School libraries which subscribe to either *Library Journal* or *School Library Journal* will already have these reviews in separate issues.

Notable Children's Books, ——. Book Evaluation Committee, Children's Services Division, American Library Association, comp. Chicago, The Association. Issued annually. Free.

> A short annual list which also appears in the *ALA Bulletin.*

Treasury of Books for Primary Grades. Mildred A. Dawson and Louise Pfeiffer, comps. San Francisco, Howard Chandler Publishers, 1960. 32p. $1.

BOOK SELECTION AIDS ON SPECIAL SUBJECTS

Lands and People

Books About Negro Life for Children. Augusta Braxston Baker, comp. Rev. ed. New York, New York Public Library, 1961. 31p. 25c.

> An annotated list of two hundred books "which give an unbiased, accurate, well-rounded picture of Negro life in all parts of the world."

Books for Brotherhood for Adults, Young People and Children. New York, National Conference of Christians and Jews. Issued annually. Single copy free.

Books on Asia for Children. New York, The Asia Society, 1961. Single copy free.

> A selected and annotated bibliography of books for elementary and junior high school.

Reading Ladders for Human Relations. Margaret M. Heaton and Helen B. Lewis. Rev. and enl. ed. Washington, D.C., American Council on Education, 1955. 215p. $1.75.

Richer by Asia. Chicago, American Library Association, 1959. 64p. $1.25.

> A selected bibliography of books and other materials recommended for promoting East-West understanding among young adults.

World History Book List for High Schools: a Selection for Supplementary Reading. Washington, D.C., National Council for the Social Studies, 1959. 119p. $1.25.

Science

The AAAS Science Book List. Hilary J. Deason, comp. Washington, D.C., American Association for the Advancement of Science, 1959. 140p. $1.

Growing Up with Science Books. New York, R. R. Bowker Company. Revised annually. 10c.

An Inexpensive Science Library; a Selected List of Paperbound Science Books. Hilary J. Deason and R. W. Lynn. 4th ed. Washington, D.C., American Association for the Advancement of Science, 1960. 70p. 25c.

The Science Book List for Children. Hilary J. Deason, comp.; Ruth N. Foy, consultant. Washington, D.C., American Association for the Advancement of Science, 1960. 139p. $1.

The Traveling High School Science Library. Hilary J. Deason. 5th ed. Washington, D.C., American Association for the Advancement of Science, 1959. 61p. 25c.

Vocations

Careers in Science: a Selected Bibliography for High School Students. Hilary J. Deason and William B. Blacklow, comps. Washington, D.C., American Association for the Advancement of Science, 1961. 23p. 15c.

Vocations in Fact and Fiction. Kathryn A. Haebich, comp. Chicago, American Library Association, 1953. 62p. $1.25.

A selective, annotated list of books for career backgrounds and inspirational reading.

SUBJECT INDEXES

Subject and Title Index to Short Stories for Children. Chicago, American Library Association, 1955. $5.

Subject Index to Poetry for Children and Young People. Violet Sell and others, comps. Chicago, American Library Association, 1957. 582p. $9.

AIDS FOR SELECTION OF INEXPENSIVE MATERIALS

Children's Books for $1.25 or Less. Lucille Menihan, comp. Rev. ed. Washington, D.C., Association for Childhood Education International, 1961. 31p. 75c.

Free and Inexpensive Learning Materials. 10th ed. Nashville, Tenn., Division of Surveys and Field Services, George Peabody College for Teachers, 1960. 252p. $1.50.

Fare for the Reluctant Reader. Anita Dunn and others, comps. Rev. ed. Albany, N.Y., New York State College for Teachers, 1952. 167p. $1.

> Compiled for the Capital Area School Development Association, Albany, N.Y.

Gateways to Readable Books; an Annotated Graded List of Books in Many Fields for Adolescents Who Find Reading Difficult. Ruth Strang and others. 3d ed. New York, The H. W. Wilson Company, 1958. 181p. $3.

Good Reading for Poor Readers. George D. Spache, comp. Rev. ed. Champaign, Ill., Garrard Press, 1960. 175p. $2.50.

High Interest Low Vocabulary Booklist. Donald De Witt Durrell and Helen Blair Sullivan, comps. Boston, Boston University School of Education, 1952. 35p. 75c.

AIDS FOR SELECTION OF CURRENT BOOKS

Most of the aids for the selection of current books are discussed in Chapter 2. Another source is the weekly book review section of most large daily newspapers. Probably the best known are New York *Herald Tribune Books* and the New York *Times Book Review.* The section "For Boys and Girls" of New York *Herald Tribune Books* is prepared by Margaret Sherwood Libby. It usually covers one page and presents from six to ten books. The juvenile section of the New York *Times Book Review* is entitled "For Younger Readers." The children's book editor, Ellen Lewis Buell, signs some of the reviews and is assisted by other reviewers whose names are indicated. The number of reviews is about the same as in New York *Herald Tribune Books.* Both indicate reading level by age, a practice which for school libraries is somewhat less helpful than indicating reading level by grade. The chief value of either is to help school librarians keep in touch with new books. Both carry a large section of reviews for Book Week and New York *Herald Tribune Books* has a special section for the Children's Spring Book Festival, discussed in Chapter 19.

INDEX